£1·99

13/3

Moses

Emil Bock

Moses

From the Mysteries of Egypt
to the Judges of Israel

Floris Books

Translated by Maria St Goar

Originally published in German under the title *Moses und sein Zeitalter*
by Verlag Urachhaus in 1935. Sixth German edition 1978.
First published in English by Floris Books in 1986.

British Library CIP Data

Bock, Emil
Moses: from the mysteries of Egypt to the judges of Israel.
1. Bible. O.T.—Commentaries
I. Title   II. Moses und sein Zeitalter. *English*
221.6   BS1171.2.

ISBN 0-86315-017-9

Printed in Great Britain
by Billing & Sons Ltd, Worcester

Contents

Joshua – the Judges – Ruth
3 Battles and Premonitions of the Messianic Future

Acknowledgements

Unless otherwise stated, all quotations from the Bible are from the Revised Standard Version with kind permission of the National Council of the Churches of Christ (New Testament © 1946, 1971; Old Testament © 1952).

Where the context required it, Bock's own translation has been translated into English. These are marked *B* after the reference.

Preface

It is not possible to describe history without having courage. It does not suffice to link external facts and events together; in themselves, they are not yet history. What moulds them into historical elements are the ruling influences of spiritual powers and entities who stand behind the destinies of individuals and nations.

The gods draw their inscriptions upon the earth; what they thus call forth into existence are the facts and events of terrestrial occurrences. This is the essence of history: it is initially written by the hands of gods. And if we human beings dare to record history, we must recognize that only to the extent that we have developed the faculty to decipher and read this primordial script of facts and to trace it in the limited letters of our thinking and speech can there be truth and reality in our representation.

Clio, who writes on stone tablets with her stylus, was considered the inspiring muse by the ancients, whom a writer of history would have to emulate. Her image was an aid, a bridge, between the gods' writing in facts and men's writing in words. How is it possible to 'write with the stylus of Clio' in our time where, in contrast to the hieroglyphs of the Egyptians hewn in stone, the cuneiform writing of the Assyrians, the Nordic runes carved in wood, writing and even its implements have become shallow and mechanical, an expression of an abstract mode of thinking?

One way would be to locate precisely the tablets on which the spirits of history inscribe their indelible letters. But where can we take hold of the Book of Life into which the gods wrote and still write with Clio's stylus? Where in historical development are true meaning and progress revealed? On the surface, the whole of history can appear as no more than the eternal rise and fall, the revolving senseless progress and regression of the various civilizations. Nowhere do we see really significant, lasting fruits carried over from a dying culture into another one unless we still hold a naïve belief in external civilization and progress. A contemplation of the external side of mankind's history can basically only lead to a pessimistic world-view such as Oswald Spengler: presented in his *Decline of the West*: over and over, the cycle of cultures recurs through the stages of germination, bloom, maturity and decline. No sense of evolution that would lend justification to the cultural sequence passes from one civilization to the next. The spirits of history appear to write with worthless ink that always fades away after a time.

In reality, those pages in the Book of Life on which indelible letters have been inscribed are to be sought today on a more inward level. The tablet on which Clio's stylus writes is *human consciousness*. One who tries to read and represent world history as the history of consciousness gains access to the aims of the gods which hold sway therein and are progressively realized. The changes of consciousness mankind undergoes are the stations of divinely willed progress; in them, the meaning of historical evolution is perceived.

This book attempts a description of history in the sense of a history of consciousness in the directions pointed out and opened up by Rudolf Steiner's science of the spirit, Anthroposophy. This must be especially emphasized in regard to a description of the age of Moses since the latter represents a particularly significant turning-point.

The history of mankind up to and beyond the age of Moses is not yet history in the sense of more recent developments, for human consciousness of those times was quite unlike that of today. What applies in greater measure to the primordial age, including the time of the patriarchs of the Old Covenant, still holds good for the age of Moses: history is superhuman and mythological, more than human and historical.[1] Coming from the superhuman realm, history in its actual sense only arrives on the human level in the age of David. The age of Moses is, however, that of the great transition. The change of consciousness that took place then is basic to the consciousness of humanity of more recent epochs; the forces that guide historical evolution indicate the actual level of man in that period.

The customary view that Moses, Joshua and the judges already belong to the purely Jewish stream frequently stands in the way of recognizing the significance the Moses age has for all humanity. Just as the universal, human element of figures such as Adam, Enoch and Noah had to be emphasized in *Genesis*, so the pre-Jewish character of Moses and his successors must become discernible through this book. Jewish history as such only originated in the age following Solomon, by means of the emergence into the foreground of the tribe of Judah from among the twelve Israelite tribes. Until then, the history of the Old Covenant still bore the stamp of the general Israelite element; the twelvefold character of the people represented a balanced quintessence of all mankind. Among other points, this should be illustrated by including parallel events in Greece. The great transformation of consciousness that permeated the age of Moses was in fact a process that took hold of and moulded all humanity everywhere.

The desire to clarify the significant turning-point of the history of consciousness, and to give a detailed description, limits this volume to the era of Moses. As far as the method of description is concerned, the reader is referred to what was stated in the preface to my *Genesis*, for it applies also to this book. In one respect, however, in the course of writing this book, I felt compelled to adhere even more to one principle: detailed quotation of Rudolf Steiner's texts appeared absolutely indispensable especially here. In Rudolf Steiner's wealth of lectures descriptions abound that throw the most amazing, revealing light on historical evolution. From a variety of premises and in many contexts, the problems relating to the age of Moses in particular are discussed in such a manner that all historical thinking can receive essential stimulation. I hope that this can be the source of new thinking and perception for many readers as it has been for me.

Emil Bock

Osiris – Akhenaton – Moses

1. Twilight of the Egyptian Gods

Michelangelo carved Moses to appear like the father of the gods, the omnipotent primordial thinker, Zeus. Filled with creative power, the hands look as if they could hurl lightning and thunder: the right, supported on the tablets of the law, fingers the long locks of the beard; the left, tensed for action, rests lightly on the lap. Yet, the main emphasis of the figure lies not in the hands but on the brow. From his forehead, Zeus gave birth to his daughter Athena, rich in thought. From the forehead of Moses two horns rise in majestic spirit-loftiness. They proclaim that here is the royal terrestrial beginning of individual human thinking.

This superhuman marble in the church of San Pietro in Vincoli in Rome, which assumes gigantic dimensions the more one contemplates it, is the classic expression for the pivotal significance of the Moses figure. There exists no period, no branch of cultural development, even to this day, that does not exhibit the characteristic imprint bestowed by the Moses impulse on the spiritual make-up of humanity: In him, as in a first beginning, awoke the consciousness which in altered form is modern-day consciousness as well. Prior to Moses, the twilight of the mysterious, revelation-filled dream spheres of mythology held mankind's soul under its spell. Moses was the greatest among the leaders towards the free expanses of awakened thought.

The beginning which took on form in the figure of Moses, was not limited to Israel. During the same era, it caused the emergence of a new humanity everywhere. Simultaneous events flashed like fiery signals across the whole world. The exodus from Egypt

13

coincided with the Trojan War. When Moses led young Israel towards its future tasks out of the confining realm of an Egypt grown old, this simultaneously was the hour when the European spirit was born. With the conquest of Troy, the genius of Greece – the first-born of Europe – cast off the tutelage of ancient Asian cultures. Like shock waves of an earthquake, movements by various peoples continued throughout the Mediterranean region, in India, even in China, and bore witness to the same universal turning-point.

1.1 The birth of a people in a foreign land

Between Joseph and Moses, the Old Testament omits four centuries. That is the period of Israel's becoming a people, which came about unassumingly in the shadow of the monumental Egyptian life. From early on, the development of the biblical nation seemed to stand under the motif of divinely willed homelessness. The times of the patriarchs, spent in secure proximity to the gods, remained embedded within the sphere of Babylonia and Egypt. Abraham's migrations only came to rest relatively late between Mesopotamia and the Nile in the Land of the Promise. Only Isaac's life, which was guided by a prophetic presentiment, had the region of the Jordan as its exclusive surrounding. When Jacob had attained manhood, he returned for only a brief time to the land of his fathers and his youth. His life, like that of Abraham, alternated between Babylonia and Egypt. The temples on the shores of Euphrates and Tigris were the background for the first decades of his adult years; the world of pyramids and the sphinx occupied the eve of his life. The twelve sons of Jacob, the progenitors of the twelve tribes, remained in the Palestinian realm for only a short while during the middle of their lives. With the exception of one, they had all been born in Babylonia and, like their father, all died in Egypt. Once we have ceased to picture all biblical narratives as images from the life of shepherds and nomads, placing them in landscapes of meadows and pastures, our view is free for an ever richer, more colourful perception of the magnificent temple environment, which is the actual religious-historical background for the first books of the Old Testament.

An abundance of cultic monuments holds the inconspicuous germ of a people. This is particularly the case after the era of the patriarchs has run its course. For four hundred years, from Joseph to Moses, it is as if the seed of future developments was completely lost in the ground of its supporting basis. Then, all at once, there stands the figure of Moses and through him we perceive that the family-like group, which had once moved to Egypt, has grown into a great people.

In the period when, for Israel, the completed process of developing into a nation becomes historically visible, the destiny of homelessness of these people is also increasingly revealed. Egypt had been a friendly foreign land when one of their own, Joseph, had occupied high offices of Egyptian government. Now, the land of the Pharaohs had become hostile, alien territory; the might of the tyrants had turned the Israelites into a despised, subjugated class of slaves.

At the time of Moses, Egypt's own character *was* no longer the same as four hundred years earlier. The dreams of the Pharaoh, which Joseph had been able to interpret, had not only been a premonition of an external famine; in them, the waning of all Egyptian spiritual life was foreshadowed. What is outwardly beheld at the time of Moses, however, seems totally to contradict this. When Moses was born, the power of the Egyptian world empire had grown to unlimited proportions. Had Pharaoh's visions of calamity been contradicted by the course of history?

The most important events and figures of those four hundred years throw light on the transformation that occurred in Egypt.

1.2 Thutmose III and the Battle of Megiddo

Around the middle of the second pre-Christian millennium — it is usually thought to have been the year 1479 BC — when the growing Israelite nation had already lived through half of its Egyptian centuries, an event occurred that shook up the whole civilized world and had a much more decisive impact than ordinary historical views ascribe to it: the battle of Megiddo. Thutmose III, the first and also the greatest conqueror among the Egyptian Pharaohs, brought the armies of the Middle East to their knees in the plain of Jezreel, lying in Galilee between Mount Tabor and the Mount Carmel, which henceforth was to become *the* battle-ground of Palestine. Not only Palestine and Syria, but all the civilized regions of Asia Minor thus came under Egyptian rule. Thutmose was right when, after the battle, he said to his victorious troops, 'The conquest of Megiddo signifies more than the conquest of a thousand cities!' A world empire came into being that consolidated into a unity regions that formerly had been the setting of great independent civilizations and cultural developments.

A historical view fascinated by the appearance of power and great empires will consider an event like the battle of Megiddo a fortunate one, entailing progress not only for Egypt's development but that of all humanity. A concentration more upon mankind's spiritual destinies shows, in that battle and its consequences, the fateful introduction into history of decadence. The appearance of the principle of conquest and power signifies the end of a spiritual life born of the wisdom of revelation. In Thutmose III the impulses continued which, centuries earlier in Mesopotamia, had appeared in the Nimrod-figures of Babylonian rulers. They had caused Abraham's renunciation, for he was intent upon an inward intensi-fication of culture. Man, for whom the light-filled sphere of super-sensory existence with the gods was diminishing, tensely reached out into the sense world and snatched up whatever he could reach. In the empire acquired through conquest under the Pharaohs of the eighteenth dynasty, Egypt found a surrogate for the disap-pearing kingdom of the spirit in which earlier it could feel securely supported. Greed for power is nothing but suppressed fear that is caused by the loss of the spirit sphere.

In the age preceding Abraham, the sister-cultures of Egypt and Babylonia blossomed side by side in genuine spirituality. Each was sustained from the well-head of revelations emanating from its temples and mystery centres, and they mutually benefited each other in their creative aims. Although Abraham's departure from Chaldea already testified to the beginning Babylonian decadence, even the migrations themselves of the patriarchs Abraham and Jacob were proof of the fructifying exchange of forces between Mesopotamia and Egypt. When now, the sister-kingdoms rose up militantly against each other with intentions of conquest, the loss of the spiritual interplay of forces became evident. The ties to the realms of the gods were lost. Thus commenced the ever-shifting political ties between earthly states under the leadership of whoever was the most powerful at a given time. Not only the vanquished, the victor too suffered a loss. As Thutmose III bound the chains of power around the Orient, he sealed the forfeiture of former existence with the gods. Although sensory illusion would demonstrate the opposite, Pharaoh's dreams of evil foreboding had now truly been fulfilled in Egypt's soul-nature.

The battle of Megiddo was more than a military event, it was an apocalyptic occurrence. It signified the break in the continuity of revelations, which the great civilizations of the old world enjoyed with the supersensory spheres. With earthly weapons, mankind fought its way out of the realm of divine revelation. A great reversal of the battle of Megiddo must one day take place in the future: with the weapons of the spirit, courageous human souls will then gain new access to the supersensory world. The apocalyptic loss related to the physical victory of Thutmose III will be offset by an apocalyptic victory. As the seer in John's Revelation in the New Testament beholds and describes this future event, it presents itself in images of the battle, which is the reflection: the battle of Armageddon (Rev.16:16), the spiritual counter-image of the battle of Megiddo. The term 'Armageddon' is nothing but an inflexion of 'Megiddo'. Moses grew up in an Egypt powerful through the conquests of Thutmose III but rushing spiritually into its decline.

1.3 Amenophis IV, Akhenaton

Approximately a hundred years after the battle of Megiddo, at the youthful age of twelve, a personality ascended the throne of the Pharaoh who, like a prophetic symbol, was in his way without equal in Egyptian history. Like a guest from another cosmic sphere, he departed the earth at the age of thirty: Amenophis IV, Akhenaton. He was the complete opposite of Thutmose III and all the other conquerors and despots on the Pharaonic throne. He was the first Utopian idealist of mankind, an avowed opponent of all quest for power and the use of force. He turned his back on the splendid royal residence of Thebes and the temples of

Karnak. Instead of siding with the priesthood of Thebes and
Karnak, corrupted by political involvement, and their gods of
black magic, he adhered to the light-filled sun divinity proclaimed
in Heliopolis. This was the quiet, ancient mystery centre which
had survived in the vicinity of Memphis, the royal city of the
Ancient Kingdom, although Memphis was already desolate and
abandoned for over a thousand years. The figure of Akhenaton
was a living protest against Egypt's decadence at a time when the
country had attained the pinnacle of earthly power and treasures
of gold. The tender youth on the most powerful throne of the
world was not deceived as to the true state of affairs by the
immeasurable wealth that year after year was amassed in the Nile
region through the payments of tribute by all the kings of the
surrounding world. An early enlightened rationalist, he was
disgusted by the religious customs of his environment, feeling that
they were terrible superstitions. All the activities of the rulers
appeared to him to be brutally inhuman. Construction of a
completely new, broadly designed royal city on the shores of the
Nile between Memphis and Thebes was to signify his break with
the hitherto existing developments and to seal his reformative
intent for a radical new beginning. Within two years, the 'City of
the Horizon', Tel el Amarna, grew out of the sands of the desert,
and when he was twenty-one years old, Akhenaton ceremoniously
moved into this new world created by him.

Within ten years Akhenaton's city was once again empty and
abandoned. The walls of the all too hurriedly erected houses and
palaces quickly crumpled into rubble and ruins. The seething
waves of lust for power, once unleashed in humanity, did not halt
before the island of humanitarianism, which an unworldly youth,
out of step with his age, had begun to construct. They mercilessly
engulfed it and henceforth ruled the world unchallenged.

It is as if a hidden symbolism in the course of world history had
tried to come to the fore when the unrests, which finally led to
Akhenaton's fall, broke out precisely in the area around Megiddo.
A few of the subjugated princes in northern Palestine and Syria
rebelled against Egypt's rule. Akhenaton, the opponent of force,
prohibited the use of arms. The rebellion rapidly grew in
proportion. To no avail, the vassals faithful to the Pharaoh, among
them the governor residing in Megiddo, called for Egyptian mili-

18

tary assistance. In no time at all, the most powerful empire broke apart. Akhenaton was hardly dead when the spirit of the victory at Megiddo reached out for a renewed and even more pronounced advance. Brief wars restored the world empire to a large extent. Reinstated Thebes was filled with gold. As proof and symbol of the reaction to the unsuccessful attempt at reform, the unbelievable gold treasures that were discovered in the tomb of Tutankhamun, son-in-law and successor of Akhenaton, confront the eyes of a fascinated world. The grasping hand of fear reaches even more greedily into the pomp and glitter of earth-existence. The warm wisdom-gold of ancient Egyptian spiritual life is replaced by the insatiable greed of cold terrestrial gold.

It must have been only a few decades after Akhenaton's death that Moses was born. As the adopted son of the house of Pharaoh, his destiny led him into the world of Thebes' recklessly unfolding reaction symbolized by Tutankhamun's gold. In a different way, suited to the new age, the will to oppose decadence, which had permeated Akhenaton's soul with the stamp of a far-off future, was to mature in Moses.

The figure of Akhenaton was overshadowed by a mystery, comprehension of which is indispensable in searching out the socio-historical conditions that the young Moses was faced with. It is more than just poetic glorification if Merezhkovsky gave his Akhenaton novel the title the 'Messiah'. The strange young Pharaoh must have affected many of his contemporaries as if he were the fulfilment of the Messianic expectations which began to pervade humanity in those days.

1.4 Expectation of a Messiah

It is commonly assumed that anticipation of the incarnation of a divine saviour did not originate until the era of the Jewish prophets at the time of Isaiah and the Babylonian exile, for it is then that it becomes clearly evident in literary expressions. At most, it is thought that the idea existed earlier in germinal form among the people of Israel and that it might have been adopted by Egyptian spiritual life when the Israelites lived under the jurisdiction of the Pharaohs. In reality, the expectation of a Messiah arose among all civilized peoples of the ancient world independently of each other and expressed itself in quite different forms. For example, from the centuries of the Middle Dynasty, before Joseph's age, a prophecy by an Egyptian priest has come down to us which speaks of the coming 'good shepherd'.

He brings relief for what burns. He is a shepherd of men.
When his flock is lost, he does not rest all day until he
has gathered them together again. Verily, he vanquishes
sin and raises his arm against it. Where is he today? Does
he perhaps slumber among you?[2]

The source of Messianic hope and prophecy among all people lies, as Rudolf Steiner's spiritual research gives us to understand, in the mysteries. There, initiates were able to foresee an event in the spiritual cosmos fraught with consequences while it was under way, and their vision could trace its actual occurrence. It is the event which was described in mythological language as the death of Osiris or Adonis.

Rudolf Steiner describes how, during the earliest Egyptian times, the temple neophyte was led in the higher degrees of the Hermes initiation 'to the shores of the universal existence' and to the entities whom he recognized as the guides of his innermost soul-spirit being through deaths and births. Isis, the great mother of all soul existence, revealed herself to visionary sight, first as the wordless silent goddess; the great riddle of human existence weighed heavily upon the neophyte's soul in beholding her. In the image of Isis, man perceived the kinship of the human soul with the soul of the universe. But is the soul element, which dissolves at death into the cosmic maternal source, man's highest member? Is it not a fact that also an individual spark glimmers in him that can never be extinguished, a germinating core of his being that can pass beyond all deaths to new individual destinies? Through the momentum of this question, Isis was then shown to the advancing neophyte as the eternal mother who gives birth to the sunlike creative universal word which consolidated into the Osiris figure. The radiant bearer of the spirit-core, Osiris, was simultaneously the eternally newborn son and spouse of Isis. To experience Osiris signified the solution of the universal riddle of man.

Then, however, an age dawned which brought with it a great

and serious change. The goddess remained silent to the one who ascended into spiritual worlds. She had become 'incapable of giving birth to the word of the worlds,' Osiris was torn from her, she had become a widow; no answer resounded to the painful riddle, the question concerning man's innermost being.

> Those who underwent this initiation and returned again into the physical world possessed a solemn but resigned world view. They knew holy Isis, but they perceived themselves as 'sons of the widow.'

The Osiris-being disappeared from the sun-radiant sphere in which it had revealed itself until then.

> If, during the later Egyptian era, a person ascended into the spiritual worlds . . . as an initiate, he experienced the gradual dying away of the god . . . He felt . . . how the god took leave of the spiritual world in order to pass over into another world . . . Gradually, out of this mood, the Osiris myth took on form.[3]

The myth relates how Osiris is torn from Isis by sinister Typhon; his corpse is carried away in a chest-like coffin by the waters of the Nile; later it is dismembered and scattered to the four winds.

From a certain time, the northern Baldur lament for the death of the fair divine youth arose in Egypt; and as Egypt mourned Osiris, the Syro-Phoenician world mourned Adonis, and Babylonians, Tammuz. Darkness moved into the sphere in which human beings had been able to gain awareness of eternity and immortality. But then, more and more clearly, a hope infiltrated the sadness: Although the god had disappeared from the sphere where we once encountered him, he has nevertheless not ceased to exist. Where is he now? In what sphere should we seek him? Perhaps he is closer now to us earth beings than previously; perhaps he is only on his way to us.

The as yet faintly grasped thought about a return of Osiris-Adonis, a resurrection of the god who has died, is the root of the Messianic idea. It awakened in Egypt and in Asia Minor and came to visible expression for all the people in the dramatic burial and resurrection cults, for example the Phoenician Adonis cult.

In reply to a question concerning the time of the great transformation in Egyptian spiritual life, Rudolf Steiner gives an answer that is significant for our considerations:

The time between the ancient initiation, when a seeker
could participate in the birth of Osiris in the ancient Egyptian
mysteries, and the time when he only met silent, grieving
Isis and could become a 'son of the widow' . . . that is
the time in which Moses lived.[4]

The age of Moses was filled with the dramatic atmosphere of a
great turning-point of time. The Akhenaton figure was already a
sign, projected down upon the earth, of the mighty upheavals
which occurred in the spiritual cosmos. When the young reformer
had an effect like a being come to earth from a distant star, and
when he began the imaginative task of replacing the hitherto
existing social order by a kingdom that was 'not of this world',
did not the question perhaps arise, consciously, or in a dreamlike
manner: he who disappeared in the heavens above, the radiant
son of the sun, has he now arrived here among us human beings?
Apocalyptic excitement must have taken hold of the people of
that period. But Akhenaton was not the one who was to come;
he was at most the distorted shadow cast prematurely and errati-
cally by a distant light. Three hundred years earlier, the young
Israelite Joseph had trodden the Egyptian soil adorned by the
Osiris-Adonis mystery as by a precious veil. The far-off Messianic
future glimmered around him like the light of an early dawn.
Akhenaton was younger at his death than was Joseph when
brought from his dungeon to high honour. He had owed his
Messianic light-aura mainly to his over-delicate corporeality. His
must have been a premature birth; he appeared at once feminine
and masculine — many an impressive hermaphrodite statue of
him stands in the museum in Cairo — and as such he was a natural
focus for an abstract anticipation of future soul-potential. In an
age and a country where intellectual thought did not yet light up
the dusky sentient soul, he had staked his life and empire on an
abstraction.

In the apocryphal legends, there is a tradition that Moses' birth
was premature. It says there concerning his mother Jochebed:
'When seven months had passed she gave birth to a son; the house
was filled with light, bright as the light of sun and moon when
they shine.'[5]

Like Akhenaton, Moses was ahead of his time. But he
proceeded in a sound manner. Thus, he gave rise to no confusion

of his person with that of the Messiah to come but on the contrary, he became his first great proclaimer and forerunner. Moreover, thinking, the mighty future force of mankind, did not dwell in Moses in unduly mature and Utopian abstraction as in Akhenaton. In Moses, the birth of head-thinking took place in dramatic, fateful form.

1.5 Rameses II and the infanticide

The age of Moses brings the birth pangs of a new world. In the Egyptian surroundings in which Moses grew up, a third Pharaoh stands before us after Thutmose III and Amenophis IV. Older traditions have always considered Rameses II as the Pharaoh of whom the Bible says that he imposed hard labour upon the Israelites. In all likelihood, one must concur in this view, which more recent historians increasingly fall back on. It may even be assumed that Rameses II was not only the Pharaoh of oppression but indeed the one of the exodus. He belongs to the nineteenth dynasty and was ruler over the Egyptian empire for almost seventy years (from 1292 to 1225 BC).

Rameses II continued the course of power expansion and pomp as embodied earlier in Thutmose III and Tutankhamun. He was truly one of the inaugurators of the Caesarean cult, which was later transplanted from Egypt to Rome, and which is also an outgrowth, albeit a coarse and materialistic one, of the Messianic idea. Considering themselves human incarnations of the deity, the despots henceforth demanded divine veneration for themselves and thus justified their insatiable greed for power. They believed they had rediscovered the vanished sphere of the gods in their own human nature on earth; the drive for conquest sprang from the wild passion-filled hallucination that a divine kingdom had to be established on earth. World empires came into being as caricatures of the increasingly disappearing supersensory world.

Rameses II not only expressed his Caesarean passion in mighty conquests but first and foremost in ceaseless building projects. He covered his realm with new and extensive temple constructions. Many of the temples still on view in Egypt today date back to him. Everywhere he erected colossal statues of towering proportions. The gigantic Pharaonic figures, for example, by the cave temples of Abu Simbel in southern Egypt near the border of the Sudan were built by him. On his orders whole cities rose from the ground to add to his glory; the subjugated nations owing him tribute were pressed into service as immense armies of slaves for the sake of his insane will to build. The Bible mentions that during construction of the two cities Pithom and Rameses, which were situated on the eastern shore of the Nile delta, the Israelites also were employed to do slave labour of the hardest kind (Exod.1:11). It is this indication that led scholars tentatively to identify the biblical Pharaoh as Rameses II.

The story of the Pharaonic infanticide is inseparably linked with these contemporary backgrounds of the biblical reports which pick up the thread of history again four hundred years after Joseph. Just like the legendary tradition of Nimrod's infanticide from which young Abraham was miraculously rescued, the report of the infanticide in Exodus is an imaginative hieroglyph requiring interpretation into historical description. Behind these images is concealed the execution of gruesome black-magical cults. In early Egyptian times, the force of Osiris had streamed into the souls of initiates as the holiest blessing for the self by means of the vision of the celestial birth mysteries, as the divine mother Isis bore Osiris. Now, Isis had become the mourning widow in the spiritual cosmos. The few who were capable of perpetuating the mysteries in a pure and genuine way through the ages of the twilight of the gods, sought out places of seclusion where they awaited the new Osiris revelation in reverent patience. But generally, Egyptian life fell into decadence. It consisted in wanting to cling forcibly to the vanishing power of former times. It rebelled against humanity's destined course. The power-hungry rulers in particular forced their way into initiations; they inaugurated orgiastic cults to bring about the incorporation of supersensory forces, notwithstanding the fact that the latter were in process of disappearing. The end permitted the means. Eerie terrestrial counter-images came into existence in place of the celestial birth mysteries. Compensation was sought in the misuse of the secrets of birth entrusted to mankind on earth. The miraculous cosmic power which, as a last paradisal remnant of the age of primordial man, inheres in women about to become mothers and which also still envelops the newborn infant, was desired by the Pharaohs and Caesars. They sought to acquire and transform it into faculties of undue influence over others.

Apparently the Pharaoh referred to by the Bible — let us assume that he is identical with Rameses II — deeply invaded the domain of the Israelite people in order to appropriate victims for his unlimited greed for power. Not only the biblical narration of infanticide attests this but also related legendary traditions. The Pharaoh reputedly forced the Israelites to immure their newborn infants in the walls of the new cities in place of bricks, if they could not produce a sufficient number of bricks; and Pharaoh Malul was bathed in the blood of slaughtered children from Israel in order to cure his leprosy.[6]

It was no coincidence that the black-magical decadence of Egypt utilized the colossal stone sculptures reminiscent of the sphinx of Giza. A hundred years before Moses, following a dream-vision, Thutmose IV, a successor to the victor at Megiddo, dug the huge figure of the sphinx out of the sands of the desert. Adjacent to the great structures of the pyramids, even then (circa 1400 BC) a monument to an almost unimaginably ancient time, the sphinx was on the verge of being consigned to oblivion. In their stern geometric regularity, the pyramids document early intensification of grave cults and death mysteries. In like manner, in its exciting incalculability, the sphinx of Giza poses the question concerning the riddle of life and the human being and is an ancient monumental evidence of the birth mysteries.

When it was uncovered in the days of the Egyptian twilight of the gods, it may well have become a stage for the decadent birth mysteries through the temple chambers within it and connected with it. Now, the sphinx's lofty enigmatic character was replaced by that of a mighty predator. It proliferated monstrosities of greed for power across the land in the colossal similar sculptures erected everywhere by Rameses II.

1.6 Moses' basket of bulrushes

The feverish pharaonic lust for power infringed the beginning of the life of Moses. As the boy Abraham was saved in a rocky cave, so the infant Moses was rescued from the threat of infanticide by the 'basket of bulrushes' floating on the Nile.

The biblical documents did not originate from external recollections and traditions but from the clairvoyant retrospection of enlightened minds; earthly historical facts, however, did not immediately become accessible to this vision of the past. Not the events in their outward course, but the accompanying soul- and spirit-processes were perceived in imaginative pictures and recapitulated as if they were external occurrences. In the days when the biblical texts came into being, interest was not directed to the outer surface of events as exclusively as it is today. There are spiritual processes that in their pictorial quality are identical with the external events embodying them; but there are also those that were in no way accompanied by corresponding physical events. The imaginative style of the biblical books does not distinguish between the two. It remains the step-by-step task of one who struggles for comprehension of the Old or the New Testament to do this and to interpret them in today's historical conceptions. The naïve position that simply assumes outward events in all pictures and stories leads to nothing but errors and dead ends.

An image especially fraught with secrets and in need of patient deciphering is that of Moses' basket of bulrushes. The story of the abandonment of the newborn infant, as related in the Old Testament, remains full of riddles if it merely depicts the outer facts; considerations quite near at hand will show that. We need only realize that the Israelites had not penetrated deeply enough into Egyptian territory for even a few of them to have arrived in the vicinity of the Nile. The land of Goshen assigned to them lay far from the Nile to the east of the delta. If the Pharaoh's daughter found the basket where the royal hills of Thebes are mirrored in the Nile near Karnak and Luxor, as must be assumed, then the biblical narration transports us to a region which, for the travelling conditions of those days, lay several weeks away from the Nile delta and the habitation of the Israelites. If nothing else, the Old Testament description presupposes that the family of Moses had some connection with the royal court, perhaps through Miriam, designated as Moses' sister. But above all else, the image of the basket that floated on the Nile is meant to direct us to spiritual facts in the Moses destiny. We have already mentioned once[7] that the Hebrew Bible uses the same word, *tebhah*, for both Noah's ark and the basket of Moses (the Authorised Version uses the same English word, 'the ark of bulrushes'); this is a term from the mysteries which is retained in the Greek version of the Old Testament as a borrowed word, θιβις (*thibis*). The corresponding Greek word is λάρναξ (*lárnax*). It indicates Deucalion's ark in the great flood as well as the coffin in which, according to the myth, the body of Osiris drifted down the Nile and across the sea all the way to Byblos.[8] We confront the symbol of the initiation coffin in which the mystical burial of the disciple of initiation took place and out of which he returned to life as one reborn after the deathlike temple sleep lasting three days. This symbol was not completely concealed within the secrecy of the mystery centres. In pictorial enactments, it was shown to the people during great cultic festivities. At special holy sites of Adonis, a statue of the radiant young god was placed in a coffin-like chest at certain times of the year, it was then carried in solemn processions to the shores of the sea or a river and subsequently submerged in the water. For three days, lamentations resounded over the god's death. Then came the morning of resurrection. The coffin was again pulled ashore, 'drawn out of the water'. The statue of the deity was again raised up and the lamentations changed to hymns of jubilation over the god's resurrection.

The most important centre of Adonis worship was Byblos on the coast of Syria. Since the Osiris myth, as handed down by Plutarch, speaks of the arrival of Osiris' coffin in Byblos, it does acknowledge Adonis worship as its continuation and allows us to recognize the identical imagery of the Osiris coffin adrift on the Nile and the Adonis chest annually submerged in the sea. Another important location for the worship of the dying and arising Adonis was situated on the island of Cyprus, where even today the harbour city on the south coast owes its name Larnaca to the Adonis coffin.

By showing us the Moses infant in the coffin-chest of initiation the Old Testament indicates that here, as a chosen instrument of

27

fate — on account of his earlier destinies — a human being at the beginning of his life is placed in a blessed relationship to the spiritual world and gifted with wisdom otherwise only attainable by man at a mature age through initiation. This is elaborated in the classic Moses lecture, which Rudolf Steiner gave in Berlin in 1911:[9]

> In the manner of ancient descriptions, the fact that in Moses we are dealing with a soul who gave the utmost that it could offer out of eternal sources is symbolically indicated to us in Moses' being enclosed in the basket soon after his birth. One who is familiar with such descriptions from religious history knows that they always are meant to indicate something significant. From earlier studies . . . we know that if man wants to raise his perception to higher spiritual worlds, he must complete certain steps in his soul development by completely isolating himself from his surroundings and awakening the most elemental forces of his soul. Now, if a person is to be depicted who already at birth brings along the spiritual treasures that lead up to the highest levels of humanity, it cannot be better described than by saying: it was necessary for this individuality . . . to undergo an experience that reached even into the physical level whereby his senses, all that he possessed in the way of gifts of comprehension, are cut off, as it were, from the physical world. It therefore sounds understandable to us . . . that the Egyptian princess, Pharaoh's daughter, fetched the infant out of the water herself and named him Moses, because she said: For I have pulled him out of the water. This implied that the representative of Egyptian culture, the daughter of Pharaoh, directed the very life-blood of this culture into a soul filled with the substance of eternity.

Anthroposophy outlines even more precisely what took place against the background of the Pharaonic infanticide in the soul of the still very young Moses through this initiation by destiny. If we venture to include such descriptions, we must depend on the reader to understand correctly the intention behind this. We do not raise the claim to prove such descriptions, much less to deduce them from the biblical text. They are mentioned according to the facts as single but yet organic components of a comprehensive world view and conviction so that the accounts of the biblical texts, the results of external historical research and the results of Anthroposophy can illuminate, support and deepen each other. The latter will naturally only be historically instructive to the reader to the extent that he is already open to them in some way. This is why I have inserted the results of anthroposophical research into the whole text in such a manner that the reader, who is unfamiliar with them, can at first simply pass over these quotations or at least leave them open to question. I believe that I am justified in doing this, because in regard to many individual points comprehension can result from the context or the accord with similar points, and one is therefore not dependent upon understanding each single explanation purely on its own.

In his lecture cycle about the Gospel of St Matthew,[10] Rudolf Steiner speaks of a profound link of destiny between Moses and Hermes, or Thoth, the inaugurator of Egyptian wisdom and culture, who lived more than two thousand years earlier. This close connection of destiny is attributed to the fact that approximately four to five thousand years before the turn of time both were incarnated as disciples of the great Zarathustra, the founder of the ancient Persian culture. This lofty teacher placed into each of the two disciples the seed for a spiritual stream required in the future. Hermes was introduced by him into the tranquil wisdom of physical space; Moses was taught the tension-filled dramatic secrets of the flow of time. But Zarathustra was not content merely with instructions; he offered up something of his own soul-being to the two disciples in such a way that it would not be lost in subsequent lives on earth before the mission, now laid into them in rudimentary form, was fulfilled by them in the decisive incarnation. The soul-body (astral body) of the great teacher was implanted into Hermes to ensure his wisdom of space; Moses received the life body (etheric body) of Zarathustra so that his wisdom of time could come to life in the most marvellous way.* What had once been implanted in Hermes and Moses of the

---

*In the description of the meeting between Abraham and Melchizedek in my book, Genesis, (p. 113f) a similar occult fact was mentioned, namely Abraham's impregnation with the etheric body of Shem and of Melchizedek as the specific bearer of this etheric body.

wisdom and being of their teacher came to life anew from early childhood in the earthly bodies in which they had to realize their great tasks as leaders of humanity in inaugurating whole cultures.

How this proceeded in the case of Moses is described by Rudolf Steiner:[11]

> This second pupil of Zarathustra was reborn as Moses, into whom, in very early childhood, the preserved etheric body of Zarathustra was incorporated.

> Religious chronicles that are genuinely based on occultism contain mysterious clues pointing to the secrets disclosed by occult investigation. To enable Moses, the reincarnated pupil of Zarathustra, to receive into himself the etheric body of his former teacher, something quite unusual must necessarily happen to him. It was essential that the miraculous legacy he was to receive from Zarathustra should be incorporated into him before impressions from the environment were made upon his individuality, as in the case of other human beings. This is narrated symbolically in the story that he was laid in a cradle of reeds and lowered into a river — an indication of a remarkable Initiation. During the process of Initiation a human being is shut off from the outer world for a certain period of time and what he is destined to receive is then instilled into him. Thus the etheric body of Zarathustra that had been preserved intact was incorporated into Moses at a certain moment while he was shut off from the outer world; and then there could come to flower within him the wonderful wisdom concerning Time, once imparted to him by Zarathustra.

The symbol of the Osiris chest as the initiation coffin is placed into the earliest destiny of Moses' life as a sign for the wondrous reawakening of an initiation undergone in a previous incarnation. And it is deeply rooted in destiny that this event occurs in Egypt, not in the land of Goshen among the Israelites but far from there in the centre of the Egyptian temple culture. Egypt has drawn Moses into its fold. It is as if only at this moment it becomes really clear why Joseph moved his people to Egypt four hundred years earlier. Hermes draws his companion of Zarathustrian discipleship to his side. Within the completed creation of Hermes wisdom, Moses can set out on his path and work. Removed from the Israelite folk-context, he grows up as the son of the house of the Egyptian Pharaoh.

Since the Bible only describes the spiritual, imaginative side, it is not easy to figure out the external historical events that surround the infant's rescue. A certain idea can perhaps be gained by a comparison taken from much later human conditions. There have been many cases of child prodigies who at a very early age exhibited remarkable gifts as if they had brought them to earth because of earlier destinies. Mozart was such a child prodigy. Even at the age of seven he performed in major concerts. To a much greater degree, something similar must have been the case with Moses, and people must have existed in his environment who, immediately following his birth, were in a spiritual manner able to perceive his special quality; they did what was necessary to protect him from the black-magical machinations of the Pharaoh.

I would like to sketch hypothetically the course of events as one might picture them from the whole context. In the vicinity of the Pharaoh's court in Thebes, but in sharp moral contrast to the spirit that ruled, there may well have existed a circle of 'the pious of the land', organized along the lines of a free brotherhood, that included among its adherents not only Egyptians but also members of other nations. Perhaps this was the rudimentary beginning of what later became the order of the Therapeutics and Essenes. The existence of such a group would then have been the reason why a few Israelite families, among them Moses' parents, belonging to this circle, lived apart from the majority of their people in the midst of Egyptian life. Even members of the house of Pharaoh must have sympathized with this circle, who, in opposition to the ambitious madness of the ruler, were at pains to support all those efforts that stood for the ideals of humaneness and purity. This is how a connection might have existed to the Pharaoh's daughter, who is called Bathia in legendary tradition. Now, when the infant Moses was born and the members of these 'pious of the land' were in agreement concerning the lofty mission that this human being would one day have to fulfil, there was no better way to protect him than to arrange to have him accepted into the Pharaoh's house. We discern from the biblical description how readily an understanding came about between Bathia and

Miriam so that Bathia adopted the baby and assigned its own mother to it as its wetnurse. Perhaps even here, the relationship of the brotherhood may have played a part. Miriam need not have been a sister of Moses in the physical sense. If she is designated as his sister — the same applies to Aaron who is known as his brother — this might well refer to a relationship of 'brothers' and 'sisters' as is customary in lodges or fraternities. (Much of the later joint activity of Moses, Aaron and Miriam would thus be put in a different light.) If such conceptions approach historical reality, it means that at the very beginning of his life, destiny placed Moses in an environment which had spiritual wisdom at its disposal and could offer him protection both outwardly and inwardly against the black-magical atmosphere of the Pharaoh's rule so that he could link up with the achievements of his earlier initiation-destiny. What was undertaken to bring about his rescue was then at the same time suitable to bring to birth and kindle the significant legacy of destiny and gift of providence.

1.7 Education through Egypt

It is seldom fully realized how very much the first decades of Moses' life were impregnated and coloured by Egypt. As the royal son, and — as some ancient writers even state — the possible heir to the Pharaonic throne, all mystery centres and honours were open to the adolescent. His nature must have held him back from the megalomania of Rameses II and its ceaseless influences. He devoted himself all the more to a thorough comprehension of the Hermes wisdom and the still remaining genuine mysteries.

In the New Testament, Stephen in his great speech (Acts 7:22) says of him: 'And Moses was instructed in all the wisdom of the Egyptians'. A sentence like this is passed over as long as there is no clear connection of the religious and historical background of the time with a conception of the biblical figures. Moses grew up as an Egyptian in all the splendour of a son of Pharaoh. Philo of Alexandria, the brilliant contemporary of the Apostles, gives a description of the education enjoyed by Moses in Egypt in his *Life of Moses:*[12]

From all the regions, teachers soon arrived; some came

without special invitation from the border countries and the Egyptian provinces, others were asked to come from Hellas for considerable remuneration. But it was not long before he surpassed them in capability — for through his natural gift of comprehension he anticipated their teachings and it seemed as if he remembered rather than learned. . . . Arithmetic and geometry as well as rhythmics, harmony and prosody and all of music . . . were taught him by the Egyptian sages; furthermore, philosophy arrayed in symbols, which they present in the so-called holy characters (hieroglyphics) . . . Hellenists instructed him in all other general knowledge, and the teachers from the border countries in Assyrian literature and Chaldean science of the celestial bodies. The latter he also acquired from the Egyptians, who primarily pursued mathematical studies.

But the introduction, in the form of initiation, into the Egyptian mysteries meted out to Moses is more significant than all scholarly instruction and, in the sense of that age, the scientific teachings which the Hellenistic philosopher Philo focuses upon. In the fragments of the Egyptian historian, Manetho, handed down in Greek, we find the report that Moses was an initiated disciple of the mysteries of Heliopolis and there bore the Osiris-name Osarsiph. Heliopolis, called On in the Old Testament, situated in the north of today's sprawling suburbs of Cairo, was the mystery centre belonging to the ancient royal city of Memphis, where Joseph had once received his initiation;[13] this was also where Amenophis IV, allied with its priesthood, had overthrown the power-greedy priests of Thebes and had undertaken his great task of reform. Heliopolis must have been a spiritual haven, where, in spite of decadence breaking in everywhere, the genuine life of the mysteries was preserved not only until the age of Moses but far beyond that era. After all, even eight centuries later, Plato still found here venerable teachers of ancient Egyptian wisdom, whose disciple he remained for over a decade. It is not without significance for the inner relationships of the evolving spiritual life that Moses passed through the same school as did Plato later on.

Among the relief pictures on the temple walls of the Pharaonic residence of that time, there is a recurring motif, for example in the mighty Ramesseum at Thebes and on a temple wall in Karnak, before which young Moses might occasionally have stood and pondered: Pharaoh Rameses II, represented as the god Osiris, sits under the crown of the sycamore tree, on the leaves of which Hermes, the divine messenger and inaugurator of Egyptian culture, writes with a golden stylus. With such representations, the Pharaoh laid claim to the primordial symbol of initiation and inspiration for himself. It is the same symbol that was later applied to Buddha in India when he was described as sitting under the Bodhi tree and which reaches into the Gospel of St John in the figure of Nathanael, of whom it is said in a significant passage that he sat under the fig tree. The fact that this symbol was externally displayed for the glorification of the ruler indicates that only misused initiations, devoid of genuine quality, were performed on the rulers.

In Moses, owing to his completely different origin of destiny, a member of the house of Pharaoh wandered through the temple structures, newly arising everywhere at that time, who as a genuinely initiated 'Hermes disciple' knew how to evaluate such images. As Osarsiph, one who had really been introduced into the Osiris mysteries, he knew that an age had dawned in which even the highest initiate was unable to attain the Osiris stage. Owing to the cosmic event of the Osiris death, the temple pupil could merely attain to the level of a 'Son of the Widow', no longer to that of the divinely enthroned son and spouse of Isis as claimed in the reliefs for Pharaoh. It was in fact the genuine Egyptian initiation in the mystery centre of Heliopolis which had to prepare Moses for his break with Egypt. If Osiris had abandoned Egypt and was only depicted there in presumptuous distorted reproductions, then one who honestly sought him in the spirit realm had to be ready to leave Egypt in order to follow him.

When Moses slew the Egyptian, the overseer who tortured the Israelites, he really slew the Egyptian in himself. He did not flee only in order to ensure his safety but to turn away from an Egypt abandoned by its gods and grown despotic and tyrannical. The imaginative description of the Bible, which only shows this one image from Moses' period of development, conceals more than it reveals in this instance. When the writings related to the Old Testament are consulted, it becomes quite obvious that one must first penetrate the veil of images to arrive at actual historical facts.

In the New Testament, Stephen, in his review of the history of salvation, mentions the three great periods in the life of Moses:[14] Moses was forty years old when he slew the Egyptian and fled. He subsequently spent forty years in seclusion until a divine revelation sent him forth to lead the Israelites. Finally, for forty years, he was the leader of the people in the desert.

The flight of Moses appears in a much more far-reaching religious-historical light if one considers that he remained away from the land on the Nile for fully four decades. He spends the most mature years of his manhood, from age forty to eighty, in the land that he chose when he turned away from Egypt. For forty years he had absorbed what Egypt's culture and centres of wisdom had to offer. The land of seclusion, veiled in mystery, his second great school, moves alongside Egypt as equally or even more significant for the reason that Moses went there to learn for as long or longer than before. We shall try later to throw more light on the profound riddle of the middle part of Moses' life, which is closely connected with the mysteries of the forty-year-long desert trek. Here, a glance at the major steps of destiny's course suffices: Through Egypt itself, Moses had matured at the age of forty for the rejection of Egypt. At eighty he was prepared for open battle and the positive overcoming of Egypt by what the middle years of his life had brought him. More and more clearly, the independent new Moses impulse which had awakened to its own potential confronted the aged Hermes culture.

1.8 Transformation of Consciousness

In order to comprehend this clash of two spiritual streams properly, we must consider yet another aspect of the great transformation and cosmic transition which gave that new age its special character. A significant change of consciousness among the bearers of that contemporary culture corresponded — as an earthly mirror image — to the death and disappearance of Osiris from the sphere that had been his until then. Osiris' death in the spiritual cosmos was paralleled by the death of the clairvoyant and magical faculties in the people of Egypt.

During the study of the age of the patriarchs, in which occurred the separation of the Israel stream from the fountainhead of the Babylonian and Chaldean culture, we repeatedly focused on the gradual extinction of Babylonia's ancient supersensory heritage and the conscious renunciation of the old clairvoyant capability by the Abraham stream. The beginning of the actual Babylonian Gilgamesh-culture fell into the 'Dark Age' (Kali Yuga), at the onset of which (around 3000 BC) a catastrophic regression of clairvoyant consciousness took place.[15]

This is why the Babylonian civilization was an exoteric culture in contrast to the marvellous pre-Babylonian culture of the Sumerians who were still esoterically ensouled with the radiance of ancient vision. Egypt's Hermes culture was older than the Gilgamesh culture of Mesopotamia. Running parallel with the flowering of Sumeria, its beginnings date back into ages which do not yet have to be designated as dark ones. Thus, the stream of the Israelite people, whose mission was in fact the purification of the human entity from the remnants of old supersensory soul forces, immersed itself in Egypt — taken there by Joseph, reader of dreams — in an esoteric magical culture that had emerged out of clairvoyant forces.

During the age of Moses, Egypt was also caught up in the process of the great cosmic twilight. With a special nuance for Egypt, a turn of time took place similar to the one that occurred when the Kali Yuga closed in upon all mankind.

1.9 The serpent symbol

To gain clear conceptions of the facts concerning the history of consciousness of that time, we must consider some of the animal symbols which dominate Egypt's cultic sculptures and also extend into the Old Testament descriptions. The serpent is of major importance here. On innumerable art works and many of Egypt's crowns for kings and priests, the Uraeus-snake raises its head with the royal neckplate that extends far beyond head and body. On the other side, we see how Moses, together with Aaron, vanquished the snakes of the magicians with his staff that had turned into a snake; we see how he erected a bronze serpent in the desert to heal the people from the bites of the fiery vipers.

In the whole antique world, this symbol was the expression for the old supersensory forces in the human being. Rudolf Steiner once said:[16] 'In ancient times there was a technical expression for this. Those who could look into the divine-spiritual world and could become witnesses of it were called "serpents".'

The symbol of the snake causes us to look at the major stages of humanity's evolution of consciousness. In pre-Christian times, human consciousness had suffered two drastic contractions. The first occurred in the course of the Lemurian epoch and is designated by the myth of the Fall. At that time, the human being lost the divine consciousness of primal revelation and, as the divine light subsequently diminished, exchanged it for the very first seed of self-consciousness. The result of this first diminution was the clairvoyant consciousness from which the inspired civilizations of antiquity were born.

The second great contraction took place with the onset of the Dark Age and brought about the twilight of ancient clairvoyance. In the now progressively darkening perceptual life, the human being could attain a new stage of egohood by means of the intellectual head consciousness.

The snake symbolizes human consciousness in the condition that existed between the two contractions. In the age of Moses and later as well,* this image was understood to represent the perpetual state which — although man already 'knew what was good and evil' and therefore possessed the beginning of 'I'-consciousness — still produced the not yet completely shrunken cosmic consciousness.

Biblical mythology traces the consciousness represented in the image of the snake back to the serpent in paradise as its inaugurator. The first great contraction of consciousness, caused by the snake in the distant past, was accompanied also by significant metamorphoses of the corporeal human being, and only through them can the snake image really be comprehended in all exactitude.

It was then that, in regard to the evolution of his body, the human being advanced from a condition of having no vertebrae

---

*In the words, for example, that John the Baptist directed to the Pharisees: 'You sons of vipers!' (Matt.3:7*B*)

to development of a spine. Two evolutionary stages of the physical human organization followed one upon the other, which, as in two cosmic images of recollection, can be traced even today in the invertebrates and the vertebrates. In one of his earliest anthroposophical lectures, Rudolf Steiner spoke about the significant difference and evolutionary progress between these two species of living beings.[17] The invertebrate animals possess only the nervous system which in man becomes the solar plexus. Therefore, they are not yet bearers of an individual consciousness but 'perceptual organs of the common earth soul'. The possibility of a separation from the common earth soul occurs where the solar nervous system is confined in the column of the spine. Thereby, on a very first rudimentary level, the possibility arises of saying 'I'. The snake is the creature in which the spine makes its appearance in the animal kingdom. The esoteric teachers told the pupils: If you look at the snake you behold the symbol for your 'I'. Moses received such sentiments while in the Egyptian schools. The Fall actually signified the incorporation of the 'serpent' into the being of man. The consciousness, which thereby came into being, was still active in its last remnants as ancient clairvoyance during the age of Moses in Egypt. How can we picture this consciousness in the configuration of the psycho-physical human organization?

When presenting the primordial age and the time of the patriarchs, anthroposophical descriptions were frequently referred to, according to which in those epochs the human etheric body still extended beyond the physical body. Only gradually shrinking in size, it came to coincide with the physical body and its organs. By virtue of the body-free part of the etheric head, the human beings of ancient times possessed the faculty of clairvoyantly seeing into the supersensory world; because the etheric body extended also at the feet beyond the human form into the earth, man was still intimately linked with the earth and its life. If a human being placed himself in a condition of perception, something that in those ages was not accomplished with the physical brain but with the etheric body, he awakened the serpent within himself. Rudolf Steiner describes it as follows:[18]

A man in that ancient time who experienced [that] . . . would say, 'The serpent has become active within me.'
His being had been extended into the earth. He felt his

physical body not as the active part of him, but that a serpent-like appendage of himself stretched into the earth and the head was what stuck out of the earth. He felt this serpent being to be the thinker. . . . So, in ancient times, to apprehend something meant: '. . . I feel my serpent nature.'

How did the extinction of clairvoyance make itself felt in the being of man?

It was to be no longer possible for man to feel himself extended into the earth through his limbs and feet. Also, feeling had to die away in his ether body, and had to pass instead into his physical head. If you correctly picture this change you will find it well expressed by saying. 'One is wounded in the feet but with his own body he crushes the serpent's head.' Which means, the serpent's head ceases to be the organ for thinking. The physical brain kills the serpent, which takes revenge by withdrawing man's feeling of belonging to the earth. It bites one on the heel.

The prophetic verse in the Bible, directed to the serpent after the Fall, 'he shall bruise your head, and you shall bruise his heel' (Gen. 3:15) is fulfilled by the transformation of consciousness that took place in the age of Moses. Although even into the Christian era, there was no lack of streams such as the Naassenes and Ophites (from the Hebrew term, *nachash*, and the Greek, *ophis*, the snake), that strove to retain the old condition of the etheric body as the only divine one and therefore worshipped the serpent, the age of the snake was really over now.

1.10 The horns of the ram

Another animal symbol that we encounter frequently in the late Egyptian culture and the Bible's picture world is the image of the ram or the lamb. In our study of the age of the patriarchs, we already had to discuss the image of the sacrificed ram in which the scene of Isaac's sacrifice culminates. Later, as the most important expression of Israel's severance from Egypt, Moses inaugurated the Easter sacrifice of the paschal lamb. Finally, Moses himself confronts us as the great ram among men, depicted as he is by painters and sculptors of all time — most mightily by Michelangelo — with powerfully raised horns of light.

On old paintings or sketches picturing Moses, we always see two luminous cones of brilliant light rays that shine forth from Moses' forehead. Because of the differing means of expression, sculptural tradition is already led to utilize a symbol of equal image quality, that of the ram's horns. Michelangelo's is the most impressive one of them all.

In the duality of the Moses representation with the cones of light rays on one hand and, on the other, the ram's horns, we confront one of the most interesting riddles of the Old Testament. In one case where the biblical books show us how Moses returns from the mountain of divine revelation with amazingly trans-formed countenance and demeanor, the Greek and the Latin translations interpret the original Hebrew text very differently. The customary English translations, even those of the Roman Catholic church which elsewhere always adheres to the Latin Vulgate, here follow the interpretation of the Greek text (Exod.34:29f, author's italics):

> When Moses came down from Mount Sinai, with the two tables of the testimony in his hand as he came down from the mountain, Moses did not know that the skin of his face *shone* because he had been talking with God. And when Aaron and all the people of Israel saw Moses, behold, the skin of his face shone, and they were afraid to come near him.

In contrast to this, the Vulgate does not say that his countenance shone but that it was 'horned'.

The puzzling anomaly of the Latin text has on occasion been relegated to an error in writing rather than one of translation. Newspaper headlines 'Writing error with consequences for thou-sands of years' popularized the theological thesis that instead of the words *facies coronata* (the countenance illuminated by a corona), somebody erroneously wrote: *facies cornuta* (the horned countenance). Here, we are dealing with more than a mere error in writing or translation. The original Hebrew text combines these two seemingly far-apart possibilities of interpretation into one, inasmuch as a close connection exists between the words 'radiate' (*qaran*) and 'horn' (*qeren*). This could well derive from the fact that this language reaches back into times when a horn was considered an earthly, solidified and hardened form of light rays. What is shaped in physical solidification and hardening as horns in the animal kingdom, for instance in the ram, appeared in primordial times on the human forehead in the two-petalled lotus flower in the form of light and rays. The spirit sense-organ that was the last to be extinguished in man, who was becoming a thinking, conscious being, was an organ of light horns.

From this viewpoint, the variance between the different Bible translations as well as between the artistic representations becomes comprehensible. When it was no longer possible to make anything of the physical horns supposedly attributed to Moses, Bible translations moved away from the possible interpretation given such compact expression in the Vulgate. The great sculptors such as Michelangelo nevertheless dared to depict Moses with ram horns.

Finally, the variance between the auric cones of lightrays and the physically tangible horns in the texts and pictures illuminates the level of spiritual history and that of the consciousness embodied in Moses. Moses was not really the representative of that human nature that still had full use of the original radiance and visionary power of the two-petalled lotus flower. In Moses, the human brain began irrevocably to take the place of the spirit organs once borne by the etheric body; thinking directed by the self came into place instead of dreamy undirected vision.

This transition may have shown itself to imaginative sight in such a way that a darkening and hardening process in the hornlike light cones became perceptible with the same compactness they have in the animal kingdom in the horns of the ram and other horn-bearing animals. The spirit-historical truth concerning the nature of Moses does in fact lie between the two variances of the Greek and the Latin interpretation and of paintings and sculptures.

Because of the Amon cult of Thebes which dominated the life of the country prior to and after Akhenaton's rule, Egypt stood completely under the sign of the ram symbol during the times of the great transition; for the god Amon, later equated with Jupiter-Zeus, was represented with the head and horns of a ram. Across from the royal city of Thebes, on the other side of the Nile, a long avenue lined with marble ram-sphinxes led from the city of priests, Karnak, to the temples of Luxor. Another such avenue of rams led at right angles to it from the Nile's shore to the huge western gate of Karnak, continuing into the temple area in a gigantic avenue of columns with high lotus capitals. Those who walked here down to the Nile looked through the hauntingly alive line of ram-sphinxes straight across and up to the splendid wide frontal flight of steps of the cave temple of Deir el Bahri, the centre of Thebes. These avenues, rich in symbols, conjure forth from the depths of the past the image of magnificent ceremonious processions of priests. We see them solemnly move forward between the closely aligned figures of ram-sphinxes that speak of the gods' doings to the passers-by like magically animated images. And among the highest dignitaries of the procession, we behold the initiated son of Pharaoh, Moses, adorned with the royal emblems. The many stone-ram idols' mysterious eyes follow the human ram as if they awaited their salvation from him.

The clairvoyant faculty of earlier mankind derived from the fact that the etheric body, which had not yet come to coincide with the physical body, allowed for body-free cognition by the soul organs, called 'lotus flowers' in the ancient world. In the human organism something took place that can be discerned with beautiful clarity from nature's similes outside. The lotus flowers that bloom in solemn tranquillity on the temple ponds of India and Egypt thrive as long as the element of water shields them from the hard earth of the shore. In like manner, the lotus flowers of the human soul-being floated, lucidly alert, on the quietly flowing mirror surface of the etheric body as long as it still freely streamed around the solid form of the physical body. But then, losing its cosmic body-free state, the etheric body bore the lotus flowers close to the shores of the physical body, where they withered and lost the power of supersensory perception.

The organ that shone in the middle of the etheric forehead — in primeval times high above the physical forehead like a star — is the two-petalled lotus flower. When the world of ancient vision still existed in undiminished form, this organ was experienced as the serpent's pair of eyes. The proudly erect head of the uraeus snake on the coronet above the forehead of an initiate gives a picture of this spiritual member of man. And it is an intensification of the picture if the twofold petal-nature of the forehead's lotus flower is once again mirrored in the duality of the Uraeus heads. When, after the beginning of the 'dark age,' the etheric body shrank and adjusted to the physical form and configuration of its organs, the etheric head of man maintained its body-free grandeur longest. The two-petalled lotus flower still blossomed into a certain light of vision when its sisters had already turned dark, but it was now experienced and perceived in a different imaginative picture. No longer was vision with this forehead-organ a condition of soul occurring at any time as a matter of course. Only through the assistance of his personal will could man still arrive at clairvoyant perception by means of the two members of the spiritual eye on his forehead. This is why the imaginative picture of the serpent-heads was replaced by that of the ram horns. When a man clairvoyantly beheld something through the body-free part of his etheric body, it was as if the ram raised its horns.

Although referring to a later age than that of Moses, when the 'I' had begun to be effective, Rudolf Steiner described this transition similarly:[19] 'Henceforth, man no longer beheld the creative forces of the etheric body in the image of a snake but in that of the lamb.'

The next step in the 'I'-development of consciousness, the extinction of even the last two-petalled lotus flower, was brought about by the coincidence of the etheric head with the physical outline of the skull. The sun-ram died on the Calvary of the human head, the lamb was sacrificed so that instead of the clairvoyance before the birth of the self, self-imbued thinking could dwell on human foreheads as the royal seed of freedom. In the future, mankind will struggle towards a resurrection of consciousness. As if borne aloft on eagle-wings, thinking will again soar to vision of the spirit. The two-petalled lotus flower will gain new life, no longer in the image of serpent heads or ram horns but that of eagle wings. Egypt therefore pictured the god Horus, in whom Osiris was resurrected, as a falcon. The path leads from the serpent to the eagle. There are crowns on Egyptian representations of gods which, in their manifoldness, reveal an awareness of the whole death and resurrection process of the human spirit. The two curved ram horns support the whole design: Above them, in the centre, rests the golden sun disc; two uraeus snakes crowned with small suns raise their heads on each side; two tall feathers of the Horus falcon proudly stand atop the large sun-disc.

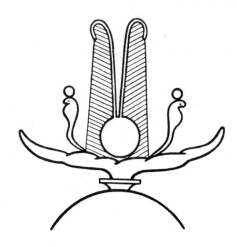

Egyptian crown of deity with ram horns, uraeus serpents and Horus-falcon wings (from Brugsch, Religion, 585).

Many temple inscriptions that have been preserved reveal the same secret. All the stages of the forehead lotus flower are linked together:[20]

Hail to thee, Min Amon, thine is a beautiful sight to see!
The two horns are standing up.
Lord of the coronet with the tall pair of feathers.
Beautifully encircled with a tall white crown,
The royal serpents of South and North belong to him. . . .

In the hymns of ancient tradition, the process of vision is always exalted in the same images:

A concealed ram rises up from the primordial waters as
the world still dwells in darkness. And it opens its eyes
in order to light up the world. The two celestial bodies,
the sun and the moon, appear: its right eye and its left
one.[21]

The sun that exists from the primordial beginning rises
like a falcon out of the centre of the lotus flower's calyx.

44

When the portals of its petals open in their sapphire
radiance of colour, night is parted from day. Like the holy
serpent, thou risest up, a life-bearing spirit that brings
about the sunrise and, formed magnificently, shines forth
in the sun's boat.[22]

The Book of the Dead, dating from an earlier age, allows still
deeper insight into the same secrets:[23]

'I am the god Amsu [Chim] in his coming forth; may his
two plumes be set upon my head for me.'

Who then is this?

Amsu is Horus, the avenger of his father, and his coming
forth is his birth. The plumes upon his head are Isis and
Nephthys when they go forth to set themselves there, even
as his protectors, and they provide that which his head
lacketh, or (as others say), They are the two exceeding
great uraei which are upon the head of their father Tem
[Aton], or (as others say), His two eyes are the plumes
which are upon his head.

'Osiris Ani, the scribe of all holy offerings, riseth up in
his place in triumph, he cometh into his city.'

What then is this?

It is the horizon of his father Tem.

1.11 The sacrifice of the lamb

We are now able to comprehend exactly what Moses' destiny and
mission of consciousness consisted of in the evening twilight of
Egyptian life. Moses was the lofty human ram; he was still in full
possession of the ram's power, the last clairvoyance, that shone
on the forehead of man. Yet he was already capable of developing
the force that was to dominate the next great epoch of human
spiritual evolution: on his noble brow, man's royal thinking was
born; he was the great guide out of the dreamland of ancient
vision into the wakeful land of thought. In order not merely to
endure the great transition of consciousness of that turning point
of time but to execute it actively so that it would be effective for
all humanity, Moses had to undergo a sacrifice. In a sense, he
had to repeat the Isaac sacrifice and carry it further.

Let us consider the sacrifice of Isaac once again. The Israelite task was to inaugurate a hereditary stream from which the remnants of the old spiritual soul-forces were increasingly eliminated. Those who, like Haran, Lot, Ishmael, Esau, and Joseph, were bearers of ancient magic clairvoyant forces, could not continue the 'chosen' line and therefore became propagators of side developments apart from the pure Israel stream. Isaac also was not immediately suited to continue the folk line since he possessed the ancient solar clairvoyance of the two-petalled lotus flower. He would have had to be sacrificed if the possibility had not existed for him to offer up the sacrifice of the spirit heritage alive in him, as the Bible describes in imaginative style. Rudolf Steiner describes this:[24]

> In place of Isaac, a ram, or lamb, was offered up. What
> does that mean? . . . It was necessary to give up all
> vestiges of dreamy old clairvoyance . . . any in-pouring of
> revelations such as exist in all other religions of antiquity
> including the Chaldean and Egyptian religions. Every last
> gift from the spiritual world had to be renounced. The
> last gift from the spirit world that still remains after all the
> earlier ones have become extinct is designated in mystical
> symbolism by means of the ram. The two ram horns refer
> to the sacrifice of the two-petalled lotus flower. In order
> to maintain Isaac's corporeality in the [desired]
> configuration, the last clairvoyant faculty, the gift of the
> ram, the two-petalled lotus flower . . . is sacrificed.

But what was distilled from the stream of the inherited blood line had to be brought back afterwards from outside into Israel's spiritual life as a cultural enrichment. In Egypt, the Israelites submerged themselves for four hundred years in a culture that was the fruit of the ancient gift of clairvoyance offered up by Isaac. The people's sojourn in Egypt was the spiritual return of the sacrifice, which had to be brought by Isaac for the corporeal development of Israel. In Moses, this return culminated. The ram, which had been killed at Isaac's sacrifice, lived again in Moses through the Egyptian initiation; its horns crowned the forehead of Moses.

But in the nature of things, nothing final could be intended with the return of that part of Isaac's soul which had once upon a time been offered up. All mankind was nearing the point where even the last remnant of the ancient spirit heritage became extinct, where the lamb died on Calvary, the place on the skull of man. The ram power that had been sacrificed in Isaac was brought back in a cultural sense only to be offered up again through Moses. The difference between Isaac's age and that of Moses is the following: Isaac lived in the midst of a world in which the forces of the serpent and the ram were still active everywhere; his sacrifice was therefore nothing more than a renunciation for the sake of a path to be opened up into the future. Moses, on the other hand, was placed into a great twilight of the gods; the old spiritual forces finally became extinct everywhere, mankind was threatened with a fearsome dark void. The sacrifice of the ram, freely made by Isaac, had no more meaning if it only took place as a renunciation, for the loss was imminent anyway. Moses had to conduct the sacrifice of the ram in the sense of a transformation; he had to change the ram's power by will into a force that could be carried over into the future.

We have already once mentioned the important parallel events of the Moses age that occurred in the dawn of Europe. The Trojan War had been preceded there by the migration, which in mythology found its expression in the journey of the Argonauts. Under the guidance of the divine bard Orpheus, the mighty leaders of emerging Europe travelled to Colchis to acquire the Golden Fleece, the sun-radiant fleece of the divine ram that found its death in the first hour of the birth of Greek life. Behind the myth, the following is concealed: The impulses for an independent Greco-European culture, which could struggle free from Asian tutelage a hundred years later in Troy, were brought from a mystery centre where the ram force had already been subjected to a transformation. When the ram has died on the forehead of man, when the two-petalled lotus flower dies down as an eye of vision, then, as a recollection of the vision, of the Golden Fleece of the ram, *thought* remains. Thinking is transformed vision. The whole of Greek culture grew out of a thinking in which the golden memory of former vision was still reflected. Even Plato still said that our ideas are recollections of what once was beheld in the spirit realm. This was the culture of the Golden Fleece.

For the Egyptian and Palestinian culture sphere, it was Moses who had to carry out the transformation of ancient clairvoyance into the power of thought. In this way, he had to continue the Isaac sacrifice.

All around him, the world of the god Amon, who bore the form of a ram, spread out powerfully and demandingly. A hundred years earlier, Akhenaton had waged his tragic and futile struggle against this world. Egypt was not ready for the Isaac sacrifice; it continued the ram worship although the ram force was dying down everywhere. A vacuum was left particularly in the Amon cult, which now could not help but fall into untruth, decadence and demonic possession. When he led the people of Israel out of Egypt, Moses set up a symbol, by means of which his people were to find the will and readiness to proclaim that they would reconcile themselves to the great turning point of consciousness, and to help in the transformation of soul forces: He inaugurated the annual sacrifice of the paschal lamb. Thereby, what had been the mystery renunciation of one individual in Isaac's case becomes a fact involving mankind.

1.12 Aaron and the sacred bull

Apart from the ram force of ancient clairvoyance, Egypt still possessed another spiritual faculty dating back to the source of ancient capabilities: the magical word. Egypt exuded a monumental static greatness that originated in the supreme authority of the priestly traditions, as laid down in the sacred scriptures and brought out suggestively by means of the still retained word-magic. Just as the last clairvoyant faculty was linked to the spiritual part of the human forehead and the ram symbol, the word-magic was connected with the spiritual part of the larynx and the image of the bull. Through training, the Egyptian priests tried to retain the condition where the etheric larynx and mouth did not yet coincide with the corresponding physical organs; consequently, the spoken word and language were not as dead as they are today, but were filled with a supersensory life that became effective in sound. The awe-filled awareness that the word of the god can resound in the word of man was kept alive in the ancient centres of northern Egypt by means of the bull symbol and the sight of the sacred Apis Bull. One need only climb down into the dark catacombs below the ground of the Saqqara sand desert to the twenty-five monumental stone sarcophagi that stand in a row there side by side with the mummies of the sacred bulls, to be touched — although these graves date from a later age — by the breath of ancient Egyptian magic that had its source in the bull-like power of the priestly word.

The bull force reaches back into older epochs and in some respects expressed the nature of Egyptian culture even more directly than does the ram. The age of the Babylonian-Egyptian culture, designated in Anthroposophy as the third post-Atlantean culture epoch (2907–747 BC), was determined by the vernal sun's rising in the sign of the bull (Taurus) from where it shone its forces in a formative way into the human organism. The formation of the specific organ, which man owes to the sun's spring equinox in Taurus, is the speech-producing larynx. Therefore, in the age of Moses, the word-magic conserved by the Egyptian priests was not only an expression of the gifts of the gods that had been received in the sacred past, but also of the ruling spirit. Only half a millennium later (in the fourth post-Atlantean, Greco-Roman period, 747 BC – AD 1413), the vernal sun would enter the sign of the ram (Aries); from there, it would illuminate the spiritual part of the human forehead and fashion it into the site of the spirit-recollecting thinking.

Moses was therefore really ahead of his time. But in regard to the zodiacal signs, the cultural epochs are not sharply distinguished from one another. By the middle of one epoch the effects of the following celestial sign are added to the effects of the preceding one. Hence, with the age of Moses, the forces of the sign of the ram begin to influence the bull culture; they receive a distorted image in the Amon cult, in Moses a pure one.

But to confront Egypt's darkened magic force, Moses found there was something lacking in him. How could he, the ram-man, be victorious over the bull-magic of Egyptian priesthood? This was the question with which he replied, after forty years of seclusion, to the spiritual power that was calling him: 'I am slow of speech and of tongue' (Exod.4:10). In order to compensate for the inadequacy, Aaron was placed at his side for Aaron shared in the word-magic nurtured in Egypt. As an aid, the bull-man stood at the side of the ram-man; beside the bearer of the future stood the contemporary man who was still to a large degree indebted to the past. Later on, Aaron would be paying his tribute to the powers of the past insofar as he abided by the desire of the people in the desert to return to Egypt; he restored the image of the golden bull-deity (the 'golden calf') and lent his hand to a relapse into the outdated magical cults of Egypt.

With the help of Aaron's magical forces, Moses overcame Egypt in the spiritual battle assigned to him. The Bible gives imaginative descriptions of the two brothers' appearance before Pharaoh and the ten plagues that they conjure up over Egypt. Such imaginative descriptions must not be misunderstood as of grotesque external miracles, but interpreted clearly into outer historical conceptions.

First we are told that by divine command Aaron throws his staff on the ground before Pharaoh and that it turns into a snake. The Pharaoh calls for his sages and magicians who also turn their staffs into snakes but the serpent from Aaron's staff devours the other snakes.

What external occurrence took place there? Moses, son of Pharaoh, who had been missing for forty years, has suddenly reappeared. It must have caused a great stir. Eighty years old, with a companion three years older, he appeared before the ruler. Let us assume that it was Rameses II, whose sharply edged facial outlines in the crumbled mummy reveal to this day the tyrannical greed for power, the paranoia, and at the same time a cold ruthlessness. Aaron begins to speak. His words have the magic effect whereby all those present are placed into the condition of visionary sight, the serpent's stirrings. The sorcerers of Egypt pit their speech against Aaron's, theirs also causes visions. But against the images of future events that Aaron calls forth, the forces conjured up by the Egyptians become lifeless phantoms. Egypt's power is extinguished.

Legend describes in a graphic manner the appearance of Moses and Aaron at the Pharaoh's court after Moses' forty-year absence. The veil of the imaginative description is often quite transparent here for the external historical course of events. It is said that the Pharaoh had just concluded a ceremonious matter of state during which all the kings had paid homage to him, when he received the report that two old men stand outside the portal. Pharaoh asked whether they wore crowns. When told they did not, he gave the order not to admit them. But at this very moment Moses and Aaron entered the hall. The lions guarding the entrance to the palace had, upon encountering them, become quiet and tame and followed behind like obedient dogs. Now, Moses and Aaron bore witness to their divine mandate before Pharaoh and his whole court. Pharaoh summoned his wise men so that they could refute Moses and Aaron. Seventy learned scribes were in service to the Pharoah, each one of them master of a different script and language.[25]

But when the scribes beheld Moses and Aaron and saw
their forms which resembled that of angels, their height
that of the cypresses of Lebanon, their eyes bright as stars
. . . their countenance shining like the sun, and in addition
the staff of God . . . and when they heard their speech
which flashcd forth out of their mouths like sparks — they
were overcome by fear and trembling . . . they dropped
their writing-reeds out of their hands and the scrolls from
their shoulders and prostrated themselves on the ground
before Moses and Aaron.

Nevertheless Pharaoh commanded that they enter into the dispute.

'Wait, I shall have the chests brought in, where, since time
immemorial, our scrolls are kept: There are letters the
first kings who existed from the creation of the earth, and
those of the first wielders of power who ruled over the
universe. I shall have them read by the scribes in all seventy
languages; perhaps there is a text among them with the
name of your god!'

The chests were brought in and the proclamation of Moses and Aaron was confronted with Egypt's ancient handed-down word. But the name, with whose power and in whose behalf the two men had come before Pharaoh was not found anywhere in the holy scripts of any of the languages. Moses and Aaron were, after all, emissaries of a completely new human principle. The Pharoah wanted to turn them away and called his curse down upon them. But now it became evident — this is related in the scene of the serpents, which is kept wholly in the imaginative style, as in the biblical report — that Moses and Aaron were also superior to the Egyptian wise men and magicians in the usage of the ancient clairvoyant forces.

1.13 The ten plagues

The biblical narration follows next with the description of the plagues: the transformation of all water into blood, the plague of frogs, and so on up to the great darkness and the slaying of the first-born. What happened is that Moses and Aaron now appeared before all the Egyptian people just as earlier they had appeared before Pharaoh. Again, it was Aaron, bearer of the word-magic, who opened the battle with the same weapon that Egypt fought with. At the shore of the Nile, he addressed a group, which need not have been a large one. A certain excitement had already taken hold of the people anyway. Some sort of dark calamity, so they all sensed, was in the air. The spiritual dusk had begun to be an instinctive experience of the people. This is why, as they listened to what Aaron had to say, the most gruesome visions arose before these people, visions of such density and fearfulness that they obtruded over all physical perception and had to be taken as tangible reality. In a turbulent way, Aaron's word once again called forth from their souls the diminishing ancient forces of vision; but the formerly clear vision had turned into hideous black vision. The images of fright spread contagiously like a virulent epidemic over the whole land. In vain, the Egyptian magicians tried to put a stop to the calamity; instead, they achieved the opposite result. They too addressed the people — the Bible explicitly states concerning the first three plagues: 'the magicians of Egypt did the same to their secret arts' (Exod.7:22; 8:7; 8:18) — but lo, the same frightening visions emerged from their words as from those of Aaron. Against their will, they fought on the side of their own opponents. They helped spread the plagues of blood and the frogs over the whole land and the people. Not until the third plague did a change occur: the word of the magicians now no longer had any effect at all; it did not even bring about the Aaron-effects; it had finally become powerless.

The supposition that the ten plagues do not deal with physical but with soul events appears to be at the basis everywhere of apocryphical tradition and is often expressed with classic distinctness. The ancient Wisdom of Solomon (17:4–20), gives us a description of the plague of darkness that broke in over all of Egypt while the Israelites walked about in bright daylight:

> For not even the inner chamber that held them protected
> them from fear,
> but terrifying sounds rang out around them,
> and dismal phantoms with gloomy faces appeared.
> And no power of fire was able to give light,
> nor did the brilliant flames of the stars
> avail to illumine that hateful night.
> . . .
> But throughout the night, which was really powerless,
> . . .
> they all slept the same sleep,
> and now were driven by monstrous spectres,
> and now were paralyzed by their souls' surrender,
> for sudden and unexpected fear overwhelmed them.
> Whether there came a whistling wind, or a melodious
> sound of birds in wide-spreading branches,
> or the rhythm of violently rushing water,
> or the harsh crash of rocks hurled down,
> it paralyzed them with terror.
> For the whole world was illumined with brilliant light,
> and was engaged in unhindered work.

In describing the last plague, the slaying of the first-born, the legends relate: 'In the houses, where the first-born had already died, the dead person appeared to his family members to die before them once again.'[26]

From this, one can easily gain an understanding of the visionary nature of the whole event.

Were these arbitrary images of fear that broke in upon the Egyptians through the word-effects of Aaron and the spiritual power of Moses? Was the sole purpose of the plagues to frighten and punish the hard-hearted Egyptians? In exact apocalyptic picture-sequence, Egypt beheld its own Last Judgment. As if they were occurrences of the external world the various acts of the drama of consciousness which played itself out in their own soul-configuration, arose before the people involved. The twilight of gods and souls and, connected with it, the ever deeper descent of the human soul and spirit into the hard physical body was completed in a way akin to a catastrophe as great cosmic horrors of night frightened the souls into themselves. The transformation of water into blood was the outwardly projected downward plunge of one's own being which up to now had been able to dwell in pure body-free streams of ether, into the depths of the blood. It all was an incarnation process resembling a roaring tempest or an earthquake. The soul could no longer hover dreamily over the body; in painful terror, it had to let itself be forced into the body. The vision of the frogs emerged everywhere out of the water as the astral body was thrown towards the solid physical corporeality, having suddenly been pressed and forced into the shrinking etheric body. People in a sickening way experienced how, now as soul embryos, they once again slipped into their bodies, and they beheld this process imaginatively in the picture of the countless frogs. All the other plagues were but further steps in the loss of the spirit and the gods, that came about through the frighteningly deep plunge into the physical body. The plague of darkness formed the sudden complete cut-off of the soul from the cosmic, astral world's light, into visionary experience. And behind the death of the first-born was concealed the fall of the 'I', the son who is born within, from the starry heights into the ghostly dark skeleton of physical man. The first earthly 'I'-experience moved into Egyptian humanity as fear of death.

One way or another, the great transformation of consciousness did take place at that time. It affected those who fought against it, wanting to cling to the old faculties of spirit, as horrifying sequences of terror. The more desperately they had held on to the ancient supersensory experience, the more vehement and fearful had to be their fall now. Moses guided his people to accept the death of consciousness willingly. What was a frightful plague to the Egyptians was willed sacrifice for the Israelites. The offering of the paschal lamb was the cultic expression for the compliance with destiny to which Moses wanted to lead his people.

1.14 The passage through the Sea of Reeds

One event stands for the most fundamental sealing of Egypt's twilight and its replacement by Israel. It is an event that is to be understood as a simple natural event, not, as is usually the case, as an incomprehensible miracle: the Israelites' passage through the Sea of Reeds and the drowning of the pursuing Pharaonic army in the sea. The biblical description of the waves that form into walls, leaving a dry passage free in the middle, is meant in an imaginative way. Legendary traditions reveal that in regard to the actual physical event, they can indeed find a natural explanation compatible with this imaginative description. They laud the tribe of Benjamin and especially one Nahshon, a member of the tribe of Judah, for the stout-hearted courage to be the first to plunge into the waves and thus to encourage all the others who are following.[27] Does this not presuppose the idea of wading through a part of the sea that can still be crossed at this point because of low-tide. But soon afterwards, as high-tide follows, destruction meets those who dare venture in. The difference that first became obvious through the great visions of terror in the ten plagues now culminated on the physical plane in a difference in comportment toward the processes of nature. The miraculous aspect in the Israelites' rescue from the flood waters of the Sea of Reeds is not found in the external circumstances but in the difference between Moses' consciousness and that of the Egyptians.

Rudolf Steiner describes the ancient clairvoyance being linked with a telling intuition for weather conditions and life processes in nature; people were capable of regulating their conduct thereby. During the rightful period of their culture, the Egyptians had been gifted to a special degree with these faculties of an instinct for nature. But along with the ancient vision, this intuitive ability was extinguished:

> for human beings were supposed to learn to see through
> the configurations of the external elements with their
> intellect and, still out of clairvoyant consciousness, Moses
> was supposed to give the impulse for this. There, we see
> Moses confronting the Red Sea with his people. And by
> means of his knowledge, which is similar to ours but in
> his case is still translated into the clairvoyant element, he

recognizes how, through the natural events (a special relationship between an easterly wind and the course of the tides of the sea) a possibility exists to lead his people through the sea during an advantageous hour . . . Moses stands there as the inaugurator of the new intellectualized world view . . . which will teach human beings anew how to bring life's practical aspects into harmony with the conditions of nature . . . The Egyptians were a people whose time was over . . . The ancient natural instincts had declined . . . and they could not find their way into the new intellectual consciousness. Therefore they faced the Red Sea, helplessly confused by their no longer appropriate consciousness, and succumbed to disaster. We thus see Moses' new element clearly contrasted against the old; we see the extent to which ancient clairvoyance had deteriorated so that it doubted itself and brought about its own downfall by no longer fitting into the new age.[28]

When the waters of the Sea of Reeds separated the two nations that had lived side by side for four hundred years, two states of consciousness separated from one another, and along with that two great epochs of humanity's history.

1.15 The coffin of Joseph

Both the biblical and the apocryphal tradition place special emphasis on one pictorial detail during the exodus from Egypt: 'And Moses took the bones of Joseph with him' (Exod.13:19). The legends show us Moses searching for Joseph's coffin. In the royal tombs of Thebes, he climbed from one crypt to the next without success. Finally, he had the idea that Joseph's coffin must be resting on the bottom of the River Nile. So he stood on the shore of the Nile and 'right away, Joseph's coffin left the bottom and floated upwards like a reed. Moses, however, lifted it upon his shoulders and went on his way with it.'[29]

Other legends relate that Moses took Joseph's cup, which once the brothers had found concealed in the grain in Benjamin's sack, and broke it into four pieces.

On one piece he carved the image of a lion, on another

one that of an eagle, on the third a bull, on the fourth a man. Then he stood by the river's edge and cast the piece with the lion into the water and called out: 'Joseph, the hour has come when Israel will be redeemed; the majesty of God, however, hesitates for your sake and the clouds of glory hesitate for your sake'.

But the shrine did not emerge. Then, Moses cast the image of the bull into the river and spoke the same words, but the coffin did not rise up. Then, Moses threw the eagle's image into the water and repeated the plea. But the ark with the bones of Joseph did not appear. Finally, he cast the image of man into the stream and lo, Joseph's coffin floated up. Then, Moses reached out his hand and took hold of the ark.[30]

Here we confront a significant imagination which rounds out the time that Israel spent in Egypt. Just as Noah once carried Adam's remains with him through the great flood into the land of the future,[31] so Moses carried Joseph's remains through the desert. Noah brought out the changing heritage of paradisal humanity. Moses carried the quintessence of Egyptian spiritual life, insofar as it was compatible with Israel's spiritual life and could appear embodied in the Egyptian-Israelite Joseph. Moses had the task of restoring in a spiritual manner those components of Israel's nature that had once been eliminated from the genetic stream. In Moses, who was capable of its spiritual transformation, the faculty once offered up by Isaac lived again. By means of his Egyptian initiation, he reversed the expulsion of Joseph, the dreamer; completing the past four hundred years, he transformed Egyptian clairvoyance into Israelite power of thought and in a changed form reinstated Joseph's dream-gift in the culture of his people. In the coffin of Joseph that is carried across the desert we have a picture 'for the Egyptian wisdom that came to an end with Joseph and returned again with Moses'.[32] It is a picture for the return of the once expelled Joseph-nature, brought about by Moses.

The legendary scenes where Moses caused Joseph's coffin to rise out of the waters of the Nile, resemble the great Osiris-Adonis cult, where the coffin of the god was brought back out of the waters of the sea or the river on the third day. In this picture, the knowledge of an important secret of history is in fact expressed. The image of the initiation-coffin, the Osiris-Adonis ark, surrounds the Egyptian part of Moses' life. At the outset, the daughter of Pharaoh lifted 'the ark of bulrushes' from the Nile river; at the end, Moses fetched the 'ark of Joseph' out of the same waters. In Joseph, the youthful deity Osiris-Adonis who still shone brilliantly from his heaven seemed to find his human reflection. In the age of Moses, Egypt stood under the sign of the loss of Osiris, the twilight that occurred because of Osiris' death, and it turned the initiates into sombre 'sons of the widow'. Osiris had left the heaven of Egypt; where did he live on? In the lecture already quoted about the death of Osiris, Rudolf Steiner gives an answer that will occupy us in more detail in the next chapter and which is also a contribution to an understanding of the image of the Joseph-coffin that is carried along by Moses:[33]

> For the karma of Egypt was fulfilled in such a way that not
> only was Moses initiated into the Mysteries of Egypt, but
> he took them with him. When he led his people out of
> Egypt he took with him the part of the Egyptian Initiation
> which added the Osiris-Initiation to the mourning Isis, as
> she later became. Such was the transition from the
> Egyptian civilisation to that of the Old Testament. Truly,
> Moses had carried away the secret of Osiris, the secret of
> the Cosmic Word!

The legends show us 'two arks' in the train of the migrating Israelites. 'Joseph's shrine moved, together with the ark of the testimony, through the desert with Israel and the nations of the world asked: What is the meaning of the two arks?'[34]

Past and future, the Osiris — and the Yahweh-secrets, are entwined in the figures of Joseph's coffin and the ark of the covenant into the journey through the desert.

The image of the altar-shrine that is carried up ahead by the priests as in a procession is already a most notable link between Israel's spiritual life and the world of Egyptian cults. The externally emerging cult of the Egyptians was characterized especially by such processions where the Osiris chest, the 'holy coffer' containing symbolic objects, was carried at the head of a procession.

Desert Journey – Jethro – Sinai Revelation

2. The Birth of Israel's Yahweh Culture

2.1 The significance of the desert

Israel's *birth as a people*, embodied in the figures of the patriarchs Abraham and Jacob, took place in foreign lands, within the spheres of Babylonia and Egypt. The *inauguration of its culture* occurred now through the creative leader-figure of Moses in the desert, in a desolate barren region of rock. The homelessness that was an attribute of these people, whose destiny was representative of all mankind, was intensified.

The forty-year-long desert sojourn by Israel appears in history as one of the most basic symbols. Every age that suffers from a difficult transitional fate orientates itself emotionally by this symbol. By becoming aware of itself and comprehending itself as involved in a 'journey through the desert', such an age is breaking through to the hopeful vista of an approaching land of fulfilment.

The weight of importance that was always attached to the image of the Israelite desert-fate could point away from the usual widely held opinion that this journey's purpose was no more than a relocation, a resettlement from the Nile area to the land of the Jordan. In order to reach Palestine from the eastern shore of the Nile delta, one would have needed forty days, not forty years.

The journey through the desert was anything but a matter of transporting people from one place to another. In it, a mysterious goal was concealed; it was a school, a trial, and at the same time a blessing; it was the stage for initiation of a people that included an innovative, far-reaching revelation. The more this journey's meaning is penetrated, the more mystery backgrounds and miracles of providence surprisingly open up.

The outward historical course of events that took place in the forty years is, to begin with, shrouded in heavy veils. Although they present a wealth of images, the biblical records, if rightly understood, intentionally add to the impossibility of easily drawing these veils away. We must slowly find our way from the clearly discernible soul aspect of the whole matter to the historical secrets.

In the rocky desert which Israel traversed, the people were supposed to find the earth, the now completely hardened sediment of cosmic evolution.

Before its age was over, Egypt had been more a land of heaven than of earth. Its whole culture derived from the insights of souls who had not yet descended completely into the hard physical corporeality and who therefore lived more in a clairvoyant observation of the supersensory sphere than a physical sense perception directed to the earthly world of objects. The people of Israel inhabited their physical bodies differently from the Egyptians. Since Abraham, a corporeality had been handed down through the generations that was characterized by the congruence of etheric body with physical body, which consequently brought about an ever more complete extinction of the old clairvoyance and an increasingly clear development of external sense perception and brain-thinking. Although organized to develop a consistent earthly consciousness for themselves, the Israelites had been surrounded and enveloped for four hundred years by an old celestial consciousness and its products. Only now, when Israel had left Egypt behind, they found an environment in the rocky, totally terrestrial desert that truly corresponded to their consciousness which had become terrestrial as well, an environment in which this consciousness could come into its own. In the desert, the Israelites were to find the earth and their own self.

2.2 Osiris, Yahweh, Christ

In the desert, the Israelites were meant to discover the divine being that belonged to them, above all else. The desert was intended to be the stage of a specific, divine revelation for them.

In order to comprehend this in a spiritually exact way, we must completely free ourselves of the present-day abstract, rigid conceptions of God that are quite erroneously applied to the biblical texts. For a world-view that includes the supersensory in a living way, the conception of the fullness of a divine spiritual world with many spheres and kingdoms of beings is not in contradiction to the thought of divine oneness. The world of hierarchical beings is an orderly one; in it, there exists at the highest level an all-encompassing being whom all the other evolving beings serve, for whom they make themselves translucent and transparent and in regard to whom they conduct themselves as do the individual limbs of the human body to the whole human being. Likewise, the idea of the eternal quality of the divine will does not actually contradict the conception that even in the realm of divine spiritual beings there exist destinies, transformations and developments. The gods too have their paths and goals; their service and activity only has meaning through the guiding will of the very highest being that leads them forward.

Out of such life-imbued conceptions of God, the theology of early Christianity could still form concepts through which the forty-year-long desert wanderings move into a wondrous light of divine purpose. It was Origen who brought the forty-two campsites, listed as the stations of the desert journey (Num. 33) into relation with the forty-two generations of Jesus' genealogy given at the beginning of the Gospel of Matthew. The campsites represent a spatial sequence, the generations a sequence in time. How can one view the spatial stations of a path as corresponding to the evolutionary stations of time in the Messianic lineage? This is possible if the image of a path is also discerned behind the sequence of generations. Early Christian theology beheld the divine Messianic Christ-being in pre-Christian times on its way from heaven to the earth, where, arriving finally, it incarnated as man in the figure of Jesus of Nazareth. On earth, in the course of time, the line of the Messianic generations moves forward step

61

by step. Each step corresponds in the spiritual realm to the Christ being's drawing nearer the earth. The ancestral genealogy from Abraham to Jesus with its forty-two names is the shadow image in time and history of the ladder from heaven to earth on which the Christ-being descends into incarnation.

Now, early Christian thinking experienced the forty-two stations of the desert journey as another reflection — condensed into forty years — of the same cosmic divine process. In order to translate Origen's symbolical manner into our modern form of thoughts more clearly and vividly one could say: The Israelites, seeking the earth in the desert, moved towards the Christ-being descending from heaven to earth in order to be able one day to receive him in their midst. This is the reason why the forty-two campsites correspond to the forty-two generations of the Messianic lineage.

Here we have touched upon a significant religious-historical relationship. We begin to approach the events in the divine spiritual world, the destinies of gods, that represent the celestial parallel to the twilight of Egypt taking place on earth and Israel's assuming the cultural leadership from Egypt.

We have spoken of the extinction of the Egyptian Osiris-life, the disappearance of Osiris from the sphere where the Egyptian initiates had formerly been able to encounter him. Osiris had ceased to reveal himself in Egypt. One who wanted to continue experiencing him had to depart from Egypt along with him. Where would he have had to go? We recall the words of Rudolf Steiner: 'When he led his people out of Egypt . . . Moses had carried away the secret of Osiris'.[35] But this indeed implies that henceforth the desert was the place where – although in a changed form — Osiris allowed himself to be found. Moses and the people of Israel ventured into the desert to follow the vanishing god. When the Yahweh deity revealed himself to them in the pillar of cloud and fire, in the fiery lightning of Sinai, they encountered the same divine power that earlier had proclaimed itself to the Egyptians in the figure of Osiris. The divine entity, whom Egypt indicated with the Osiris name, had come a step closer to the earth. Once, it had dwelt in the sun's heights; now, on its way to the earth, it has moved into the sphere of the earth's forces, the realm to which the migrating people were supposed to acclimatize themselves in the rocky desert.

Whether we say that Israel followed the god who left Egypt's heaven, or we say that Israel was wandering towards the god who was on his way from heaven to earth: either way, however falteringly, we try to express the same mystery. The same divine entity, who later arrived in the world of men and incarnated in the human being, Jesus of Nazareth, appeared in ancient times as Osiris to the Egyptian initiates and subsequently as Yahweh to the Israelites. Now it might seem that we want to lend support to a simple equation between Osiris, Yahweh and Christ. This is not the case. As a highest spirit being, the Christ-being undertook its journey to earth through the millennia of the ancient world, thereby passing from sphere to sphere. In each one, different hierarchical beings offered themselves to it as servants and sheaths. For ancient Egypt, a being of the higher angelic realms shone forth: Osiris; but Osiris was not Christ himself. The Christ-being appeared through and in him. Because the Christ is sun-luminous, and the Osiris being gave itself to him in a completely transparent manner, Osiris shone forth brightly for one cosmic hour on the spiritual firmament.

Then the Christ-being moved on, drawing closer to the earth. The Osiris light became dim and faded. Another entity now offered its service and gave itself as a sheath to the Christ, thus lighting up: Yahweh. Being a member of a higher hierarchy, however, and manifesting to a greater measure as an individual being, Yahweh, unlike Osiris, was not transparent for the Christ; he reflected the light which fell on him as the moon reflects the light of the sun. But it *was* the light of the same exalted lord of the sun, which, for the Egyptians, shone sunlike out of the Osiris sphere and, for the Israelites, shone moonlike out of the Yahweh sphere.

In the desert, the people of Israel were supposed to find the earth and at the same time the divine being who had moved into the domain of the earth forces, namely the Christ, revealing himself through Yahweh.

> Through the great cosmic events, this lofty being drew ever closer to the earth sphere. Increasingly, clairvoyance could sense Christ's approach to the earth, as it were. His approach could be perceived more and more distinctly, and was unmistakable in the fiery lightning on Sinai. What

did Moses behold in the burning thornbush and in the fire on Sinai? The Christ. But just as we call the sunlight, when we see it mirrored by the moon, 'moonlight,' so the Christ was called 'Yahweh' or 'Jehovah'. Hence, Yahweh is none other than the reflection of the Christ before he himself appeared on the earth.[36]

Here, by means of an important example, we become acquainted with the religious-historical survey that becomes possible through science of the spirit. The pre-Christian religions did not stand side by side as isolated systems. Since they all originated from actual spiritual vision, they also addressed themselves to the same facts and beings of the spiritual divine world, although they gave them different names. On the other hand, it can never be exactly the same divine being that is referred to in the various religions, for the beings of the spiritual world never remain static; in a different age, they themselves have become different. Especially in reference to the age of Moses, Rudolf Steiner expanded the religious-historical survey by a glance at the gods of the Indian heaven, which also helps us to comprehend more exactly the relationship of Christ to the gods of the pre-Christian religious movements.[37]

We come to a number of spiritual beings who do not descend as far as the physical world, who express themselves in this world through the air . . . And the most powerful . . . is the one who in ancient India was given the name Indra . . . To this same entity . . . must be attributed the phenomena of lightning flashing through the clouds and the rumble of thunder as well as the beneficial effects that accompany thunderstorms . . . There is a certain time in the earth's evolution . . . where it appears to clairvoyant sight as if rays of light were falling on Indra from a completely different being; through this light that falls on Indra, he himself is illuminated; he is thereby elevated to a higher level of his own development . . . The god Indra is present in the soul world at a time when, for earth evolution, the Christ is not yet visible, but where the light emanating from the Christ already falls on Indra . . . This light, which as yet does not itself shine on the earth but is only reflected by Indra and therefore does not allow direct perception of the Christ — as we perceive sunlight when it is reflected by the moon, is the light that was proclaimed by Moses to his people; and he called the Christ light that is thus reflected Yahweh or Jehovah . . . The Christ proclaims himself ahead of time and Yahweh is the name for the Christ light reflected and thrown back by an ancient deity who prophetically proclaimed the Christ.

2.3 The geological nature of the Moses revelation

As long as one approaches the Old Testament with the rigid abstractions of the modern concepts of God instead of the life-imbued views of the transformations of the divine beings and the changes of human consciousness linked with them, not only is the relationship between the divine experiences of the Israelites with those of other nations misunderstood, but the fact is also ignored that the divine was experienced in quite different regions of exist-ence and provinces of consciousness at the different times of Old Testament development.

The Yahweh experience at the time of Moses was fundamentally different from that of the later age of the Jewish people and their prophets. Nevertheless, the picture of the divine concept of the whole Old Covenant that people most often arrive at is primarily orientated to the later prophetic proclamation, for the latter seems to harmonize most readily with the basic religious concepts of recent times. Only at the time of the prophets, beginning with Elijah, but increasingly in the figures to whom the prophetic books of the Old Testament are traced back, the Yahweh religion advanced from outside to within. The divine was no longer found and experienced in the elemental kingdoms of nature but only in the soul within. It was therefore the prophetic proclamation that insisted upon a radical abolition of even the last remnants of a nature religion and pressed instead for the nurturing of a purely inward devotion of soul. But with the concepts valid for the age of the prophets as an approach to the religious element of the Moses age, the way is open to the most portentous errors.

The militant reform carried out by the prophets was not merely directed against the religious cultic world of the surrounding tribes but also against that of their own past. The revelations of the

Moses era still flowed out of sources which — half a millennium later — were radically rejected, and rightly so for their time, by the prophets.

The struggle of the prophets was directed first of all against the 'heights', the ancient nature-sanctuaries on holy hilltops. Moses, on the other hand, still received his revelation on a holy summit, Mount Horeb-Sinai. The prophets placed themselves in the most conscious opposition to the spiritual forces that rule in the elements of the kingdoms of nature, in wind and waves, in clouds and smoke. To the utmost extent, they were opposed to all activities of oracles and sibyls that dominated the ancient world even as far as the late Greco-Roman times, for these derived their revelations from the realm of the elements and presupposed almost everywhere that its representatives submerged themselves in somnambulistic, mediumistic soul conditions in order to receive revelations. The prophets created the unbridgeable chasm between sibyls and prophets[38] and thereby between pagan and Jewish civilizations. Yet Moses still heard the voice of God in fire, smoke, clouds and lightning.

A polarity similar to that between sibyls and prophets held sway between Moses and the prophets. But what was still justified and right in Moses' age had to be fought against already as wrong and demonic by the prophets. In Moses' time, the Yahweh being still spoke, after all, from outside, from the realm of the elements. During the age of the prophets, the journey of the divine being that was on its way to human incarnation had progressed another step. Yahweh now spoke only in the inner province of the human soul. On the same holy mountain, where Moses received the divine revelation in fire and smoke, lightning and thunder, Elijah had to come to the realization four hundred years later that Yahweh no longer dwelt in the rushing of the wind, in the quaking of the earth, in the flaming glow of the fire, but that he had moved into the still small voice of the inner being (1 Kings 19:11f). Herein lies the greatness of the Old Testament: it allows us to sense the breath of history like no other document of mankind. It encompasses the greatest contrasts of divine and world experience, for it traces the dramatic transformations that have taken place in heaven and on earth, in the gods' existence and in men's consciousness.

2.3 THE GEOLOGICAL NATURE OF THE MOSES REVELATION

In Moses' time, the earth-sphere with its elemental force-effects was the sphere for the Yahweh-Christ revelation. Rudolf Steiner expresses the difference between divine spheres in the various cultural epochs and national streams in a clear-cut formula.[39] He designates ancient Persia's world-view as that of chronology, astrology as that of the Egypto-Chaldean time, that of the Greeks as meteorology, and that of the Israelites as geology. The transition from Egypt to the Moses culture is denoted by the step that leads from astrology to geology. The divine reveals itself in the realm of the earth's forces, no longer in the spheres of the stars.

In a unique way, the desert passed through by the people offered the possibility to meet the divine guiding power in the sphere of earth forces. On one hand, because of the absence of any vegetation, the world of minerals, of hard stone, exclusively dominated everything. Wherever the thick cover of plants spreads over the mineral substance of the ground, the forces of the planets and fixed stars reach in with their effects and cover up the earth influence. On the other hand, in the area of the Israelite desert journey, the process of earth's coming into being had not completely come to an end. It would be wrong to explain the miracles of the desert related by the Old Testament in a symbolic way. Real events of nature, processes in the domain of earth forces, are indicated by the images of the burning thornbush, the pillar of cloud and fire, the thunder and lightning in the fiery smoke clouds billowing around the summit of Sinai, and the miracle of the spring. As a sphere of the most alive, active earth forces, the rocky Sinai desert became the site of the most abundant divine revelations for Moses and his people.

Rudolf Steiner describes the geological background of Moses' proclamation:[40]

> We know . . . If we look at the doings of Moses in the
> right light, we find them constantly related to activities of
> the Earth. Moses goes to the rocks with his rod and makes
> water gush out. Moses goes up the mountain. Above and
> below, the mountain is connected with Earth-activity. For
> we must think of this mountain as a volcano, or at least
> as vulcanic. It is not the Sinai generally imagined; the Earth
> is active in it. The column of fire in which Moses stands
> is akin to what happens when we burn a piece of paper in

the sulphur hills of Italy and smoke comes out. So does
fiery smoke, telluric activity, come out of the mountain. In
front of them went the pillar of cloud or of fire – telluric
activity! . . . What Moses proclaims is Geology!

. . .The Hebrews felt themselves in close relationship to
forces rising from the Earth below and bound up with the
Earth. Yes, even the sufferings of the Hebrew people come
from the desert, where the Earth-forces prevail. Geology
dominates the destiny of the Hebrews.

2.4 The location of Mount Sinai

The more clearly we perceive the sphere of earth forces and their
activities as the basis in nature for the Moses revelation, the more
'Mount Sinai' must turn into a problem for us. The towering
mountain range in the south of the triangular Sinai Peninsula with
its gigantic rock formations that rise up above 2500 metres (above
8000 feet) consists of Pre-Cambrian rock, granite and gneiss. Here
we may well face a centre around which roared the most varied
processes of earth evolution; all cosmogonic evolutionary
processes of the planet earth may have left their traces around so
that the Sinai Peninsula in its triangular shape appears like a
primordial image and prototype of all continents of the southern
hemisphere.[41] But the southern mountain range itself stands as
an unchanged witness of earth's beginnings, having long since
completed all processes of development, a resting pole and pivot
in the midst of all transformations of the earth's surface from the
beginning of the Lemurian age. In no way can these mountains
of Pre-Cambrian rock be identical with the still fiery, simmering
mountain region of the biblical Mount Sinai.

Rudolf Steiner also points this out in connection with the
already quoted descriptions of the geological character of the
Moses revelation:[42] 'Above and below, the mountain is connected
with Earth-activity. For we must think of this mountain as a
volcano or at least as vulcanic. It is not the Sinai generally
imagined.'

The Sinai problem has already given rise to much concern for
theological thinking of the last century. The biblical description

of the occurrences on the mountain during the revelation of the commandments made it increasingly mandatory to consider the geographic and geological conditions of the Sinai region referred to there:

> On the morning of the third day there were thunders and lightnings, and a thick cloud upon the mountain, and a sound arose as of mighty trumpets. All the people who were in the camp trembled. Then Moses brought the people out of the camp to meet the revelation of God; and they took their stand at the foot of the mountain. And Mount Sinai was wrapped in smoke, because Yahweh revealed himself there in the fire; and the smoke of it went up like the smoke of a kiln, and the whole mountain quaked greatly. (Exod.19:16-18B).

From these words of the Second Book of Moses it was felt safe to conclude that the biblical Sinai had been a volcano. Now, it seemed certain that it was only due to a mix-up that the tradition could have arisen that Moses had received the revelation of the commandments on the granite mountains of the southern Sinai Peninsula. The search for the true Mount Sinai commenced. If it were to be found among the mountains that were or are actually volcanos, a nearly insurmountable difficulty presents itself. Neither on the Sinai Peninsula nor north-east of there, in so-called Arabia Petraea, have volcanos ever existed. But this is the region between Egypt and Palestine which, to begin with, one would want to assume to be the site of the Israelites' desert wanderings. Regions of predominantly volcanic character are not encountered until south-east of Damascus which is, however, located far too much to the north to come under consideration as Mount Sinai of the Bible. Furthermore, ominous volcanic eruptions called 'harras' are found in this region and on the eastern edge of the Jordan Valley. While some have looked for Mount Sinai in the unlikely volcanic region east of the Red Sea, identifying it with Hala-el Bedr which rises on the eastern slope of a range called Tadras, in Arabia, other historians hit upon the idea to place the biblical Sinai on the northern end of the savagely ravined, Arabian lava-fields, at Jebel Druze.[43] Already the tradition, which viewed the Sinai of the Bible as the one in the southern Sinai peninsula, presupposed that the forty-year-long desert fate of Israel entailed a nomadic moving about with many detours; after all, the presumed holy mountain is by no means located on the direct path from Egypt to Palestine. Now, theologians had to resort to the assumption of much more complicated and far-fetched travel routes. The geographic puzzle became ever greater and the veil of secrets that conceals the events of Israel's forty years in the desert became more and more impenetrable.

In actual fact, with its descriptions of the Sinai region, the Bible refers neither to the Pre-Cambrian mountain range of southern Sinai nor to a regular lava-spewing volcano after the manner of an Etna, a Vesuvius or a Stromboli.

A formidable obstacle on the way to the solution of this basic problem of biblical geography is the very one-sided conception held generally today concerning the nature of volcanic activities. Only where specific volcanic rock formation is discovered in the ground, be it in the form of basalt or in a less solid, altered state due to weathering, is the conception of fiery evolutionary processes arrived at. The prototype and start of all volcanic telluric activity is, however, the blazing flame which in pre-Atlantean, Lemurian times caused the southern half of our planet to seethe violently everywhere, and finally, simultaneously with the origin of the present-day continents, brought about the destruction of large parts of the earth's surface through conflagrations of gigantic dimensions.[44] As they subsided more and more, the Lemurian fires from the earth's interior continued to flicker and to be active in the most varied forms on the broadest base possible. Where the telluric fire expels solid rocks out of towering volcanos, we merely confront the most vehement offsprings of the Lemurian flames, those that interfere most profoundly in the realm of the elements. The upward-pushing evolutionary force of fire did not subjugate the hardest and densest of the elements everywhere. Instead of the solid mineral substance, it flung out water, smoke, steam and flamelike substances elsewhere. Mud, water and smoke-volcanoes, steaming fissures and gorges, rifts of flame and fire pits fed by pitch and sulphur, undoubtedly existed in countless numbers in the ancient world where no real volcano was anywhere nearby, and today no volcanic stone formation is found.

People should take much more into account how fundamentally

the countenance of the earth has changed in regard to volcanic and semi-volcanic processes just in the past two- or three-thousand years. If even the majority of 'fire-spewing mountains' have become completely or almost extinct in the most recent telluric epoch, those fire processes, working in the less dense elements of water, air and warmth, came to rest in infinitely greater measure. Above Pozzuoli in Italy is a more unusual example where the crater Solfatara lies, which has given its name to this type of volcanic activity. There, one walks across a crater-like depression over light chalky rocks warmed by the subterranean heat. At some spots, the intensity of the heat is so increased that boiling mud sputters and spews out of a small mud-crater which a person can closely approach. Everywhere in the ground, held down in an unstable balance by the atmospheric pressure, however, there lurk quantities of sulphuric vapour and smoke. If a piece of paper or a torch is lit, columns of steam and smoke immediately rise out of the ground, following the heated air that billows upward. And this does not occur only in the vicinity of the lit fire. If, anywhere, the restraint is loosened that binds the subterranean forces, the ground at once starts to steam and smoke in innumerable spots all the way up to the topmost rim of the mountain slope. According to the large number of traditions, the earth must have steamed solfatara-like out of many cracks, vents and rifts until the time of early Christianity. The Castalian gorge near Delphi on the majestic slope of Mount Parnassus can be cited as a classic example. The mythological, visionary age experienced the smoke vapours arising there as the fearsomely coiling pythic dragon; tamed by Apollo, they billowed around the sibyl's oracle seat.

If the elemental basis of nature for the Sinai revelation is pictured in the form of solfatara-like earth force activities, as fire and smoke processes similar to those in the gorge of Delphi, the way is open to answer the question concerning the geography of the biblical Sinai.

Earlier, we have mentioned the fact that the great rift through which the River Jordan flows today — this deepest depression in the earth's surface — remained the source of fiery evolutionary processes into late epochs, being an important border-zone of mighty fissures.[45] Particularly in the southern continuation of the Jordan Rift, with the Dead Sea and the Wadi el Arabah (or Arava

Valley, the desert which leads southwards to the Gulf of Aqaba)
the last flickers of Lemuria's fire came to rest only very late.
The fire catastrophe, which the Old Testament describes in the
destruction of Sodom and Gomorrah, occurred because the Lemurian fire-forces underneath this great rift-scar of the earth once
again concentrated together into a large eruption and tore open
the depths in which subsequently the lye of the Dead Sea
collected.

After the Sodom cataclysm, all sorts of semi-volcanic, solfatara-
like processes of fire and steam must have abounded in varying
degrees especially in the area of the Arabah between the Dead
and Red Seas. The names with which the surrounding volcanic
mountainous regions were denoted, the 'Hauran', the 'harras'
formations, still evoke an idea of the character of the whole area,
for they all mean 'hot land'. Even the book of the prophet Isaiah
calls forth images concerning the land of the Edomites — the
Arabah and its surroundings — that refer in classic clearness to
the subterranean threatening forces that slumber there in the
ground. In this passage, we have an invaluable key for the
geological and geographic riddle of Sinai:

> And the streams of Edom shall be turned into pitch,
>> and her soil into brimstone;
>> her land shall become burning pitch.
> Night and day it shall not be quenched;
>> its smoke shall go up for ever.
> From generation to generation it shall lie waste;
>> none shall pass through it for ever and ever. (Isa.34:9f).

According to the conceptions now gained, the Sinai referred to
by the Bible may outwardly have been much more unassuming
than the granite giants in the south of the Sinai Peninsula or a
crater-volcano like Mount Etna. It is a significant corroboration
of the line of thought we are pursuing that legendary traditions
know of Mount Sinai as an outwardly not particularly striking
peak. Mention is made there of a contest between mountains.
Carmel, Tabor and Sinai compete to be allowed to be the site of
the great revelation. But 'the mountain on which God had the
desire to dwell is none other than Mount Sinai, for it is the least
among them.'[46] If Moses' mountain of God was lower in altitude
than Tabor and Carmel, neither being even 600 metres (2000 feet)

high, then Sinai's greatness could not have been due to physical size but to its sphere of forces.

The Bible knows two names for the mountain of revelation in the desert: it calls it Sinai one time, Horeb another time. That both designations refer to the same holy mountain-peak is clearly shown by those Old Testament passages which use the name Horeb precisely where otherwise the term Sinai is employed. The texts of Chronicles speak of the tablets of the commandments, 'which Moses put [in the ark] at Horeb' (2Chr.5:10); the text of Malachi which forms the conclusion of the Old Testament states: 'Remember the law of my servant Moses, . . . that I commanded him at Horeb' (Mal.4:4). But perhaps the two names are not simply interchangeable designations for one and the same mountain. Perhaps the assumption is correct, which theologians of older schools often hit upon,[47] that two different peaks of one mountain were referred to with the names Sinai and Horeb. Then, it could have been that the two peaks were divided by an oracle-gorge similar to that of Castalia, and that Moses received the divine revelation out of the columns of smoke and fiery flames that arose out of this ravine. This conception even appears to be supported by certain descriptions in the Bible. The voice of God said to Moses: 'Behold, there is a place by me where you shall stand upon the rock; and while my glory passes by I will put you in a cleft of the rock, and I will cover you with my hand until I have passed by' (Exod.33:21f). Even if the image of the oracle-gorge between Sinai and Horeb is taken hypothetically in the sense of a possibility, it can serve to clarify the geological Sinai milieu.

Let us now try to approach the biblical descriptions with the above acquired views in order to search in them for indications and reference points for the geographic course of Israel's journey and particularly for the location of Sinai-Horeb.

First of all we realize that the sequence of stations and camp sites through which the forty-year long trek passes is determined by the revelation-filled fire and smoke phenomena of the territory's nature there. The ark was evidently put down at such spots where the columns of fire and smoke billowed forth out of the earth-forces' sphere, or where they could be produced out of the ground by means of the performance of incense offerings:

On the day that the tabernacle was set up, the cloud

covered the tabernacle, the tent of the testimony; and at
evening it was over the tabernacle like the appearance of
fire until morning . . . And whenever the cloud was taken
up from over the tent, after that the people of Israel set
out; and in the place where the cloud settled down, there
the people of Israel encamped . . . as long as the cloud
rested over the tabernacle, they remained in camp. Even
when the cloud continued over the tabernacle many days,
the people of Israel kept the charge of the LORD, and did
not set out . . .

   . . . and the ark of the covenant of the LORD went before
them . . . to seek out a resting place for them. (Num.9:15-
19; 10:33).

The travel route therefore follows a line of localities whose special
feature consists in the fact that active processes of earth evolution
could still be encountered there. The trek appears to follow a rift
in the earth's surface.

But a closer geographical determination of the marching route
meets with odd difficulties now. A labyrinth of contradictions is
before our eyes when we pay heed to the indications of location
and time of the camp sites. Is this only caused by the fact that
the Bible does not merely want to describe an external journey,
but simultaneously stations of inner development?

A special geographical mystery is concealed, which can only
gradually be unlocked by the key of compositional considerations,
viewing all details together. We shall focus especially on those
segments of the journey to which the puzzles and contradictions
refer.

By far the greatest part of the description given us by the Bible
of the travels through the desert relates to the first two years. The
remaining thirty-eight years are more obscure. The dates that
bring us into the second year of the journey extend into the Fourth
Book of Moses (Num.9:1; 10:11). Then, the forward movement
came to a halt at a significant point. Moses sent out the twelve
scouts and awaited their return. And since the people allowed
themselves to be shaken in their devout sense of purpose by the
message they brought back, a forty-year time of waiting and
serving was imposed on them: 'And your children shall be
shepherds in the wilderness forty years' (Num.14:33). Then it

appears that this waiting period receives its meaning by the fact that the king of Edom refuses the Israelites passage through his realm, necessitating their circling around it on tedious routes. In its looking back, the Fifth Book of Moses (Deuteronomy) lists the time between the departure from the site where the scouts were dispatched and the approach to the Jordan region as thirty-eight years (2:14). But in the important list of the forty-two camp sites (Num.33), a completely different picture surfaces. The date of Aaron's death, which occurs soon after the departure from the place where the scouts were dispatched, is determined: 'And Aaron the priest went up Mount Hor at the command of the LORD, and died there, in the fortieth year after the people of Israel had come out of the land of Egypt' (Num.33:38). According to this indication, only an exceedingly short part of the forty years is left to circle around Mount Seir in Edom, namely the remainder of the last year; and we realize that the whole thirty-eight years between the first two years and this brief final segment are passed over in silence.

The Bible, however, wants to tell us something through the language of contradictions and riddles. It leads us to the conclusion that the Israelites spent a full thirty-eight years in the vicinity of the site where the scouts left them and returned again. If nothing special could be said concerning this place and the people's long sojourn there, there would be no reason to veil the long halt of the journey of Israel so consciously.

Moses indicates a profound mystery of the years in the desert, when, in looking back in Deuteronomy, he says: 'So you remained at Kadesh many days . . .' (Deut.1:46). Kadesh is the mystery-enveloped central point and main site of the Sinai trek. The biblical description also points this out by placing a number of the most important events there in spite of relating almost nothing concerning the major part of the forty years. Aside from the dispatch and return of the twelve scouts, it concerns in particular the rebellion of the Korah adherents and Miriam's death.

If attention has at last been drawn to the riddle of Kadesh, many other questions begin to be answered. The veil is even slowly lifted from the mystery of the location of biblical Sinai. The Bible speaks through the sign language of composition, and we comprehend its indications by considering two scenes together that represent a kind of frame for the whole biblical description of the journey. They are the two great miracles of the springs of water that Moses performs. The first is related immediately after the passage through the Sea of Reeds: The people demand water, long for the return to Egypt, and vex Moses with their anger. Moses receives a divine instruction:

> And the LORD said to Moses, '. . . take in your hand the rod . . . Behold, I will stand before you there on the rock at Horeb; and you shall strike the rock, and water shall come out of it, that the people may drink' . . . And he called the name of the place Massah and Meribah [testing and finding fault], because of the faultfinding of the children of Israel, and because they put the LORD to the proof . . . (Exod.17:5-7).

Note that here the site of the spring, Massah and Meribah, is placed quite near Horeb-Sinai. At the very beginning of their journey, we find the Israelites in the vicinity of Sinai. Towards the end of the description that the Old Testament gives of Israel's fate in the desert, during the story of the last water-miracle, the Bible refers back to the first site of the spring: 'These are the waters of Meribah, where the people of Israel contended with the LORD . . .' (Num.20:13). The Israelites are still in the Sinai region. And now, in continuation, the biblical text gives a point of reference for a closer determination of that site of the spring: 'Moses sent messengers from Kadesh to the king of Edom ". . . here we are in Kadesh, a city on the edge of your territory. Now let us pass through your land . . ." And they journeyed from Kadesh' (Num.20:14-22).

If, during the first water miracle, the site of the spring Meribah was placed in the vicinity of Horeb-Sinai, now, in the case of the latter miracle, it is placed in the neighbourhood of Kadesh. It follows from this that there can be no great distance between Sinai-Horeb and Kadesh. With this we have found the key to the Sinai problem: Sinai is closely connected with the area of the thirty-eight-year-long sojourn: the area surrounding Kadesh.

What does Kadesh represent? The Bible places it in the desert of Paran (Num.13:26). And the assumption is probably correct which has for a long time identified Kadesh with the site of an oasis in the Wilderness of Paran, east of the Ramon mountain range. Until the nineteenth century the bedouin who lived near the oasis Ein Qadeis fearfully kept the location, which they even considered to be a sacred one, secret from Europeans. In 1842, Rowlands brought back the first report concerning it, and in 1881 the oasis was explored and described in more detail by the American, Henry Clay Trumbull. This Kadesh is located where the Sinai peninsula merges with the Negeb Desert, south-west of the Dead Sea, 75 km (47 miles) south of Isaac's city Beer-sheba, hence not far at all from the region which is the stage of later developments.*

The mountains around Har Ramon on the western ridge of which Kadesh is located, belong to the mountain ranges that in the west frame the broad desolate valley Wadi el Arabah, the continuation of the Jordan Valley between the Dead Sea and the Gulf of Aqaba. In the east, on the other side of this primeval rift in the earth, across from Har Ramon, lies the mountain range in Edom called Mount Seir, and on its western edge, approximately on the same latitude as Kadesh, ancient Petra is located, which in the last decades has received much attention due to the continuing extensive excavations.

The name of this city, 'Rock', expresses the character of the whole desert terrain, after which western Arabia is designated as 'Rocky Arabia', Arabia Petrae. The remains of Petra are situated between fantastically shaped mountains of stone. A 'sacred city', consisting of numerous elaborately decorated rock-tombs and places of sacrifice, certainly at the site of ancient sanctuaries, has been uncovered there. During the last pre-Christian times, the capital city of the Nabateans, an esoteric branch of the Arab people distantly related to the Essenes, stood there. The most splendid ruins of graves and temples from the Hellenistic period are located where a steep, rocky gorge, resembling a tear in the earth's crust, widens into a broad canyon. Perhaps we find ourselves there in a former oracle-gorge at one of the places where, long ago, the earth forces were active in a special way,

---

*It is not quite clear from Bock's German text where he is referring to, as maps of that area have until quite recently been unreliable. Following Trumbull's description, the oasis which this explorer visited appears to be what is now marked on the maps as Ein Qadeis, 30 km (20 miles) west of the Israeli settlement of Mizpe Ramon, just on the Egyptian side of the border. This location has been used in translating this chapter and naming the locations.

giving vent to fiery smoke-steam from the earth's interior and sending sibylline oracles into human souls. This narrow gorge is called Wadi Musa, the 'Valley of Moses'. Local traditions state that the brook that flows there is the water that Moses struck out of the rock (Petra). And the *Targum*, the Chaldaean translation and paraphrasing of the Old Testament, equates Petra with the biblical Sinai.

While this identification is instructive it remains unlikely. On the other hand, the tradition, already mentioned by Josephus, that the highest mountain of Petra, the Jebel Harun (1336m, 4383ft) is the biblical Mount Hor, the camp site following Kadesh, seems to be affirmed. On the summit of the mountain, where remains of a pre-Nabatean, Midianite sanctuary have been discovered, Aaron died, and since ancient times his grave has been shown there and greatly venerated.

With the two localities, Kadesh and Petra, on both sides of the Wadi el Arabah, we have gained an approximate idea for the position and topography of the Sinai-Horeb, which, as the Bible leads us to believe through its compositional element, must be looked for in the surroundings of Kadesh, although its more specific contours will remain shrouded in obscurity. The surprising part of this result is that the Sinai region moves into very close proximity with Palestine as well as Egypt. According to this, Israel's journey took a much straighter route than was previously assumed, for the 'Sea of Reeds' that was crossed in such a miraculous way may well refer to the region of the Bitter Lakes that were linked to the Red Sea where today the Suez Canal cuts through the land. The Israelites did not cover great distances in the outer sense during their wanderings. The main content of the forty years was an inward development that was gone through during outward rests and stops in the Kadesh-Sinai region.

The confusion between the biblical Kadesh-Sinai and the momentous granite mountains in the south of the peninsula goes back far in history. Perhaps it became possible because the Pre-Cambrian mountains also harboured a sanctuary dating back to ancient contexts other than those linked to Israel. Numerous inscriptions by pilgrims from long ago as well as from more recent times, found there on the rock walls, seem to indicate this.

Through this error concerning Mount Sinai the interpretation

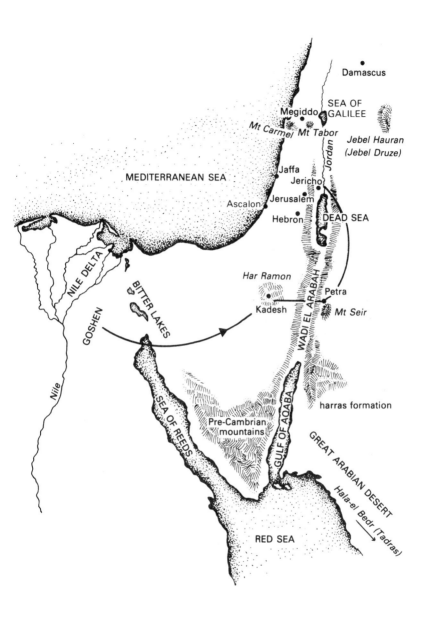

Map showing the position of Mount Sinai in the region of Kadesh. The line from the Nile Delta eastward is an indication of the journey of the Israelites.

given to the whole Old Testament was in many respects mistakenly directed. The confusion was sealed by the Byzantine emperor Justinian, who ordered the establishment of the monastery below the majestic granite summit. It may be no coincidence that this happened under the same emperor who, elsewhere too, did so much to extinguish and obscure ancient knowledge and wisdom, for it was he who, in AD 529, closed the Academy at Athens, and had the writings of Origen declared to be heretical by the councils of the Church.

The fact that alongside the established confusion the correct traditions concerning Sinai remained alive quietly is demonstrated by some old maps. In the work, *Notitiae Orbis Antiqui* by Christophorus Cellarius from the year 1732, we find that Mount Sinai is indeed placed in the area of Kadesh.

2.5 The mystery centre of Jethro

Why does the biblical description spread a veil of secrecy so elaborately and firmly over the long sojourn of the children of Israel in Kadesh, the central site of the whole desert trek?

The name Kadesh means 'sanctuary.' It must have been a cultic site in the midst of the desert that attracted and held the Israelites spellbound for a long time. Even in the Psalms that praise the divine that reveals itself in the thunderstorm, the recollection of the sanctuary re-echoes, that was dominated by the awesomeness of the desert (Ps.29:7f *B*):

> The voice of Yahweh flashes forth flames of fire.
> The voice of Yahweh shakes the wilderness,
> Yahweh shakes the wilderness of Kadesh.

Again we have arrived at a point where the mystery principle emerges from the hidden background and becomes involved in Old Testament history. Out of the mist of the past a mystery centre takes on form. What is concealed and occurs within it is something we cannot immediately discern. But two significant sites of its wider domain lie more clearly before us: the storm-enveloped mountain height of Horeb-Sinai and the oasis of Massah and Meribah. Perhaps the site of the spring stood in a similar relationship to Sinai's summit as did the Castalian spring to the temple hills of Delphi above the Pythian gorge, as a place of tests and purification from where one was at last permitted to ascend to the site of revelations. The name of the spring Massah, 'temptation,' suggests this conception. The Israelites would not 'test' the divinity here if, earlier, they themselves had not been guided by the latter into a test and temptation. They do not pass the test; they quarrel with the divine will. Not only once does this site of trials, Massah and Meribah, verify its meaning in a tragic way. In the same place, the people fail when the twelve scouts return, and for a long time they are denied the crossing of the threshold into the promised land. Even Moses is destined not to pass the test that is concealed behind the story of the last miracle of spring water. For thirty-eight years the people must remain in the domain of the desert, circling around the stern, mysterious sanctuary; and Moses must die before having set foot on the ground of the longed-for future.

The mystery centre of Kadesh bestows the inner meaning on the Israelites' desert journey. The forty years there is a school for the people, not only in the sense of an education through destiny but quite concretely in the sense of the guidance and instruction by a great initiate of humanity. In Kadesh, Israel encounters the teacher before whom Moses too bows as a disciple. Kadesh, the hidden sanctuary in the Sinai desert, is the mystery centre of Jethro.

When, at the beginning of its route, the travelling people arrived in the vicinity of the Horeb and had experienced the first water miracle in Massah and Meribah, Jethro — who is designated as a priest in the land of the Midianites — came forward to greet them, and Moses bowed down before him and kissed him. Jethro conducted a solemn sacrificial rite, and Aaron along with all the elders of the people stepped forward to receive the consecrated bread from his hand (Exod.18:7-12). And before Moses received the revelation of the law from the lightning fire of Sinai by means of which the life of the people was given order and form, Jethro was engaged as a wise adviser ordering the social configurations by establishing, through Moses, the office of judges and the council of the Sanhedrin (Exod.18:13-27), thus preparing the social order of Yahweh.

Although the biblical description makes little and veiled reference to him, through the figure of Jethro the image of the desert journey is filled out with unexpected historical concreteness. Simultaneously, what had remained obscure until now in the structure of Moses' destiny is lit up: the middle portion between his fortieth and eightieth year.

When Moses had turned away from Egypt and had fled into the desert, what destinies awaited him there? He had become the disciple of the priestly sage Jethro. The Bible mentions his stay in this second lofty school of his life with but a few words that conceal more than they reveal. What unheard-of treasures of fate and spirit he must have encountered there that made him, who, as a son of Pharaoh, had already graduated from Egypt's mystery schools, remain for four decades — the time of active fulfilment of life between forty and eighty years of age — with his new teacher who lived in obscurity!

He had become a man of advanced age, when, at the end of his Jethro-discipleship, he hearkened to the divine task heard in the fires at Mount Horeb and returned to Egypt. And what did he do, when, jointly with Aaron, he had brought the great turning point of time and spirit transition to the awareness of the Egyptians? Here we come upon the close connection between the middle and the final part in the life of Moses, upon the direct motivating link of the people's forty-year-long journey with the preceding forty-year-long concealment of Moses: Moses now led all his people to the school that had prepared him for his very own mission, namely to Jethro.

Originally, a total severance of Israel from the Egyptian context does not seem to have been within the scope of his intentions. He asked Pharaoh for permission to lead the Israelites into the desert for the purpose of celebrating a cultic festival (Exod.5:1; 7:16). Perhaps he only wanted to lead his people for a brief time into the domain of the Jethro sanctuary in order to let them partake of certain divine revelations. But destiny caused the people to remain a full forty years in the surroundings of the Jethro sanctuary, exactly the same span of time that Moses had earlier spent here as a single disciple of Jethro.

As once with the reports concerning Abraham, here also the Old Testament moves aside for an instant the curtain that conceals the sphere of the mysteries active in the background and the great initiated leaders of mankind. The meeting between Moses and Jethro and between Jethro and all the people of Israel belongs in the same category as does the solemn meeting between Abraham and Melchizedek.

Abraham and Moses are the great patriarchs and leaders of the people. But there are still greater, before whom they do homage. Just as Abraham bowed before Melchizedek, so Moses bowed before Jethro. The solemn scene where the priest-king Melchizedek carried forth bread and wine to Abraham corresponds exactly to the one in which Jethro approached the travelling people in the Sinai desert, celebrated the sacrificial rite and established the office of judges. And just as Abraham had earlier been a disciple of Melchizedek according to the traditions outside the Bible, so, as we hear from the Bible itself in this case, Moses had previously been Jethro's disciple.

In his lecture on Moses, Rudolf Steiner describes Moses' coming to Jethro and thereby shows how the imaginative style of the Old Testament weaves together outer events and soul experiences without distinguishing the images from one another:[48]

What we read in the Bible concerning the destinies of Moses and what he experienced and suffered in regard to the bondage of his people in the land of the Egyptians, we can view as a description of external conditions. But then the narration passes . . . over into a description of Moses' inner soul experiences. This occurs where Moses takes flight and is led to a priest, the Midianite priest, Jethro or Reuel. One who can recognize such a description from the conventions of ancient spiritual depictions, discovers, even to the extent of the names, that here the narration passes over into the representation of soul experiences of Moses. This is not meant as if Moses had not in fact undertaken such a journey to a temple site, a place of priestly instruction; but the representation is skilfully rendered in such a way that the external is interwoven with experiences that Moses' soul undergoes . . . What is indicated in the figure of Jethro? One can easily gather from the Bible that he is one of those individualities to whom we are directed again and again when we study the evolution of mankind, who, to a high degree, have

struggled through to an all-encompassing perception . . .
Moses was to be stimulated for his mission by . . .
becoming the disciple of one of these mysterious figures
who withdraw from the rest of humanity with their
contemplative life and are exclusively the teachers and
leaders of men.

The extraordinary penetrating spiritual influence and leadership
that the people of Israel experienced at the hand of Jethro is made
visible by the Bible in only a few passages as if through a parting
in a curtain. Aside from the scene of the inauguration of the
council of judges, one passage in particular allows us to discern
its significance because of the veiled quality of the text. When the
departure from the Kadesh region is already being prepared, it
says:

And Moses said to Hobab the son of Reuel the Midianite,
Moses' father-in-law, 'We are setting out for the place of
which the LORD said, "I will give it to you"; come with
us . . . Do not leave us, I pray you, for you know how
we are to encamp in the wilderness, and you will serve as
eyes for us . . .' (Num.10:29-35).

Ancient Jewish traditions are in agreement that Hobab is only
one of the names of Jethro or Reuel himself and that the words
of Moses were therefore directed to Jethro, who elsewhere is also
mentioned as Moses' father-in-law.[49] Moses beseeched Jethro to
be Israel's eye. He wanted his people to share in the fruits of
seeing into the spirit worlds, something that Jethro was capable
of. In particular, Moses called upon Jethro to be the guide through
the mysteries and stations of revelation in the region of the wilderness. If the sites for putting down the ark that was carried ahead
and the establishment of the forty-two campsites were selected
according to the fire and cloud columns that rose out of the ground
(Num.9:15-23), and Jethro was addressed as the one who was
familiar with and knew about these outward and inward stations,
we realize that Jethro had been the teacher through whom Moses'
eyes were opened for the divine revelation holding sway in the
realm of geological forces. Jethro had led Moses — and thereby
all of Israel — to Yahweh. He had guided them into the sphere
of existence in which, at that time, the light of Christ shone forth.

In the course of the profound inner development of the Israelite folk destiny, the initiation, which Moses received from Jethro and in which, afterwards, he allowed all his people to participate through the Sinai revelation, has a special significance. It says that Jethro had been a priest in the land of the Midianites. He himself, on the other hand, was not a Midianite; he was not a descendant of the sons born to aged Abraham by Keturah. He was an Ishmaelite,* a member of the stream that had been diverted from the Israelite folk stream by the expulsion of Hagar and her son Ishmael, the stream from which, later on, the Arabian peoples and Islam emerged. It is known in history that Ishmaelites and Midianites lived side by side in Arabia Petraea and were therefore in many instances mentioned interchangeably.[50] Just as a reabsorption of the Joseph element had been brought about through Moses' Egyptian initiation, so, through his Arabian initiation, that of Ishmael was accomplished. The streams that had been excluded from the formation of the Israelite-Jewish hereditary line are now spiritually brought back from outside through the contributions they bestow on the enhancement of Israel's spiritual life and culture.

Rudolf Steiner, who frequently described the law of physical rejection and spiritual reabsorption of ancient clairvoyant streams as significant for Israel's history, once related the encounter between Moses and Jethro in the following way:[51]

> Moses brought with him to the wisdom he acquired from his Egyptian initiation something of a quite different nature . . .
>
> What, then, is the revelation on Sinai? What was vouchsafed to Moses there . . . could well be grafted into the stem of this people because it was related to them in a very definite way. In times past the descendants of Ishmael had wandered away from their country and had settled in the regions now traversed by Moses and his people. Moses found in the Ishmaelites, among whom there was Initiation of a certain kind, those attributes and qualities which had been transmitted to them through

---

*Eduard Meyer in *Die Israeliten und ihre Nachbarstämme* shows there that the name Jethro, which means 'the outstanding one', 'the only one', is of Ishmaelite origin and occurs among the Nabataeans as the second name of several ancient kings of Sheba.

Hagar, qualities which were derived from Abraham, but in which were preserved many elements inherited from the ancient past. Out of the revelations that he received from this branch of the Hebrew people, it became possible for Moses to make the revelation of Sinai intelligible to the Israelites. In regard to this there is an ancient Hebrew legend that in Ishmael a shoot of Abraham was cast out into Arabia, that is, into the desert. What sprang from this stock is contained in the teaching of Moses. On Sinai, the ancient Hebrew people received back again, in the Mosaic Law, what had been cast out from their blood: they received it back *from without*.

As Rudolf Steiner pointed out, St Paul disclosed this same secret in the Letter to the Galatians (4:25), where he equated the Law of Moses, the testament of slavery, with Hagar: 'Now Hagar is Mount Sinai in Arabia'.

In the seclusion of Jethro's sanctuary a meeting and spiritual reconciliation took place between Israel and Ishmael. The Israelite culture received an Ishmaelite-Arab impulse through the Mosaic Law.

It was no coincidence that this spiritual reconciliation and agreement between two lineages diverging originally from two brothers happened to have the mystery region of Kadesh-Sinai as its stage. Kadesh was an important sanctuary not only in the time of Jethro. Its history goes back far into the past and also reaches clearly into the fabric of tales about the Patriarchs and into the sphere of life of the step-brothers Isaac and Ishmael. During her flight from Sarah, Hagar, Abraham's Egyptian maid-servant, rested at a holy spring, Beer-lahai-roi, the 'well of one who sees and lives', which, according to Genesis, was located 'between Kadesh and Bered' (Gen.16:14). There, in an angelic vision, the birth of her son Ishmael was foretold to her. This is an Old Testament analogy to the Annunciation scene in the New Testament, which occurred later at the well in Nazareth, when the Angel Gabriel appeared to Mary. Kadesh is like an Arabian Nazareth. After his expulsion, then, Ishmael, the progenitor of all Arabian-Ishmaelite peoples, dwelt in the Paran Desert where Kadesh is located. It is therefore understandable that Kadesh was always a central sanctuary of the Arabs, not only into the days of Jethro and Moses, but into late

Muslim times — proof of which is the fact that the location of the oasis of Kadesh was kept a secret for so long. In the very centre of the land of Ishmael, then, the spiritual return of Hagar and Ishmael was brought about by virtue of Moses' Jethro-initiation and the Sinai revelation.

At Beer-lahai-roi, the 'well of one who sees and lives', where Hagar received her prophecy, important scenes from the life of Isaac also took place — Isaac, whose step-brother was Ishmael and whose dwelling place Beer-sheba was located not far from there, seventy-five kilometres (50 miles) north of Kadesh (Gen.24:62; 25:11).[52] The Kadesh region, therefore, reaches quite near the locality of early Hebrew history. Close to the confines of the land of the patriarchs, the events of the forty-year-long desert journey took place.

From the most diverse directions we are led to the realization that the external distance and physical framework of the Israelite journey were less extensive than is generally assumed. The outer path of travel definitely recedes before the one that was inwardly completed — which is the one the Bible endeavours to describe in the first place. The 'exodus from Egypt' was above all else a spiritual separation, an inner withdrawal. In addition, it must also be taken into consideration that in the time of Moses the whole southern part of Palestine belonged politically to Egypt. In the sense of outward conditions of sovereignty, the Israelites, therefore, remained in Egypt despite the exodus. On the other hand, the people as a whole had previously not been living in Egypt proper, which unfolded its civilization along the Nile. The land of Goshen to the east of the Nile delta had been assigned to Israel. As the Book of Joshua (10:41) indicates, this land of Goshen extended all the way to Gibeon north of Jerusalem. Accordingly, in a certain sense, the journey of Moses led externally neither out of Egypt nor Goshen. The more the outward picture of the journey shrinks in regard to the territory it covered, the more the inner course of events stands out brightly.

The figure of Jethro is shrouded in many mysteries, and in the legendary traditions outside the Bible there is much puzzlement and pondering concerning the riddles arising from it. In the Book of Judges he is designated as a Kenite (Judg.1:16). The ancient

Bible interpreters explain that Jethro was called this, 'because he descended from Cain; in Jethro, Cain was absolved of his guilt.'[53]

Perhaps it was in reference to this passage from the Book of Judges that the apocryphal tradition arose which held that in Jethro, Cain was reincarnated, in Moses, Abel.[54] The legends that speak of this feel that certain scenes in the lives of Abel and Moses correspond to each other. When Moses covered his countenance in Sinai, they see in this a reflection of Abel's experience when he beheld the glory of God during the sacrifice. They bring the mystery-filled death of Moses into connection with Abel's death at the hand of Cain. They want to rediscover the twin-sisters of Abel in Bathia, the daughter of Pharaoh, who adopted Moses as her son, and in Zipporah, Jethro's daughter and wife of Moses. Even though these opinions are not based on fact, they do underline the historical significance of the encounter between Jethro and Moses. Through the meeting of these two personalities, two streams of humanity that had already moved far apart renewed contact with each other.

2.6 Jethro's daughters

Where the Bible mentions the first meeting between Moses and Jethro with but a few words, the veil of imaginative picture language spreads over the physical events. A sequence of images weaves through the historical report, referring to supersensory and inner soul experiences of Moses, not to external happenings. A scene out of a mystery drama is enacted. Cryptic sentences lead from the physical to the soul realm; by their style they finally reveal that Moses is in a condition by means of which his soul begins to see supersensory forms: 'But Moses fled from Pharaoh, and stayed in the land of Midian; and he sat down by a well' (Exod.2:15). Seven maidens approach him. They are designated as the daughters of Jethro, the priest of Midian. They come to fetch water at the well for the herds of their father. Suddenly, antagonists appear, the shepherds of the flocks. They chase the seven virgins away. Moses confronts the shepherds, helps the maidens draw the water and aids in watering the cattle. Through the seven daughters, then, Moses comes to Jethro and remains with him (Exod.2:16-21).

In the first place, these pictures indicate that the king has turned into a shepherd; instead of the royal splendour, the son of Pharaoh is surrounded by a world of shepherd-like tranquillity. But if we try to make the soul images transparent for the outer historical events, thus translating the imaginative description into a historical one, this transition in Moses' life remains effective only in regard to his innermost soul existence; seen from outside, Moses remained in the same sphere of life to which he belonged earlier, the sphere of priests and initiates. From Egypt's royal priesthood which had become decadent through politicization, Moses moved into an outwardly inconspicuous, pastoral mystery stream of priests.

In the midst of the loneliness of the wilderness, Moses entered upon the sacred confines of a sanctuary. The proximity of this source of wisdom evokes the vision of a well in his soul. In order to understand Moses' initial experience, it is not necessary to assume that he arrived at the site of a spring in the physical sense. He felt the nearness of a source from which streams spiritual life. But from the context of the view we have formed of the Kadesh region, it is nevertheless possible that Moses arrived at one of the holy springs in the oasis-region of Kadesh; perhaps, he came to the 'well of the one who sees and lives', where long ago Hagar had beheld the angel and where Isaac had often stopped; it could, however, also have been the 'well of testing', Massah and Meribah, that was to be so important later on. The spiritual experience is stimulated and supported in this case by the physical site that corresponds to it in its picture-quality. But the site is so alive in its sanctity that it unlocks the world of vision to the soul of Moses.

The figures who approach him are spiritual, not physical forms. He beholds genii-like beings similar to those pictured by the Greeks when they spoke of the Muses or the Graces. They are willing to offer man the water of life from the well of the spirit. Rudolf Steiner, who singles out this scene to demonstrate the difference between the physical and the supersensory soul events in biblical reports, says concerning the daughters of Jethro, in his lecture on Moses:[55]

To comprehend the deeper meaning of such a story, one

must . . . remember that in the mystical description of all the ages, what the soul can develop of higher knowledge and forces in itself is depicted by the symbol of feminine figures — down to Goethe's words at the end of *Faust* concerning the 'eternal feminine'. In the seven daughters of Jethro, therefore, we recognize the seven soul forces that were at the disposal of the wisdom of the priestly sages . . .

Today, we speak of the human soul and its forces, as having these forces of thinking, feeling and willing within ourselves — and it is correct from the stand-point of the intellectual consciousness to put it this way . . . Ancient man thought differently under the influence of the clairvoyant faculty . . . He felt as if given up with his being to the macrocosmos . . . and he experienced the individual soul forces as if in a relationship with specific divine spiritual beings . . . More and more, the faculties of the soul turn into abstract concepts . . . and thus, we can still recognize what the seven daughters of the Midianite priest and sage symbolize for us as the seven living spirit forces, active in the sphere of the soul in the medieval 'seven liberal arts.' There, we see the seven arts emerge vividly from the human soul. This is the last abstract remnant of the awareness that seven faculties express themselves in the soul's life.

The ancient commentators of the Torah point in an abstract manner to the unison of seven soul forces expressed imaginatively in the biblical picture of the seven maidens, inasmuch as they ponder over the seven names attributed to Jethro. In the philological interpretation given to the seven names, the inwardly necessary structure and form, still present in the imaginative picture of the seven daughters, becomes blurred, but a faint trace of it is nevertheless retained:[56]

He was called by seven names . . . *Jethro*, for he practised good deeds so much; *Hobab* because he was dear to the Lord; *Reuel*, for he was a friend to the Lord; *Heber*, for he had become like a companion to the Lord; *Putiel*, because he refrained from idolatry; *Keni*, because he was

zealous of the Lord; [?], because he had attained the
Torah.

The mystery drama at the well progresses. Moses is disturbed
in the vision of the seven genii-like figures by the priests of that
temple site. The imaginative description of the Bible indicates this
in the picture of the antagonistic shepherds. Moses realizes that,
instead of being the mediators of the genii for human beings, the
priests place themselves between them and men. So he confronts
the priests with the power of his own priestly spirit. In ancient
non-biblical traditions faint traces have survived to show that the
apparently unimportant shepherd scene deals with an important
religious and historical encounter. Thus, Philo describes how
Moses vanquishes the opponents by the power of his word:[57]

When he spoke to them in this way — for in his speech he
had transformed himself completely into a prophet and he
spoke in rapture — they were overcome by the fear that
he could fling significant oracle incantations and curses
against them. So they admitted defeat and withdrew from
the scene.

Owing to Moses' priestly action Jethro's daughters can once
again draw near, and the drink from the well of the spirit is once
more served to human beings. By this experience, as if he had
passed a test, Moses is accepted into Jethro's discipleship in which
he remains a full forty years. The Bible leaves us in the dark
concerning what it was that comprised the content of this period.
It only states in one short, hieroglyphic sentence: '[Jethro] gave
Moses his daughter Zipporah' (Exod.2:21). In the picture of the
marriage to one of the Jethro daughters, the imaginative soul
description continues.

We would be on the wrong trail if we interpreted Moses'
marriage in a physical sense. Just as the picture of Joseph's
marriage to Asenath, the daughter of the high priest at On-
Heliopolis, refers to Joseph's Egyptian initiation,[58] behind the
image of a union between Moses and Zipporah — even if an
actual marriage might have *also* taken place — the whole result
of the instruction and initiation that Moses received from his
teacher Jethro is concealed. The sequence of the images allows
us to perceive an important step taken by Moses under Jethro's
guidance. Confronted with the sevenfold genii-like beings he

chose only a single one of them, he united himself with a quite specific soul force. This decision, which determined his whole being, later found no approval among those with whom he fulfilled his mission. Aaron and Miriam, themselves still devoted to ancient clairvoyant soul forces, quarrelled with Moses at important stations of the great migration, because he had wed a person of black skin, a negress (Num.12:1). What secret is concealed behind the figure of Zipporah?

The change and decision that took place in Moses in Jethro's mystery centre can perhaps be clarified by means of an experience that the great Dominican teacher, Albertus Magnus, had in his youth. At the point of despair over himself he suddenly felt himself surrounded by a brightly shining light from which three maidenly forms approached him. The one in the middle with features like the Virgin Mary spoke to him of the great task awaiting him and, pointing to the figures at the right and at the left, placed before him the choice: Do you want to fulfil your work out of divine wisdom, or out of your own human intelligence? With self-confidence, Albertus Magnus decided in favour of human wisdom, valuing freedom of his own thinking more than divine inspiration that would hold him back on an immature level.

The still clairvoyant world of Egypt had placed the cosmic manifoldness before Moses. This diversity of soul forces, still nourished on ancient treasure, was experienced as the light-filled earthly reflection of the diversity of gods. Through the Egyptian legacy in his soul, Moses was capable of the encounter with the sevenfold variety of the gift-bestowing genii at the well in Midian. As many soul capabilities were open to him as divine forms appeared to him. Through Jethro he was directed towards taking hold of his specific task of destiny, which was not possible without great self-restraint and conscious renunciation. The break with Egypt was now completed by relinquishing all clairvoyant as well as artistic faculties and systematically deciding in favour of the shadow world of the brain-bound intellect, lacking in light. Among the seven maidens Moses chose the darkest, who, among the planets, corresponds to the moon with her borrowed light, and, among the seven liberal arts, to dialectics. Moses rested his being on that force in the soul which limited him to the contours of his single personality and made him ego-bound. The 'I'-force, promoted by the head thoughts, was the oneness that, for Moses, superseded the manifoldness at Jethro's place. We witness how:

> Moses stood with his soul-being before the totality of the seven human soul forces, but had the task above all to imbue human evolution with a single one of them . . . This was the soul force that gathers the other soul forces, previously pictured separately, together into uniform inner soul life, into a life of the 'I' . . . 'I'-consciousness, intellectuality, rationalism; reason and intelligence that are directed towards the outer sense world were to be established in humanity in place of the old clairvoyance . . . What mankind of later epochs owes to Moses is the power to unfold reason and intellect, to be able to think intellectually about the universe out of self-awareness in a fully awake state of mind.[59]

The result of the forty-year-long Jethro discipleship, condensed into the image of marriage to one of the seven daughters, is basically a coming-into-its-own of the Moses personality: Moses finds his 'I'. But he does not find it without sacrificing the old clairvoyance of the spiritual cosmos. The 'I' is alone, lonely and homeless; it separates the human being from all maternally supporting elements of the world and casts him back upon himself. Hence the Bible says that Zipporah bore Moses a son whom he named Gershom, 'For I have been a sojourner in a foreign land' (Exod.2:22). The 'I' is the inner son in man, the son of man, and the destiny of the son of man is homelessness, through which alone he can find himself and freedom.

2.7 The burning bush

Just as the experience at the waters of the well stands at the beginning of the forty years that Moses spent with Jethro, so at the end stands the divine revelation out of the mountain's fire which flamed forth from the thornbush. Here too, the pastoral image is woven into the imaginative biblical description. This says that while keeping Jethro's flock, Moses had approached Horeb (Exod.3:1). Gently, the legends reveal the imaginative character of this description, explaining at the same time how the rocky desert devoid of any vegetation could become the scene of a shepherd's existence by revealing that Moses ventured into the wasteland and near Mount Horeb in search of a lost sheep.[60] Thus, Moses is not a shepherd in the outer sense. He stands before us as the *pastor bonus*, the Good Shepherd, representing the bridge from the Egyptian ritualistic images of the great Hermes, with the recovered lamb on his shoulders, to the Gospels, in which Christ himself appears as the Good Shepherd with the lost sheep.

How should we picture the spiritual experience that Moses was privileged to have before the burning thornbush? Here it is the opposite of the scene at the well; here, it would be wrong to imagine a revelation lacking any basis in nature. Moses found himself on a holy mountain summit, inasmuch as even in the Bible Horeb is designated from the beginning as a 'mountain of God'.

It is the main mountain sanctuary, a sacrificial site, in the region of the Jethro mystery centre of Kadesh. The fiery evolutionary process of our planet earth was still active there. The Saturnian fire out of which the earth had begun to form itself long ago blazed forth here from the interior in fiery smoke. The Horeb-Sinai summit was an altar of stone on which the sacrificial fire did not yet need to be lit by human hands. The primal fire of creation itself burned there. In sight of the physical flickering flames a supersensory vision kindled in the soul of Moses. For him, the physical fire became transparent for a spiritual etheric fire element, which now flamed forth towards him from the whole mineral surroundings and the scant, mineral-like thornbush vegetation as well. Through the symbolical images he looked into the spiritual etheric archetypes, passing through the world's creation in reverse order. He beheld 'the external objects . . . in such a manner that they appear permeated in the background by the archetypes out of which they grew forth.'[61] In the description Philo gives of the burning thornbush, he comes close to the spiritual-physical set of facts:[62]

> There was a thornbush covered with thorns, of very meagre
> growth . . . Without anyone having set a fire, the bush
> suddenly bursts into flames and yet remains intact despite
> being engulfed by bright flames from its roots to the
> top . . . as if it were of insensitive material and in itself not

a substance for fire; rather, as if the fire were serving it
as nourishment.

Physical fire needs to feed on materials from the earth, but there
is a spiritual fire element in all living things which itself nourishes
the substances of the earth and brings about their growth.This is
the etheric body in plant, animal and man that at the same time
bears the spiritual archetype, the primal phenomenon of the being
to which it bestows life. It is a vision of the etheric world, which
the Horeb-Sinai fire evoked in Moses' soul.

But this form of vision is already totally different from the
etheric clairvoyance that had dominated ancient humanity well
into the Egyptian age. Ancient clairvoyance beheld the spiritual
manifoldness of the cosmos. In Moses, the clairvoyant faculty was
in the process of changing into intellectual perception and therefore accompanied and directed by systematizing thinking that
seeks for unity in plurality. Although the thought-imbued vision
and visionary thinking alive in Moses no longer possessed the
colour and brightness of ancient clairvoyance, it nevertheless
penetrated more deeply into the world of beings of the spirit. To
the human spirit that is becoming ego-like, the cosmic 'I' reveals
itself behind the many beings of the spirit realm:

> People of former times looked up to the plurality of
> universal forces as influencing the human soul so that the
> individual forces present a manifoldness, where the soul is
> merely their stage. Moses was now to perceive a universal
> spirit, revealed not merely to a single soul force as a spirit
> of equal rank with other spirits. He was called upon to
> recognize the universal spirit that only comes to expression
> in the deepest, most holy centre of the soul's life, that
> holds sway only in the 'I' itself, where the soul becomes
> aware of its central core . . . That universal spirit which
> can be comprehended with the same intellect which
> combines the various phenomena of the world, can be
> seen as the essential unity which is the basis of the
> universe.[63]

As in the vision of the seven daughters at the well, Moses is led
here also, through the experience at the burning thornbush, from
plurality to oneness. We learn to know this through the three
names that the divine entity gives itself as it becomes manifest.

95

MOSES

First, the divine name of the Elohim resounds to Moses. The round of the seven creator-spirits, revered by the faith of the ancient Hebrews, manifests behind the fiery flame and the angelic countenance that lights up within the latter: 'I am the God [Elohim] of your father, the God of Abraham, the God of Isaac and the God of Jacob' (Exod.3:6). As in a far-reaching view back over the past, Moses beheld what was known in ancient times as the sevenfold host of the deity.

Moses is not content with what is revealed to him. He has to inquire after the present name of the deity: 'If I come to the people of Israel and say to them, "The God of your fathers has sent me to you," and they ask me, "What is his name?" what shall I say to them?' Now he is given the mighty reply, the clarion call of a newly dawning age: 'I AM THE I AM! . . . This is what you are to say to the Israelites: "I AM has sent me to you".' (Exod. 3:14 B).

The one central being of all existence, the universal ego, becomes visible behind the veil of terrestrial and celestial manifoldness. The human 'I' springing forth within the soul because of the head's thinking, is the organ for the divine universal ego. The era of egohood commences in heaven and on earth, and Moses with his royal forehead is its great herald and first-born among men.

Moses has always been denoted abstractly as the inaugurator of monotheism, as the one who pointed the way from a still barbaric level of polytheism to a refined conception of God. But prior to Moses, the view of divine plurality corresponded to world reality. Monotheism is not an eternal absolute truth. Only due to the fact that during an important cosmic turning-point of time the divine being of the universe — capable of bringing to expression the holy oneness of the universe's foundation — ventured from the distant heights of existence into the earth's vicinity and began to communicate itself as the germinal force of egohood, could the idea of the one god be born.

But the multitude of beings in the spiritual world is not extinguished because the I AM, the universal 'I', the Lord, begins to manifest. What does take place is merely a division between spirit entities. A number of beings make themselves transparent for the one, become his servants and organs, and thereby bearers of progress and the future. The others cease to be vessels and revealers of the higher guiding powers; they become beings of deception and nothingness.*

Moses is given the task to direct the souls of the Israelites to an entity who, for this age, is to a special degree the bearer and manifestation of the universal 'I', the Lord. That is the significance of the third name which the deity calls from the fire of the thornbush: 'Say to the people of Israel, "The LORD, the God [Yahweh Elohim] of your fathers . . . has sent me to you".' (Exod.3:15).

The Yahweh name contains a secret that makes it unutterable for the Israelites. Philologically related to the sacred primordial statement, I AM THE I AM [*ehyeh asher ehyeh*], it harbours within itself the 'I'-name, the ego's name. One of the loftiest servants and bestowers of the 'I' is designated by the name Yahweh. But how can man dare to say 'I' to God? No being can apply the 'I'-name to other than his own self. The universal 'I' does not as yet dwell within the human being. Approaching the earth, it only casts its shadow because of the dawning of self-awareness in the thinking human soul. As the name Yahweh could not be uttered by the Israelites, the ancient name of God, Adonai, which means 'Lord', and is synonymous with the Phoenician *Adonis* and the Greek *Kyrios*, was used. In Hebrew only the consonants, which are of a corporeal sheath-like nature, are written. The soul-like vowels were only indicated at a later time. The unutterable consonants 'YHWH' had the vowel indications of Adonai added. This led to the erronous pronunciation of 'Jehovah'.

Who is Yahweh-Elohim? Anthroposophical research describes[64] how the seven Elohim, lofty Spirits of Form, who are called Exousiai in the language of the New Testament, caused the genesis of the earth out of the cosmic night; first, as a harmoniously co-operating group, then more and more clearly under the concentrated leadership of the central one of the seven entities, Yahweh. Through Yahweh, the sevenfoldness is merged into a oneness, into a personality of higher rank. Yahweh becomes the common ego of the Elohim and thus facilitates the in-pouring of the loftiest

*The Old Testament has a specially apt term for these beings who have become untimely, which, because of its similarity with the name for the deity, Elohim, possesses special emphasis: it calls them *Elilim*, the 'nothings' or 'nonentities'.

creator being, the Kyrios Christos, to whom the sevenfoldness of the Elohim offer themselves up as divine sheath and organ. From the very beginning of creation, therefore, Yahweh-Elohim is the one who prepares the way in heaven and earth for the one, the messenger and bearer of egohood.

The first of the three divine names that Moses hears, Elohim, recalls the ancient plurality of the gods; the third expresses the arising unity and egohood of God in the form comprehensible to humanity of that age. The middle name is like magical thunder and lightning itself, whereby the curtain is torn away from the inner core of the universe, thus initiating the age of egohood.

Here we fathom the wisdom-treasure, mysteriously veiled by the Bible, that Moses acquired during the forty years between the experience at the well and the vision in the fire of the mountain through Jethro. The first books of the Bible, foremost the creation story of Genesis, are an essential part of it.

If we understand the kind of vision at which Moses arrived in front of the burning bush at the end of the forty years, we also comprehend the spiritual source of the Books of Moses, especially that of Genesis, the mighty history of creation at the beginning of the Bible. Out of the soul of Moses there still emerged a spiritual faculty of seeing, but this vestige of clairvoyant sight was nothing but the enveloping sheath out of which thought pressed forth towards light on Moses' forehead. We can understand this visionary thinking and thought-imbued vision that lived in Moses' soul as a transitional consciousness, by means of the nature of our faculty of memory. Today, thinking and memory are far removed from one another. Thought has paled completely and has become abstract. Only memory has retained something of the picture quality and plasticity of ancient vision. The thinking of Moses was still completely one with memory and therefore embedded within an imaginative, visionary element. For this reason, the faculty of spiritual retrospection still indwelled the thought-filled vision of Moses; his personal capability of memory expanded to cosmic memory: through the outer phenomena he penetrated to the primal phenomena, through the sense images to the archetypes, through the present to the beginnings, through the creatures to creation and the creative beings. The fire of Horeb that burned forth out of the thornbush became transparent for him as the remnant of the ancient Saturn fire;[65] the divine genesis of all existence arose before his backward-looking soul. Just as Moses advanced from the name of God for the many, to that of the one, we also discern in the great creation myth how the creation of the Elohim is superseded and continues further through the creative deeds of Yahweh-Elohim and Yahweh.

Theology of the past hundred and fifty years was believed to have made a momentous discovery when it hit upon the idea that the divergence of the two names for God, Elohim and Yahweh, might be caused by the fact that the Books of Moses were composed of several textual sources. Depending on the title employed, several authors were construed and one was designated an 'Elohist', another a 'Yahvist'. Even logically this is an extremely flimsy theory. If the person, who later on combined the texts into one, tolerated the different names side by side and let them stand, why shouldn't an author for the whole text be assumed who employed the two names side by side? Although this theory is to a large degree 'scientifically acknowledged', it is based on the greatest abstraction possible, namely on the opinion that the various names for God have always referred to the same spiritual reality. In face of a view of the world that is familiar with concrete beings in the spiritual world and therefore knows how to distinguish between the various real entities who have been designated by the names Elohim and Yahweh, the whole theory of distinguishing the source material, the so-called pentateuchal criticism, disappears into thin air.

2.8 The staff of Moses

When Moses beheld the fiery revelation at Mount Horeb, the divine voice asked him, 'What is that in your hand?' Moses replied, 'A rod' (Exod.4:2). This is the rod that became a serpent and finally resumed its former shape. By means of its power, Moses overcame the world of Egypt. What does this staff indicate? Legendary traditions outside the Bible clearly sum up in this image the fruits of the mystery-discipleship of the Jethro years.

It is said that once, having arrived at a significant turning point of his development, Moses was in prayer in Jethro's garden:

> And as we was praying, he beheld a magnificent staff across from him, covered with sapphires, growing out of the ground. He moved close to it and lo, the undisguised name of God was carved into it. He uttered the name, grasped the staff, and tore it out of the ground as easily as one pulls up a plant.[66]

Before he had acquired it, the staff of Moses belonged to Jethro. How had he come into its possession? Here, the legends describe a course of descent that is strongly reminiscent of the imagery surrounding the primordial revelation that streams through the ages, the traditions of the 'Book of Adam' and the 'Garment of Adam'.[67] In the symbol of the staff of Moses we also behold a secret retained since paradisal times:

> It was the staff with which all divine works had been accomplished; after the creation of heaven and earth and all its hosts, of seas and streams and the fish dwelling therein had been completed. For after God had driven the first man out of the Garden of Eden, Adam took this staff in his hand and tilled the ground from which he had been fashioned. Adam gave it to Enoch; from Enoch it passed over to Noah who passed it on to Shem and his descendants until it came into the hands of Abraham, the Hebrew. When Abraham handed all that he possessed over to his son Isaac, he also gave him this staff. After this, it came to pass that Isaac's son, Jacob, fled to Mesopotamia; he had nothing but this staff when he crossed over the Jordan. He then returned to his father, but he did not forget the staff and took it along when he journeyed down to Egypt. He presented it to Joseph as something more valuable than what his brothers received . . .
>
> After Joseph's death, the princes of Egypt entered the house of the regent and his staff came into possession of the Midianite Reuel-Jethro. He then transplanted it into his garden.[68]

A concealed symbol passed through the generations of mankind. It was Moses who awakened it to reality. In Jethro's garden the staff awaited the one for whom it was destined. There were many who tested themselves against it and tried to tear it from the ground in order to make it their own. But it neither moved nor bent, as if it had roots to the centre of the earth. But when the hand of Moses touched it, it could be moved without effort. Moses lifted the spell of the magic staff; he was able to awaken the slumbering power that, until then, had been passed from epoch to epoch.*

The staff of Moses must not be conceived as an external object. Moses did not carry it outwardly in his hand but inwardly, as a basic component part of his own being. We shall be able to decipher this imaginative sign, if we find a way to bring into our view the supersensory nature of man as embodied in Moses. As on a map, we can look for and determine the 'staff's' shape and position; but it must be kept in mind that the staff has not simply been there always. Moses was the first to acquire it as a new force. Therefore, we must at the same time try to view the supersensory image of man in its evolution, in the great metamorphoses that it undergoes in the various stages of the history of consciousness.

In ancient times, when the clairvoyant faculties of human nature were still fully active, the supersensory image of man was determined by the size of the etheric body, which still extended far beyond the physical body, and by the chain of luminous organs — resembling a row of sparkling precious stones — through which the astral body shone forth from the flowing elements of the etheric body. The etheric body, which as yet did not coincide with the physical body, carried the 'lotus flowers', the perceptual organs of the astral body, through flowing activity into the light of vision.

Then came the time when the sparkling, diamond-like lights became increasingly dim. The etheric body, which was shrinking down into the physical form, carried the lotus flowers, floating freely until then, into the zone of the earthly body where, withering and hardening, they lost their mobility and their bright faculty of perception. The soul organs turned blind in favour of the sense organs and brain-bound thinking. In the future, the

---

*In connection with the old Nordic sagas, Richard Wagner creates a similar imagination, inasmuch as, in the *Valkyrie* he has Siegmund pull the sword Notung, intended for him by the Father of the Gods, out of the tree's trunk.

lotus flowers of the astral body must and will once again circle
and blossom radiantly. This presupposes intensive inner work of
man on himself. It is easy to imagine that producing changes in
one's astral body and the lotus flowers must be accompanied by
one-sidedness and dangers; for only by attaining a new body-free
condition for the etheric body can the astral body also be lifted
out of the physical body's zone of hardness and darkness.

We now have the main outline to gain an exact conception of
the transformations undergone by human nature in the course of
the evolution of its consciousness, insofar as the symbol of the
staff of Moses relates to it. In order to build up the image of
supersensory man concretely and in detail upon this outline, we
take into consideration the description given by Rudolf Steiner.

In his book, *Knowledge of the Higher Worlds and Its Attainment*, in the chapter, 'Some Results of Initiation,' exercises of
purification and strengthening that are suitable for brightening
and opening up the various organs of the astral body are described
in intimate differentiation. At important points of the chapter, to
which we must pay special heed to resolve this question, indications are interspersed concerning fundamental transformations
that have to take place in the etheric body, if the reawakening of
the slumbering astral organs is to be a healthy one. The causative
sphere for the ancient clairvoyance was located in the physical
body which, in its perviousness and soft plasticity, still left the
etheric body free. For a healthy clairvoyance of the future, the
causative sphere must move more to the inner being. The 'I' must
become capable of directly taking hold of the etheric body and
loosening it from the spell of the physical body, with which it has
become identical in outline. Thereby, the soul or astral body will
simultaneously be lifted up into a body-free condition. The body-
free state of old derived from without; it came about by itself as
a fact of nature. The new state comes from within, as an achieve-
ment of human striving for the spirit; it originates from the activity
of the strengthened ego, which learns to loosen the formative
forces body (the etheric body) from its bonds to the physical
element:[69]

> The development of the soul-body . . . permits of
> perception in a supersensible world, but anyone wishing
> to find his way in this world must not remain stationary at

this stage of development. The mere mobility of the lotus
flowers is not sufficient. The student must acquire the
power of regulating and controlling the movement of his
spiritual organs independently and with complete
consciousness; otherwise he would become a plaything for
external forces and powers. To avoid this he must acquire
the faculty of hearing what is called the *inner word*, and
this involves the development not only of the soul-body
but also of the etheric body . . .

. . . For, at a certain stage, development consists
precisely in adding to the unconscious currents and
movements of the etheric body others that are consciously
produced and controlled.

Continuing further in the descriptions, Rudolf Steiner enumer-
ates how, through correct inner training, certain centres in the
etheric body develop as emanating points of rays and movement.
The goal is 'the formation of a kind of center in the region of the
physical heart, from which radiate currents and movements in the
greatest possible variety of colors and forms. The center is in
reality not a mere point, but a most complicated structure, a most
wonderful organ.'

One day, the faculty of the 'inner word' will be linked to this
organ. But one cannot begin at the goal. The centre of freedom
in the heart's region is not the source and point of departure of
freedom, it is its culmination.

From the age of Moses onwards, it is of increasing importance
for humanity that all spiritual training proceeds from the purification and strengthening of thought:[70]

A simple start is made with a view to the deepening of the
logical activity of the mind and the producing of an inward
intensification of thought. Thought is thereby made free
and independent of all sense impressions and experiences;
it is concentrated in one point which is held entirely under
control. Thus a preliminary center is formed for the
currents of the etheric body. This center is not yet in the
region of the heart but in the head, and it appears to the
clairvoyant as the point of departure for movements and
currents. No esoteric training can be successful which does
not first create this center. If the latter were first formed

in the region of the heart, the aspiring clairvoyant would doubtless obtain glimpses of the higher worlds, but would lack all true insight into the connection between these higher worlds and the world of our senses. This, however, is an unconditional necessity for man at the present stage of evolution. The clairvoyant must not become a visionary; he must retain a firm footing upon the earth.

From this point of departure, the liberation of the etheric body takes a most significant, vivid course. 'The center in the head, once duly fixed, is then moved lower down, to the region of the larynx . . . Then the currents of the etheric body radiate from this point and illumine the astral space surrounding the individual.'

Along with moving the centre downwards, man attains the capability of freely moving the etheric body. 'This faculty is effected by currents . . . centered in the two-petalled lotus in the region of the eyes . . .' And finally, '. . . the time has come to give the complete system of currents and movements its center situated in the region of the heart . . . and at this point also the stage is reached when the student becomes gifted with the inner word.'

We gain an important conception through these descriptions: the centre of freedom travels in the human being from the forehead to the heart. But we must not imagine that the centre of freedom on the forehead is extinguished when it moves towards the heart. This freedom, once acquired in the 'place of the skull' by means of the strengthened body-free thinking, is not forfeited or exchanged for the liberation of the etheric heart. In reality it is not a *centre* of freedom that is developed but a *line* of freedom, a staff of freedom. Here we arrive at the point where we can understand the biblical imagination of the staff of Moses exactly.

The meditative directions by Rudolf Steiner, which aim for the formation of the freedom-axis in the etheric body, indicate an evolution of human consciousness that reaches into the far-off future. Despite that, the mission of Moses signifies a real beginning of this process. A force was born in Moses to which the greater number of human beings can only aspire in a distant future, maturing for it through many destinies and efforts. The staff of freedom has rested in human nature since primordial beginnings. Moses took hold of it at that point from which it can

truly become a factor in humanity: at that starting point situated
on the forehead of man, where the ram's horns of the two-petalled
lotus flower dwell and where — by the sacrifice of the lamb, the
death of the last vestige of clairvoyance — the birth of thoughts,
the resurrection of consciousness in thinking, grows forth. The
two-petalled lotus flower is the last astral organ that goes out. But
out of its tomb on the skull thought arises as the first beginning
of freedom. Moses with his royal, Zeus-like forehead took hold
of the staff at the end that points upward. He led into the evolution
of consciousness that takes hold of the human being from above
to below and makes freedom possible for man, thereby returning
divinity to him.

The Bible shows us that the staff of Moses could change into a
serpent. Once again, the transformation of consciousness comes
to expression, that occurs particularly in the age of Moses. Intellectual thought, which was only now entering fully into humanity's
development, the pole at which Moses took hold of the staff of
freedom, still appeared for the time being in the garment of
clairvoyant power. The staff of thinking replaced the serpent, the
ancient condition of the etheric body; it was a metamorphosis of
the serpent, of ancient ego-devoid vision, ascending from below
along the human spine. But as yet, the transformation was still in
the balance: the serpent turned into the staff, but the staff could
also revert once again to the condition of the serpent.

Even the age of the serpent had its premonition of the power
of the staff. But the staff of ancient mankind was not the staff of
freedom, but of magic, arising out of the dark depths of uncon-
sciousness. In order to clarify this, we must point to a significant
segment of hatha yoga, the magic yoga of India.* There, the
human being is presented in the following way. Three vertical
streams of forces course through man; each can be brought into
magic activity through certain exercises. The path to be followed
is that of the middle, Sushumna, between the two streams Ida and
Pingala. How is this accomplished? At Brahmadvara, Brahman's
portal at the lower end of the spine, the serpent Kundalini, the

*Similar material concerning this symbolism could be cited from all ancient
cultures. I owe this reference to hatha yoga to Hermann Beckh.

young mourning widow, sleeps tightly coiled between the two streams. By means of the exercises to be undertaken, the serpent raises herself up 'like a staff' and enters the path in the middle, the occult, etheric spine. Successfully to execute the exercises signifies, pictorially speaking, to grasp the snake by its tail: then, from below to above, it turns into the staff of magic perception and actions. It is just this picture that makes it clear that the ancient path of the serpent took the darkest, most unconscious forces of human nature as its starting point. The partially gruesome exercises recommended by Hath yoga, which extend into the sphere of animalistic instinct, confirm this.

The serpent is the ruler of the ancient rod symbol, being itself the old staff, the staff of magic symbolized in the physical spine. It comes to life on the path, bound to nature and sensuality, that leads from below to above. The staff of Moses signifies dominion over the serpent. It takes hold of the serpent at the head; it takes its course from above to below, taking its point of departure from the clearly conscious thought element and not permitting any step through which the clear consciousness of thinking-experiences are interrupted. Thereby it is the staff of freedom and egohood. When it comes more and more clearly into man's possession, it develops — as one discerns from Rudolf Steiner's indications — into a spiritual frontal spine in the supersensory human form, which, because of the row of freedom centres in the etheric body and the astral lotus organs arranged upon them, shines forth brightly as if adorned with precious stones. The power of supersensory cognition and action leaves the spine in the back in which it was active as the serpent, and passes into the luminous frontal spine, the first germinating beginning of which is indicated in the image of the staff of Moses. Legends do indeed offer us an exact imagination when they relate how Moses grasped the staff in Jethro's garden and pulled it out of the ground: The staff is adorned with brilliant precious stones and on it one can read the letters of the undistorted, inexpressible name of God, Yahweh, which contains the ego-mystery, the sign of freedom.

Rudolf Steiner added indications that serve as keys for unlocking the secrets of the occult figures that he published in calendar form in 1912. The sentence concerning the sign of Cancer refers to a distant future of mankind: 'The lotus flowers develop into a radiant frontal spine, the spine in the back vanishes.' What he said concerning the necessity to develop a spiritual backbone, or spine, belongs in this context. Along with the demand to proceed everywhere in meditative schooling from the clear awareness of thinking, the other, which asks that all meditative exercises be accompanied by the striving after moral ego-envigoration, is closely connected:[71]

> It must be emphasized that . . . this development of the
> lotus flowers . . . should not take place while ignoring the
> means for strengthening morality . . . What is developed
> as strengthened ego-feeling is inward firmness, which
> could be termed an elemental spine. Both must have been
> developed correspondingly: lotus flowers, so that one can
> transform oneself; and something like a spine in the
> physical world, an elemental backbone, so that one can
> develop one's strengthened 'I' in the elemental world.

2.9 The bronze serpent

Once, in the course of the destinies that tested the people in the desert, Moses openly placed the secret of his rod, which was that of the vanquisher of the serpent, in classic grandeur before the people in a symbolic sign: he erected the bronze serpent.

The people objected to what the desert signified and, as before, longed to return to Egypt. They were not merely growing tired of the deprivations and longing to return to eternal fruitfulness and nourishment. The spiritual character of Egypt with its pre-egotistic legacy of supersensory talents had offered a much more supportive environment than did the infinite, stark homelessness of the desert. Thus, the backward-looking desire for naturally-bestowed soul contents awakened a re-emergence of ancient forces in the Israelites. Atavistic elements made themselves felt in the fire and smoke phenomena of the region they had traversed. But the angelic 'I'-deity whom Moses was able to perceive in the fire did not reveal himself to the people; instead, through the fire, the serpent, the ancient atavistic force of clairvoyance belonging to the etheric body, was awakened in them in a demonic manner, causing disease. The Bible describes this as the sudden and frightening appearance of fiery serpents who caused great devastation among the people (Num.21:4-9).

It was not brought into awareness by clear experiences of images that the etheric bodies reverted to a condition no longer timely. Illnesses of epidemic proportions, accompanied by visions of fear, appeared; many people even died of them. This is what is meant when the Bible speaks of the bite of fiery serpents.

The nature of illness, of being ill, to which mankind had to succumb increasingly since the times of the Flood,[72] appears in a specific form. Ancient spiritual faculties, from which a bright perception of the spirit realm blossomed forth in their own time, recoil into the physical body and there cause illnesses in times when the etheric bodies have already shrunk down. Many diseases are displaced atavisms. Healing forces for such illnesses will become available to the human being when he is able to bring the forces, unconsciously active in his soul and etheric body, under the control of his innermost self, to master the serpent through the power of the staff.

Following the divine command, Moses erected a symbol that in a powerful way addressed the egohood's inner will to be well in those who looked upon it; it was the staff on which a serpent was crucified. No longer only a hidden form of the serpent itself, it was the staff that overcame and lifted up the serpent. The snake curled itself around the staff on which its head was fastened. Moses erected a symbol of humanity which we encounter among all the peoples who wrested themselves free of the disease-causing influence of the past epoch: the Staff of Mercury or Asclepius, the symbol of medical doctors to this day.

Greek traditions contain an exact parallel to the imaginative biblical scene of the fiery serpents. When Greece liberated herself from the spell of Trojan-Asiatic spirituality and the city of Troy was already doomed to perish, giant snakes, so it is said, crept out of the ocean onto the shore and coiled themselves around the bodies of the priests who wanted to perform their sacrificial service there. In vain, Laocoön and his sons fought against the deadly pressure of the snakes' bodies. The Laocoön statue in the museum at the Vatican in Rome expresses in classic tragedy a last revolt of the perishing, atavistic spirituality, similar to the image of the fiery snakes that tormented the people of Israel, when they were supposed to free themselves finally of the spell of Egyptian life. The bronze serpent is therefore exactly the same as the serpent-staff of the Greek Asclepian sanctuaries: the symbol in which the 'I'-endowed spirit is victorious over the sick soul remnants of the past.

The snake, crucified and erected by Moses in the desert, addressed the upright posture of the human form as in a symbolic mirror. The snake that creeps across the earth reflects what is given man only by nature and belongs to his lower being. By virtue of his upright form he is predestined to overcome the snake. But prior to the dawn of the epoch of the 'I', the serpent still ruled over the human being, for, from below to above, it could become the staff of ancient clairvoyance in his spine. Increasingly, it emerged as the serpent of temptation and doom on the tree of man's being. Beginning with Moses, man could freely grasp the staff of his upright form at the forehead above and thus force the serpent into his service. Henceforth, he could lift the lower elements, given him merely by nature, into consciousness and thereby transform them into spiritual strength. Now, man himself was the Staff of Mercury on which the snake was crucified.

In this way, Moses created two sublime symbols of sacrifice: the sacrifice of the lamb in the feast of Passover, and the sacrifice of the snake in the symbol of the staff. As the leader out of the old, unaware spirituality into the new, freely conscious spirituality, Moses inaugurated both.*

An ancient tradition relates that the wood of Moses' rod came from the Tree of Life that stood in paradise as well as the beams of the cross later erected on Golgotha. What is the significance of this pictorial concept? We see three major stages of humanity's soul evolution and development of consciousness in three fundamental symbols. In paradise, the serpent coils itself from below upwards around the Tree of Life and thereby turns it into the Tree of Death. On Golgotha, the cross stands as the Tree of Death, but the spiritual glory of the body of Christ that is nailed upon it turns the wood of the cross into the new Tree of Life. In

---

*Moses' Staff of Mercury, the bronze snake, was kept and revered in the Temple of Jerusalem until King Hezekiah, the contemporary of Isaiah, destroyed it (2Kings 18:4). At the time of the prophets, a new step had to be taken once again in the changes of consciousness; therefore certain spiritual directions of the Moses age had to be opposed.

the middle between the old and the new Tree of Life stands the image of the bronze serpent in the desert. The rod of Moses, around which, fastened at the head, the snake is coiling, is the Tree of Freedom. It opens the path in man's being from the Tree of Death to the new Tree of Life.

2.10 The miracle of the spring

One of the Old Testament scenes that we encounter most frequently in early Christian pictorial representations, in catacomb paintings and sarcophagi carvings and so on,[73] obviously valued from early on as a prophecy concerning the Christ, is the miracle of the spring: Moses points his magically powerful rod at the rock and lo, a spring pours forth. What spiritual and historical events do we look into through the images of the so-called 'miracles of the desert journey'?

Amidst lightning-bolts and thunder, like a roaring spiritual tempest, the 'I'-impulse made its first entry into earth history in the age of Moses. Apocalyptic birth pains of the new ego epoch shook the world, frightening Egypt with visions of doom, liberating Israel by merciful glimpses of a future salvation and guiding it to itself. The miracles that the people of Moses experienced in the desert were the actual reversals of the Egyptian plagues. Ancient texts, such as the Wisdom of Solomon, employ this as an exact principle of their description inasmuch as they set each of the ten plagues over against one of the blessed experiences of the travelling Israelites.

The 'I'-impulse, which flashed down from heaven like a bolt of lightning, carried actual premonitions into mankind, early manifestations of the higher being of man that were prophetically ahead of their time, and for the real fulfilment of which long distances of fate still had to be traversed. We understand the miracles of the desert, if we recognize the light of which they are the earthly silhouettes: the future image of man with the three higher members of his being.

Anthroposophy pictures the human being as consisting of firstly the physical body; secondly, the etheric, ether or life body; thirdly, the astral or soul body; and fourthly, the ego or the 'I', the inhabitant of the three sheaths. Through processes of evolution and transformation, a higher threefoldness is added to this lower fourfoldness. Once the 'I' has begun to be active, once the age of ego-man has dawned, soul body, life body and physical body do not remain unchanged from the way in which nature and destiny have fashioned them for man. The 'I' penetrates through the sheaths to the germs of its higher nature that slumber behind them. From the concealed inner essence of the three lower sheaths, it elicits three higher spirit members. Rudolf Steiner describes the development of the upper threefoldness in the following manner:[74]

> The ego has become master within the soul-life. This can be carried so far that no desire, no enjoyment can gain entrance into the soul without the I being the power that makes the entrance possible . . .
>
> . . . This astral body, overcome and transformed by the ego, may be called the *spirit self*. (This is what, in connection with oriental wisdom, is called 'manas.') . . .
>
> Just as the human being conquers his astral body by penetrating to the hidden forces standing behind it, so, too, in the course of evolution, does this happen with the ether body. The work upon the ether body is, however, more intensive than the work upon the astral body, for what is concealed in the former is enveloped by two veils, while the concealed in the astral body is veiled by only one . . . The work extends to the ether body if the ego applies its activity to the changing of its traits of character, of its temperament, and so forth . . . The strongest impulses producing this change in ordinary life are the religious ones . . . The influence of true art has a similar effect upon the human being . . . But from these it is evident that hidden within man there is another member of his being that the 'I' gradually develops. This member may be called the second spiritual member, the *life spirit*. (It is called 'buddhi' in oriental wisdom.' . . .
>
> . . . If through the activity of the I, changes take place in man in respect of its influences upon the physical body, the I is actually united with the hidden forces of this physical body . . . It can be said, then, that the I, through

this activity, works upon the physical body . . . Then the fact emerges that there is still a third spiritual member in man. It is what may be called *spirit man*, in contrast to the physical man. (In oriental wisdom this spirit-man is called 'atma.')

The earthly realization of the upper threefoldness lies in the future. Today, only the first beginnings of the spirit-self (manas) already extend into the being of man. At most, the very first, faint rosy dawn of the life-spirit (budhi) shines towards us from afar. Spirit-man (atma) is the essence of distant future ideals. Nevertheless, the three spirit members of the human being already hover above us, as it were. This is the reason why, at certain times, light rays and traces of their forces fall perceptibly into the stream of humanity's history. The age of Moses was such a time. The young human 'I' was still far from being capable of bringing forth the golden treasure of the higher threefoldness from its entombment in the three earthly sheaths. But the tempestuous nascent state of the 'I'-impulse tore revelations and force transmissions of manas, budhi and atma from heaven down to earth as a first instalment of future realizations. In the feeding with manna, the people of Israel experienced a foretaste of manas, of spiritualized soul existence. In the miracle of the spring, brought about by the rod of Moses, the Israelites were touched by budhi, the higher eternal life of the spirit-permeated etheric body. In the shining form of Moses — when he had been privileged to receive lofty revelations – they distantly sensed something of the majesty of spirit-man, the spirit-pervaded physical corporeality.

The miracles of the years in the desert were largely linked to the miracle of Moses' personality. What mankind can only realize in the future, lives in advance in the great personalities of its leaders. In Moses, the second of the three spiritual members of the human being, budhi or life-spirit, found an early realization incurred by destiny. The etheric body of Moses not only carried within itself the illumination which Moses' 'I'-force could bestow on it owing to its Egyptian and Arabian initiation. Moses' etheric body was, after all, permeated and elevated by the etheric body of Zarathustra, the most sunlike etheric body ever borne by an earthly human being (see Chapter 1.6). The etheric body of Zarathustra allowed the life spirit, which otherwise would have remained concealed for a long time, to shine forth brightly from the etheric body of Moses. The rod, or 'staff of Moses' is in itself a symbolic expression for the budhi element, which, as a special gift of destiny, Moses carried within himself. For the line of freedom, the row of force-centres, that develops from the forehead to the heart in the etheric body of man, by the ego's efforts, is none other than the location where the natural and the transformed life bodies, etheric body and life-spirit, permeate each other. When Moses turned to the people, when he spoke, acted or blessed them, the people already gained a share in the higher life, the life spirit, that he carried within himself.

They felt how he gave them the 'water of life'. In the midst of the stormy signs of the time, this experience must have intensified apocalyptically when Moses accomplished certain deeds that outwardly may well have been quite unassuming, but which were directly symbolic of the higher ethereal element streaming out of him. His thought-filled sense of sight and his clairvoyant thinking enabled Moses to have a very special relationship to nature. It was a combination of instinctive sense and intellectual, attentive observation. This mastery of viewing nature had proven itself in a classic way by the Sea of Reeds. It must have continued to stand the test in the course of the ensuing forty years, since Moses was able to lead the people to places in the arid wasteland, where springs gushed forth, constantly or intermittently, or where, with some searching and digging in the rocky ground, water could be unearthed. The rod of Moses resembled a consciousness divining rod. When Moses gave the thirsty people water to drink, they sensed not only the radiant life-spirit of Moses in the outer occurrence, but it was as if, high above their heads in the clouds, the life spirit of all mankind, awaiting a distant future, were already raining down upon them, evoking premonitions of a future new, etheric clairvoyance.

It might have been similar in the case of the wondrous feeding with manna. The miracle did not consist in the fact that, counter to the laws of nature, the open country was covered in the morning with sweet morsels of bread rather than dew. The miracle occurred rather in the soul experiences that accompanied the eating of a certain food available in the territory the Israelites were passing through. Along with their physical bodies their souls must have

felt sustained in a miraculous way and the sensation of being
inwardly nourished must have been linked with the feeling of an
expecially merciful divine blessing and supersensory peace. The
dream-blessing of the nights was projected into a waking dream
during the gathering and eating of manna. During the actual
eating, the people became aware as in a blissful memory that at
night their souls had been nourished by angels. Thus, the people
partook of a living premonition of the spirit-self, the manas
element that spread a gentle spiritualized light over the realm of
the soul's stirrings.

Concerning the outer facts, the Bible certainly suggests a natural
conception of manna in its description:

> Now the manna was like coriander seed, and its
> appearance like that of bdellium. The people went about
> and gathered it, and ground it in mills or beat it in mortars,
> and boiled it in pots, and made cakes of it; and the taste
> of it was like the taste of cakes baked with oil. When the
> dew fell upon the camp in the night, the manna fell with
> it. (Num.11:7-9).

It must have been a phenomenon that was closely connected
with the special nature of the Sinai terrain, with the spontaneous
activities of the geological forces behind which Moses beheld the
manifestations of divine powers. Perhaps an edible substance was
produced through the action of dewlike precipitation on the partly
volcanic soil and fast-growing plant forms. The astonishing fact
that in an environment of nature, which everywhere appeared to
be only consuming everything with fiery might, something
nourishing now presented itself, turned the external occurrences
into a symbol and stimulus of an inward event for the Israelites.
In a picture-image, there seemed to stand before them a higher,
lavishly giving soul-nature that reached into the self-consuming
lower soul life.

The atma secret, the distant mystery of spirit corporeality, only
shone momentarily from the Moses form into the souls of the
Israelites. Before the burning bush Moses had received the power
of the white hand. His hand could shine with such a white light
that it seemed as if, physically, it had passed over into insubstan-
tiality and only existed spiritually as light (Exod.4:6f). For the
people, this mystery became visible above all in the moment when

Moses returned from the mountain of revelation. His countenance shone with such a bright light that Aaron and the people were frightened and were not capable of facing the sight of him. They all experienced that here they confronted the effects of a spirit who possesses and bestows the sovereign power to transform physical earth substance; here, a spiritual word-power wrote directly into the hard stony matter of earth corporeality. The stone tablets of the Law that looked as if the finger of God himself had etched the deep runes of the commandments into them, signified the same thing as the earthly form of Moses that had become luminous. The mystery of 'spirit-man' who, from within, is lord over matter, announced itself.

In this way, many forms of premonitions of 'I'-perfection merged with the beginning of 'I'-development. The sovereignty that the 'I' was destined to attain over its bodily sheaths was foreseen in preconfigurations of the three higher members of man's being.

Henceforth, the people bore a holy seed for the future with them on their journey. The Letter to the Hebrews (9:4) reveals that from that time onwards three symbols were concealed in the Ark of the Covenant which the people carried through the desert: a golden urn with manna, the staff of Aaron newly turning green, and the stone tablets of the Commandments. With these three holy signs the Israelites built themselves a bridge from the miracles in the desert journey into the future that is to bring to birth the threefold higher being in man. The miraculous food addresses the spirit-self in man, the higher soul being that nourishes itself from above; the staff, which brought forth water from the rock and restores the dead to life, is the sign of the life-spirit by means of which the dying, withering being of man turns once again into the budding Tree of Life; the stone tablets of the revelation point to spirit-man, who has emerged into sovereignty over physical creation.

Signs evoking confidence of future salvation, presentiments of Christ passed through the souls during the wondrous morning sustenance on the ground of the desert, during the miracle of the spring and with the tracing by God's finger of inscriptions into hard stone.

2.11 The revelation at Horeb-Sinai

The greatest miracle in the desert was the revelation of the Commandments themselves. Here, the loftiest gift of a higher world and the culmination of the task of a great human being merged into one. Moses became the Zeus-like inaugurator of the Law, inasmuch as he stood in more ways than one on the dividing line between two worlds. Here more than elsewhere, he combined the beyond with what is of this world; here, empowered by the last clairvoyant forces of mankind, he broke through in the most momentous way into the new world of thinking and egohood.

Insofar as its origin is concerned, the establishment of the Law of Moses can in no way be comprehended by comparisons with that of laws of more recent times. In order to understand it, we must look back into ages of humanity's evolution that Moses moved out and away from. If we want to use a mythological concept, we can say that the Law of Moses had replaced the law of Demeter.

The figure of Demeter, the great mother, leads back far into ages preceding the birth of 'I'-consciousness, when outer and inner world were still a unity for man. The human being was not yet closed off within itself; the life of nature with its divine harmonies still reached completely into the souls, and the spirituality of nature found an organic dwelling place in human nature which was still gifted with divine clairvoyance. As yet a dependent member of nature, man obeyed the same laws in his moral and social actions as that followed by the life of the plant kingdom and the seasons of the year. Natural law and moral law were one and the same. Demeter-Ceres was the bestower of laws on both nature and man.

> [Demeter was] an archetypal form which points to a time when the life of the human brain was not yet cut off from the general bodily life, a time when nutrition by external foodstuffs and thinking through the instrument of the brain were not separate functions. When the crops were thriving in the fields it was still felt at that time that thinking was alive there, that hope was outpoured over the fields and penetrated the activity of Nature's wonder like the song of the lark. It was still felt that along with material substance spiritual life is absorbed into the human body,

becomes purified, becomes spirit . . . The name of
Demeter points us back to those far distant times when
human nature was so unified that all bodily life was at the
same time spiritual, that all bodily assimilation went hand
in hand with spiritual assimilation, assimilation of
thought . . .[75]

. . . There were at that time no laws in the later meaning
of the term, there were no commandments outwardly
expressed, but since man was clairvoyant, it dawned in him
clairvoyantly how he ought to behave, what was right,
what was good. Thus in those very remote times he saw
Demeter, who gave him his food, also as the cosmic power
of Nature who . . . gave him his morality, his rule of
conduct . . . This Demeter of old was a law-giver, giving
law which did not flash up into consciousness, but which
was self-evident, impelling the soul.[76]

The Law of Moses addressed a humanity to whom the innocence
and conformity with nature of the Demeter-age had been lost.
Ancient clairvoyance had been extinguished; barely a last trace
of it glimmered as natural instinct or in the stirrings of conscience,
giving man directions for his actions. In place of it, the ego slowly
began to grow forth and to venture out on the paths of self-
perception and decision. But did the human being already know
good and evil by virtue of his youthful ego, for the sake of which
he had left paradise?

The sustenance for the journey, which man received during the
final departure from the Demeter-homeland on the threshold of
the age of homelessness, was the law of Sinai. The Law of Moses
was the last fruit of old clairvoyance, but it was formulated and
intended for the humanity that was no longer clairvoyant. This is
what gave this law its transitional and bridge-like character.

Only from this standpoint can the world-historical paradox be
understood, which basically characterizes the Mosaic Law. It
relates to the sphere of attitudes, the inner being of man, by
giving rules for the religious, moral and social life. But it does
not derive from the form of revelations that are received within
the soul; it originates from the divine voice that speaks out of
nature's realm of earth forces. On the same holy mountain where
Moses had once looked through the flame in the thornbush back

into the primordial Saturnian fire and the divine beginning of creation, the Law was now made manifest to him in lightning, smoke and clouds of thunder. Out of the sphere of natural law, he deciphered the moral law of his time. While the era was already over, when, under the guidance of the motherly goddess Demeter, outer and inner world, nature and human soul, were one, Moses was nevertheless allowed to work out of a consciousness that still had a share in the harmony and unity of nature and spirit. As bearer of an especially blessed etheric body, he had, on one hand, the retrospective vision into the time when nature and morality were still identical. On the other hand, the budhi-sphere was already open to him in the glory of an early dawn, which in the future will hold sway among men by means of a new moral conception of nature and a morality that is close to nature.

Rudolf Steiner, who called attention to the geological nature of the ancient Hebrew world conception, also characterized the Mosaic Law from this direction:[77]

> Thus the Jewish soul could look into nature; it could allow the glory of the phenomena of the elements to work upon it; everywhere it could divine the existence of its God and Lord; but directly within itself it could not find Him.
>
> . . . The most significant thing Moses had to impart to his people through the mouth of Jahve was the Ten Commandments. He had received them out of the power of the elements from which Jahve spoke to him. Moses did not descend into the depths of his own soul; he did not ask in lonely meditation: 'How does God speak in my own heart?' He went up the mountain and through the power of the elements the divine Will revealed itself to him.

In another place, Rudolf Steiner showed the position of Moses' revelation between the ancient cosmological view directed to the external cosmos, and the later, purely inward conception:[78]

> . . . the Hebrew teachings formed such a wonderful complement to the cosmological knowledge of the Persians, for they introduced the element of morality into revelations given from without, thus making it possible for the concept of 'guilt', of 'human guilt' to be imbued with meaning . . .

Thus the moral code was given to the ancient Hebrew people as a revelation from without — like the revelations concerning the kingdoms of Nature. This could only come about because Zarathustra had made provision for the continuation of his work . . . by passing on his etheric body to Moses . . . Moses was thereby endowed with the faculty to perceive, as Zarathustra had perceived, the forces at work in the external world; but instead of experiencing neutral forces only, Moses became aware of the *moral* power holding sway in the world, the power that can take the form of *commandment* . . . A personality such as Buddha could not have appeared within the Hebrew people. The Law could be apprehended only through enlightenment from without . . . To give birth to the Law from their own hearts was beyond the power of the Hebrew people.

Moses was the great interpreter. Because of his share in the diminishing clairvoyance, he was able to read in the open book of the supersensory world in the fire and smoke of Sinai. Because of his share in the ego-endowed power of thought, which was emerging, he was able to put the supersensibly perceived revelation into order and to translate it into the language of a no longer clairvoyant humanity.

Just as the mountain where Moses received his revelation has two names that point to an inner duality, Horeb and Sinai, so, the work that proceeded from this revelation shows an important inner duality. Moses not only brought down from the mountain the stern pronouncements of the Decalogue and the subsequent establishment of the Law but also the abundant wealth of images, according to which the tabernacle and the ritual of Aaron were formed.

The Horeb-Sinai revelation that we find in the Old Testament is divided into the more visionary picture element and the more thought-imbued word element. In *ritual* and *law*, the fruits of two opposite attitudes of consciousness, which yet emerge from one source, stand alongside each other. The inauguration of the ritual is still interwoven everywhere by the last warm glow of ancient vision; from beginning to end, the inspiration of the law breathes the stern coldness of the moonlike thought element. Perhaps, the

Horeb and Sinai summits of the holy mountain were actually dominated by a polarity — as has occasionally been assumed — which bore a distant resemblance to the difference between solar and lunar nature. Perhaps, the supersensory world spoke differently to Moses in the course of revealing itself, depending on whether Moses stood on one or the other side of the gorge, the Horeb or the Sinai elevation. In any case, in the duality of Moses' work, the step taken by mankind's consciousness in the soul of Moses becomes known: the ritual originated from clairvoyant capability which, in him, as the last, was still alive; the Law unlocked the portals to intellectual thinking into which he, the first, was already able to enter with a part of his being.

In Moses, two poles of spiritual life united. Later on, in Greece, they were once embodied classically by the figures of two philosophers, Plato and Aristotle.

One could speak of a Mosaic Platonism ensouling everything that Moses contributed to the image-like structure of the Hebraic ritual and priesthood of Aaron. Likewise, one could speak of a Mosaic Aristotelianism in the more abstract configuration of the Law.

In the inauguration of the cultic ritual, the clairvoyant as well as the 'geological' character of the Moses revelation is more clearly recognizable than in the establishment of the Law. The Platonism contained in it re-echos in a remarkable way in the Letter to the Hebrews (8:5 *B*) in the New Testament. It is expressed there inasmuch as Moses is shown to us as the one who, on the mountain, beheld the archetypes, the primal images, called 'ideas' by Plato. It says there that in the ritual 'the images and shadows of the heavenly things hold sway according to the divine oracle that spoke to Moses, when he was to build the tabernacle, "See that you make everything according to the primal pictures which you beheld on the mountain".'

To a special degree, Philo, the neo-Platonist, has been able to sense the Platonism in the work of Moses. In his writings we therefore discover interesting contemporary parallels relating to the above passage from the Letter to the Hebrews:[79]

> Moses was instructed by divine words of guidance about
> the erection of the tent on the mountain, where, for the
> future construction of corporeal objects, he beheld

incorporeal pictures in the spirit. From them, as from an
archetypal sketch and purely spiritual patterns, sense-
perceptible copies were to be fashioned . . . The form
imprinted itself into the spirit of the prophet, duplicated as
to shape and form in invisible, non-material ideas; the
structure was then completed in accordance with the above
form inasmuch as the artist faithfully reproduced these
impressions in materials suitable for each object.

We come upon a reflection of the 'geological' character of the
Moses revelation, if we recognize that the ritual of the tabernacle
and its continuation in Solomon's Temple consistently represents
an exact inversion of the external cosmos, a translation of outer
creation and nature into the more inward realm of the soul's
worship. Moses reproduced the world's creation in building the
first temple of his people. The seven working steps in the construction of the tabernacle correspond precisely with the seven days
of creation at the beginning of Genesis.[80] The tabernacle was a
microcosmos that had been made as an inward replica of the
macrocosmos.

The cultic details were all like the external world transposed.
Just as the people themselves were, by virtue of the twelve tribes,
like a reflection of the starry heaven with the twelve constellations
of the zodiac, so, within the cultic realm, was the table with the
twelve show-breads. The seven-branched candelabra was like the
round of the seven visible planets including sun and moon. Finally,
the four multi-coloured materials, of which the curtain of the
tabernacle consisted, represented the world of the four elements,
again forming a link between the outer world and that of the soul.
Ancient traditions still knew very well that cultic matters were
transcribed from the archetypes of the kingdoms of nature. Hence,
Philo said about fashioning the curtain out of the four elements:[81]

As materials for the fabrics of the curtain for the
tabernacle, he chose the finest from innumerable others,
corresponding in number to the elements from which the
universe was created and which the former point to: earth,
water, air and fire. For byssus comes from the earth, purple
from water, the hyacinth-coloured fabric resembles the
air . . . the scarlet-red fabric, the fire. It was natural that
if human hands were to erect a sanctuary for the Father and

Ruler of the universe, the same substances were chosen
with which He had fashioned the universe.

The actual Law was translated much more emphatically into
the abstract element of thought and the sphere of 'I'-conscious-
ness. The cosmic numbers seven and twelve had been replaced
by the more abstract number ten, belonging to the ego-endowed
human being. In the Law, Moses spoke as the great, stern
educator to human egohood. With the Law, in itself still a gift of
revelation, he consciously closed the gates of revelation. The
prohibition of images, 'you shall make no images nor any like-
nesses', shut the Israelite stream off not only from the sphere of
ancient clairvoyance but from the whole wealth of visual arts,
painting, sculpture and architecture. The law pointed sternly into
abstraction, into the exclusiveness of intellectual consciousness.
If, for every detail of life, the commandment relative to it had to
be considered and followed, a consistent intellectual attentiveness
and awareness had thereby gradually developed, and wrested the
ground away from under the naïve, unconscious dream-state of
life.

The individual laws were in the form of commandments.
Thereby, they addressed the ego's will. The 'thou shalt' stamped
the character of severity on them. As yet, the 'I'-impulse in
humanity was young and weak. The human ego was not yet
mature enough to make free decisions concerning what is good
and what is bad in concrete questions of life. The Law therefore
made the decision for it by ordering the good and prohibiting the
wrong. As judge who instilled fear, the Yahweh divinity stood
behind the Law. But in order to comprehend the judicial spirit of
the Mosaic Law, one cannot merely take the one-sided meaning
into consideration that the concept of judging and the judge have
assumed today. The languages of antiquity combine a spatial and
moral meaning of the word 'to judge' more clearly than our
modern languages. In the first place, 'judging' signifies 'giving
direction', as can even be seen today in the German language
where *richten* retains this double meaning. This positive meaning
outweighs by far the negative implication of atonement and
punishment. This is the specific nature of the Mosaic Law in
contrast to other bodies of law of the ancient world: It interpreted
the laws inherent in the nature of the earth forces so that the ego

was given its direction during the first stage of its path, where it was only on its way to freedom. The fiery seed of the 'I' was sown when Moses stood before the burning bush on Mount Horeb, and when he was surrounded by the lightning flames of Sinai. The spark of man's ego was enkindled for all mankind in Moses when the cosmic ego revealed itself to him in the fire's brilliance. A time will come when the Sinai revelation will be antiquated. Then the Old Covenant of the Law will be replaced by the New Covenant of love and freedom, and the volcanic Sinai fire will make room for the quiet inward flames of Pentecost.

But along with the revelation of the Mosaic Law, mankind nevertheless did receive the first instalment of future freedom. The ego impulse settled, like the crown of a coming, inner royal state for all men, upon each individual person. The holy name Yahweh resounded not only from outside to man in the Law; in each human being rested the name 'I', which one day will be able as a genuine echo to answer to the Yahweh name. The legends describe this invisible, prophetic process that spiritually accompanied the inauguration of the law on Sinai:[82]

> When the Lord came down to give Israel the Torah, sixty thousand angels descended with him, (as many as there were persons among the journeying folk). Each held a crown, engraved with the holy name, in his hand; and they crowned the children of Israel with them.

2.12 Trials and temptations

The Old and the New Testament are related to each other by quite definite architectonic correspondences of form. Like a biography of a higher kind, the history of the people of Israel proceeds through the same stages and crises as the life of Jesus of Nazareth. At each stage, a biography unfolds before us that does not continue from one coincidence to the next but is 'canonical' in the highest sense of the word, transparent for spiritual laws of progressive levels, for an inwardly necessary, spiritually dramatic sequence of events.

Passing through the Sea of Reeds, the people complete the same stage that, in the life of Jesus, is denoted by the Baptism in the Jordan. In the destiny of the people, the forty-year-long wandering through the Sinai Desert corresponds to the forty-day-long temptation of Jesus in the desert of Judea. In truth, it is not only a chain of miracles and revelations that pervade the forty Sinaitic years. Just as the clear sequence of three temptation-experiences dominates the forty days after the Baptism in the Jordan, a clearly discernible line of temptations and trials also surfaces within the journey of the Israelites.

Two scenes at the 'well of the test' at Kadesh (Massah and Meribah — testing and contention) represent the pivotal points in the drama of purification about to be undergone: the first concerns all the people, the second their leader.

We have already mentioned the first one in which the people as a whole were put to the test. Moses had sent ahead the twelve scouts. They were not only to explore the physical condition of the country, at the threshold of which Israel had arrived, but the spirit that held sway there as well. After forty days they returned to the people, who impatiently awaited them at the waters of Kadesh. The large cluster of grapes that they carried, an image of Dionysian egohood, symbolically expressed the same thing as their message: a land of mighty tensions of soul, of troubles and conflicts lay on yonder side of the threshold. The people were frightened; they longed to return to the tranquillity of the ancient wealth that prevailed in Egypt. The past was more enticing than the future with its militant unrest and uncertainty. The Israelites' 'I' was as yet not so strong that it could imbue them with Dionysian courage and daring.

Thus, the people showed that they could not yet measure up to their predestination. Although they may well have changed their minds superficially and decided in favour of entering the land of strife, they were still denied passage across the threshold for many years. They had not passed the test.

The divine judgment that became effective at the 'spring of testing' was more severe than would appear at first. The thirty-eight years that must pass before entry into the land of the future were not only a period of waiting and probation; they were a time of dying away. Of those people who departed from Egypt and were frightened upon the return of the twelve scouts, not a single one crossed the threshold in reality. Even of the twelve scouts, ten died before the people set foot on the promised land. The two scouts from among them who had tried to instil courage into the people, Joshua and Caleb, were the only two to survive the whole desert journey. They alone passed through both the Sea of Reeds and the Jordan. Those who, under their leadership, entered the land of their fathers, were not yet alive when Moses led the people out of Egypt and through the Sea of Reeds. They belonged to the generation that was born in the desert. So, in this sense too, the forty Sinaitic years signified a radical shedding of the Egyptian past inasmuch as they had brought about a complete rejuvenation of the people. The divine decision at the 'well of the judgment' at Kadesh was in fact a death sentence for the whole Egyptian generation of Israelites. Only the younger generation, in which the magnetic recollection of the world of Egypt no longer stood in the way of the budding 'I' impulse and which, from birth, had instead absorbed the landscape of homelessness and egohood, was in a position to enter the land by the Jordan.

The second trial at the 'well of decision' was directed at the leaders, at Aaron and Moses themselves. The people grumbled, filled once again with dissatisfaction because of their backward longings. Moses and Aaron proceeded to the sanctuary of the tabernacle to question the deity. The words of the oracle that came to Moses out of the fiery radiance ordered him to give water to the people from the rock. Moses and Aaron obeyed, assembled the people, and the miracle of the spring took its course. Twice, Moses struck the rock; water in abundance poured forth and quenched the thirst of men and beasts. 'And the LORD said to Moses and Aaron, "Because you did not believe in me, to sanctify me in the eyes of the people of Israel, therefore you shall not bring this assembly into the land which I have given them." ' (Num.20:12). Here, the biblical text poses a difficult riddle. How is it possible that such a severe divine judgment was pronounced on the almost ninety-year-old Moses and on Aaron who was three years older? Had Moses not followed the divine direction most faithfully and did water not flow in abundance where he struck the rock with his rod? The miracle of the spring had taken place; nevertheless, even Moses must somehow not have passed a test at this 'spring of judgment', the water of railing against God! The judgment that had been pronounced over all of Israel here, now also struck him: he was turned away at the threshold; he would not set foot in the promised land.

A sequence of deaths arise before our soul that reveal a deeply mysterious tragedy. The three who went at the head of the people died one after the other in the desert: Miriam, the sister, died in Kadesh; Aaron, the brother, died at the next large campsite at Mount Hor, the Petra of today; and finally, at a hundred and twenty, Moses died in the mythological seclusion of Mount Nebo, from where he was allowed to look down into the longed-for Jordan lowland. Others completed the task that these three began. What secret of Moses' destiny is concealed here? We leave the question open for the time being.

Around the two tests at the well of Kadesh are grouped a number of temptations to which the Israelites were exposed in the desert. Obvious polarities show that these comprised a major component of the spiritual guidance that directed the destiny of the people.

Two dramatic scenes belong together in polarity, of which one follows the Sinaitic revelation, the other the return of the scouts: the erection of the image of the golden calf, and the revolt of the company of Korah.

Already, the stone tablet utterances of the Decalogue were translated from the sphere of revelation in lightning and thunder and coined in human words, among them the sentence: Thou shalt make no image. Impatiently longing to go back, the people built a golden image of the holy Egyptian Apis Bull under Aaron's leadership. While, on the mountain, Moses was sunk into archetypal contemplation of the cosmic, supersensory ritual that he was supposed to transpose into the form-world of earthly priesthood, the great relapse into the cultic ritual of Egypt took place at the foot of the mountain. The spirits of the past with their impressive magic greatness gained power over the souls of the Israelites more readily than the stern forces that were to lead to egohood through the chilling desert and subterranean fire-tempests. A great number of the people succumbed to the temptation of the Egyptian relapse. Even Aaron did not resist it. Returning from the holy mountain, Moses pitted himself with unrelenting severity against the attraction of the past as if he were the human incarnation of the cosmic fire of wrath that had blazed around him. He toppled the image of the bull and, with the aid of the Levites, who were destined to be the bearers of the new priesthood, eliminated the last traces of the Egyptian cultic mood in the lives and souls of the people.

The biblical descriptions are permeated everywhere with the kind of imaginative elements that have no direct physical correspondence and must therefore be understood as soul pictures. When it says that three thousand people were slain by the swords of the Levites (Exod.32:28), this should not immediately be taken as physical fact. The numbers are used more in a qualitative sense. Egypt represents the third cultural epoch. Human beings, who inwardly were attached to the spirit of Egypt, represented the three thousand, even if they were few in number. (Similarly, in the New Testament stories of the feeding of the four thousand and five thousand, it is not a matter of exactly four or five thousand men, but of human beings of the fourth — at that time the present — and of the fifth cultural epoch — at that time, the future.) It was a spiritual eradication of Egypt that was accomplished by the Levites. Naturally, this is not to say that nobody lost his life during the Levite vengeance. Certainly there existed also a physical set of facts; but the biblical description refers first of all to the inner, soul-like set of facts and thereby obscures what actually took place on the physical plane.

The opposite temptation arose, when, after the return of the twelve scouts, the people drew back in fright from crossing the threshold. In face of the hesitancy of the many in regard to the future, a smaller group, led by the Levite, Korah* developed a fanatic will for the future that overshot the mark. Not only the past, the future also made its appearance as a tempting power. The followers of Korah made demands with which they wanted to anticipate a distant future of the ego's life in an abstract manner. They were Utopians, revolutionary advance guards of a democratic principle that could not as yet be fulfilled historically.

---

*Korah means 'bald'. The 'company of Korah' must have referred to the members of an extreme sect that was the opposite of the Nazirites. Just as the latter despised any sort of cutting of the hair of the head and beard in order to conserve certain cosmic-clairvoyant possibilities, the Korah members, anticipating the principle of tonsure, must have shaved their heads and beards in order to speed up the hardening process of the organism. See also the explanations concerning the story of Samson (Chapter 3.9).

So, demanding equality, they rose against the leadership and addressed Moses and Aaron: 'You have gone too far! For all the congregation are holy, every one of them, and the LORD is among them; why then do you exalt yourselves above the assembly of the LORD?' (Num.16:3).

Moses did not stand up against Korah and his group. Their refutation had to occur differently. They had to reduce themselves to absurdity. In consequence of their viewpoints, they laid claim to the same possibilities of receiving revelation for themselves as were open to Moses and the others who stayed with him in the blazing flames of the holy mountain. Moses now actually allowed them to enter into the cultic intercourse with the oracular earth forces. A dramatic scene ran its course that once more affords a look into the mysterious play of geological power that was the background of nature for the revelation to Moses.

Ordinarily, Moses and Aaron entered the realm of the tabernacle alone when it was a matter of questioning the deity. Now, in the area of the tabernacle, Moses allowed Korah's followers to light the incense in their censers, and lo, the earth opened her horror-filled mouth; dreadful calamity befell those performing their incense offering.

What took place here? Let us transport ourselves once again into the landscape of unfinished evolutionary processes and activities of the earth forces, as we have pictured them similar to the Italian solfatara. This still dominated the character of the area around the broad fault of the Arava Valley desert between Kadesh and Petra. In the ground, alternating between marly soil and rocky ravines, smoke and fiery forces slumbered everywhere. From time to time, flames and steam flared forth. But they could also be aroused by the actions of men; through igniting smaller or larger flames, columns of steam and fire and whole volcanic eruptions could be enticed out of the earth's interior.

It was in such a world that the wandering Israelites found themselves in the Sinai territory. Rising from deep gorges clouds of smoke, with thunder and lightning, stormed around the mountain above. Below, near the campsite, there were solfatara-like spots. The tabernacle with the Ark of the Covenant must have been carried to such a location, so that the fiery steam of the earth itself mingled with the incense that Moses and Aaron ignited there. Through these columns of steam and fire, Moses was able to perceive and hear the divine power.

Now, the company of Korah's Utopians were confronted with the quite concrete consequences of their views. The incense that had been lit up on their censers unleashed violent tempests of the earth's interior. It was as if the forces raged once again that Sodom and Gomorrah fell victim to in prehistoric time. The Bible says that the earth tore assunder and, swallowing the offenders in the jaws of hell, eradicated even the last traces of presumption with the fiery flames of cosmic wrath. Here again, imaginative elements are most likely mixed into the description. A catastrophe of nature broke in upon them: heaven's answer to the aberration of the fanatics. An external, total annihilation of the men of Korah with all their goods probably did not take place, for, in later ages, when their ideals were no longer quite so untimely, we encounter the children of Korah again, namely as the singers of numerous psalms. But an extermination of soul elements, namely of the error of Korah, was occasioned by the elements that were conjured forth.

Still another duality of temptations rose in the path of the people. This happened when the Israelites finally left the desolation of the desert behind and entered the territory of the promised land. Magical atavisms determined the religion and attitude of its inhabitants, filling the atmosphere of the area in which they dwelt. The mood of superhuman soul potentials of old exuded a suggestive effect that the Israelites could not completely escape. This stirred up in their soul and bodily organisms what they themselves bore within as remnant and residue of ancient clairvoyance despite the stern discipline that they had been subjected to. It became apparent that the atavisms continued their destructive influence in the human organization in two different disguises: disease and sin were the ominous left-over metamorphoses of the old supersensory experience.

Mention has already been made of the first form of atavistic assault: at the edge of the desert, the fiery snakes appeared. Feverish visions were ignited in this demonically charged border-zone and continued as processes of illness in the etheric and physical bodies. Moses erected a barrier against the demons of illness with the symbol of the serpent-staff, signifying the power of the future; with it, he appealed to the free spiritual ego-force that is capable of being the ruler over the lower nature of man. The second atavistic temptation was carried intentionally into the ranks of the people of Israel by the enemy, namely the Moabites of the eastern Jordan land, into whose sphere the Israelites now wanted to enter. The Bible relates that Midianite women were dispatched as seductresses into the camp of Israel in order to unleash a storm of orgiastic, sensual passions. The sensual desire, to which a part of the people actually abandoned themselves, was only another form of the once spiritually orientated faculties of soul that had now fallen into the sphere of earthly bondage to the body, and could only be turned into a positive direction in the future through inner self-control over them.

The fact that this stratagem of the Moabites was not merely a physical diversion becomes apparent by the biblical report that the Israelites, who had succumbed to the whoring, simultaneously joined in the religious cult of the Moabites, the veneration of Baal of Peor. The atavistic character of the spreading infection of sensuality is clearly evident. The Israelites came into the sphere of influence of decadent Babylonian and Near Eastern sexual cults. They encountered nations among whom orgiastic, sexual sensuality was part of the religious, cultic domain of life. The ecstasy of carnal desire was the decadent remnant of ancient holy union with supersensory worlds. It must have been cult prostitutes, designated in the Old Testament as *Qedeshot* 'those ordained for the temple' (Deut.23:17), through whom the Israelites were led into sinful temptation. Proceeding from the opinion that the figures of Jethro's daughters were physical human beings, the question has repeatedly been asked: How can it now be represented to the Israelites as such a sin to unite with Midianite women, if Moses himself had taken a Midianite as his wife? In reality, the people's temptation by the Midianite cult prostitutes was the complete opposite of Moses' encounter with the daughters of Jethro. Herein lay the severity of the aberration; namely, that an experience, which at one time had its truth in the spirit realm, was now dragged down to the level of physical existence. The people not only abandoned themselves to any kind of sensual excess, but to one that was at the same time a caricature and

130

perversion of a formerly spiritual experience. Illness and sin were the calamitous shadows that remained of the light of clairvoyant antiquity.

Two figures represented the Moabite temptation: Balaam and Phinehas. Before the Moabites attempted to draw the Israelites under the spell of their sultry decadence, they called on the magician who had power over the ancient magic force of the word and the old dreamlike clairvoyance. He was supposed to cast the magic curse over the approaching alien nation. Once more, we look into the properties of ancient supersensory forces, but strange things happen. Just as the Israelites were led into temptation by their arrival in the realm of the magic of old, so, conversely, through Israel's approach, a bright benevolent spirit light fell into the sphere of bleak decadence. Whether Balaam queried the nocturnal oracle of his dreams (Num.22:8,19) while his soul dwelled outside his body, or whether he descended during the day into its depths, where he was also able to hear spiritual voices — the Bible describes this condition in the imagination of riding on the she-ass (Num.22:21-35) — or whether, finally, he uttered ecstatic, prophetic words out of the smoke of the altars on the holy heights of the land: a stern spirit barred his way, reversing his and the Moabite king's intentions into their opposite. He blessed where he was supposed to curse; finally, a wondrous prophecy concerning the Messianic future of the people of Israel poured from his lips (Num.24). An antagonist was to be advanced against Jethro, but against his will Balaam had to serve the same spirit.

After the attempt of cursing Israel had been unsuccessful because of the resistance of the spiritual world, the Moabites resorted to their orgiastic sexual cults. Here, the flame of a spirit flashed forth from among the Israelites in which we perceive right away that it was a herald and bearer of the future. The youth Phinehas from the high-priestly house of Aaron, stepped forth and thrust his spear through a whoring couple; he stayed the plague of sensuality with the spearlike might of the spirit that rules over soul and body. The brazen snake of Moses overcame the plague of the feverish visions and illness. The pure grail-lance of Phinehas triumphed over the plague of sensual intoxication and sin.

Not much mention is made of Phinehas but what is said of him is fraught with significance: 'Behold, I give to him my covenant of peace; and it shall be to him, and to his descendants after him, the covenant of a perpetual priesthood' (Num.25:12f).

Moses could not complete his task himself. Joshua, the warrior, led the people across the Jordan. Aaron still belonged in many respects to the perishing old world and therefore failed; his grandson Phinehas, however, salvaged the future of the Aaronite priesthood. Mighty in spirit, he ignited the holy flame on the altar for all future times.

Talmudic traditions probe their way closer to the mystery of the Phinehas-figure: 'The name Phinehas was unto the Lord as was the name Elijah the Thisbite, and he bestowed on him temporal and everlasting life.'[83]

Through his modern spiritual research, Rudolf Steiner revealed this mystery in a clearly discernible way: in Phinehas, the same spirit-ego was incarnated that later was reincarnated in the figure of the prophet Elijah.[84] Just as Elijah later toppled the Phoenician cult of the priests of Baal on Mount Carmel, so, here, Phinehas overturned the seductive Moabite cult of Baal of Peor at the threshold of the promised land. A spirit made its appearance in youthful form by the side of the hundred-year-old Moses, that one day would inaugurate a new, important era of the spiritual development of Israel. In the act of rejecting the Moabite temptation, the first indication was given of the advance from Moses to Elijah that history would have to make in the future.

2.13 The death of Moses

We return to the riddle of the test imposed on Moses at the spring of Kadesh. How did Moses fall short of the stern demand of the spirit and what imposed on him the tragic need to die on this side of the threshold to the longed-for land?

Among all humanity, Moses is perhaps the mightiest among those who, with their own fate, had to seal the destiny of a turning point of time. Such figures have the mission of bringing about a new age with great emphasis, but they can do it only by being related still to the dying, bygone age. Their nature is not of the new age; they are only paving the way for it.

In the parallel between Israel's history in the Old Testament and the life of Jesus in the New Testament, the death of Moses and the death of John the Baptist correspond. Just as the tragedy of John stood behind Christ's first activities after the Baptism in the Jordan, so the death of Moses stood behind the people's entry into the land of the fathers. Just as the Baptist spoke, so spoke Moses through his destiny: He must increase, but I must decrease.

The element that caused the tragedy of the Moses figure was the same that gave him his superhuman, sublime nature. By means of his own etheric and astral configuration, his ego worked among men blazing the trail from the world of ancient clairvoyance into the kingdom of clear thought. But destiny had gifted him with a power that extended far beyond his own ego. Since Moses was the bearer of Zarathustra's body of formative forces, a superhuman field of force enveloped him, realizing ahead of time a segment of mankind's future. Effects emanated from Moses, in which the created work surpassed its creator by far.

The aura of Moses' work that is larger than life exposes the struggle of consciousness and the drama of soul that his personality underwent. His consciousness was involved in the attainment of the ego-like thought impulse, but it could not harbour it within itself save in the garment of the ancient clairvoyant soul-forces. Thereby, Moses himself was drawn into the evening dusk that held sway over his age.

How must we picture the form of perception available to Moses? The thought-imbued visionary faculty of Moses' perception was most active in face of the fire and cloud elements. In the image of the pillar of clouds and fire that moved ahead of the people, phenomena of nature are indicated, signs that were decipherable by Moses' spirit. They designated the route through the great rift valley in the earth's surface that is like a cosmic fissure of primordial time and runs through the Arava Valley northward to the Dead Sea.

Through the Lemurian fire that must have blazed forth from the earth's interior in those days in many different locations, Moses looked back into the Saturnian beginning of the earth and the countenance of the creator-beings themselves. The element of fire ignited in him the grandiose retrospective vision to which we owe the biblical story of creation. For him, the divine being,

creating, giving direction and judging, dwelled in fire itself. Philo
points to this mystery:[85]

> A cloud that assumed the shape of a very tall column
> moved at the head of the multitude of people, radiating light
> that was like the sun during the day and like fire at night,
> so that they would not go astray on their way but could
> follow it as their natural guide. Perhaps it was also a servant
> of the great king, an invisible angel, a divine guide
> enveloped in the cloud, whom earthly eyes were not
> permitted to see.

The cloud, formed of the elements of air and water, did not
confront the soul of Moses with such utter transparency as did
that of fire. It cast a veil for him over the divine powers of creation
themselves. But this veil was woven of the archetypal images of
all earthly creation; for the cloud element unlocked the etheric
world and the reflection, contained therein, of the ancient sun-
earth, to the soul-eyes of Moses. He was at home in the etheric
world insofar as he had a share in the last etheric clairvoyance of
the old world. Philo relates:[86] 'It says of him that he entered in
upon the clouds where the deity dwelled; this meant moving into
the formless, invisible, body-free archetypal essence of things,
where he perceived what is imperceptible for mortal nature.'

As the remainder of the watery, dense atmosphere of the Atlantean epoch, the cloud element was the stimulus and image of
nature-linked etheric clairvoyance for human beings of ancient
times until the age of Moses. This was not true only of the dense,
physically visible cloud formations in the sky and the mists and
steam-clouds of the earth's surface. In the sense of a qualitative
world view, the cloud is an element that is present everywhere.
The atmosphere, even if the sky may appear clear and cloudless,
is in itself 'cloud', for as well as air there is always some humidity,
the element of water, present. There is 'cloud' in every plant,
animal and human being, for, in all organisms, there occurs a
concurrence of fluids or blood with air or the breath. No living
being exists that does not dwell within a 'cloud'. The etheric
bodies of plant, animal and man are closely connected to this
cloud. The omnipresent element of the clouds is the delicate
physical veil of the etheric world.

It is an indication of the etheric clairvoyance, still existent in its after-effect during the age of Moses, that the campsite of the people in the desert was described as being surrounded by seven clouds: one was in front, one in the back, two each covered the two sides, and one hovered above the heads of all the Israelites.[87] A last flashing-up of clairvoyance took place among the people especially at the beginning of the journey through the desert: 'In the days of the exodus from Egypt, a lowly maiden beheld things that even Ezekiel and the other prophets have not seen.'[88]

The soul of Moses must have entered into the bright light of vision least of all in face of the solid earth element. It remained for him a dark, powerful feeling that a divine spiritual power was also concealed behind the sense impression of mineral rock formations. The motif of Petra or the rock was for him barely more than a symbol for the firmness of the divine will. Here, the veil that the physical world draws before the supersensory sphere remained impenetrably dark and impervious. Although the psalm-like hymn, with which Moses prepared himself for his death, returned seven times to the image of the divine Rock, the 'Rock of salvation' (Deut.32:4,13,15,18,30,31 and 37), particularly this emphasis seems like a constantly recurring knocking on a door that would not open. Finally, the stone tablets of the commandments themselves stand in Moses' destiny as a symbol for a riddle that had not been completely solved.

The clairvoyance in face of fire and cloud had eventually to go out. Following the Bible, legendary tradition is able to indicate the moment when visionary sight ceased in Moses and the people: 'When Aaron had died, the cloud of the glory vanished.'[89] The legends relate Aaron's death like a leave-taking of the etheric world. Moses stood by the bedside of his dying brother and helped him strip himself of the earthly garments. Aaron said: 'I see nothing strange; only the divine cloud envelops the limbs from which you take off the covering.' Following this, when Aaron had taken his last breath, the cloud detached itself from him; the last 'cloud' departed the earth.[90] Now vision of the etheric corporeality had been extinguished. The cloud and fire pillars appeared no longer, either to the people or to Moses alone. The rock formation, the inanimate stone desert itself, became the more impenetrable.

Now we can try to comprehend the puzzling scene at Massah

and Meribah, the 'well of testing'. Moses was able to call forth the miracle of the spring in wondrous abundance. The budhi or life spirit of the future poured forth generously. Not only water streamed forth that quenched thirst; 'streams of the water of life' were experienced. But here, what worked in Moses was something that towered above his own personal 'I', namely the gift of Zarathustra. The half visionary, half thought-filled consciousness of the Moses 'I' lagged behind the gift that radiated out of his blessed being. His ego did not penetrate the rock from which the spring streamed forth. While it did sense holiness and the deity's nearness, it could not recognize him, who in reality bestowed his streams of life. Moses looked as if into a mirror, sensing the dark outline of a being, but he did not behold the being itself. Although Moses had taken hold of 'the rod' of an ego-pervaded etheric body at the point of the forehead, the time was still distant when the point of freedom would move from the forehead down to the heart, where it would awaken an organ that could perceive 'face to face.' The mobility of the heart organ is called 'faith' by the Bible. This is why — despite the fact that in his actions Moses revealed the hidden deity — the divine judgment sounded forth to him, saying: 'Because you did not believe in me . . . you shall not bring this assembly into the land which I have given them' (Num.20:12).

In his First Letter to the Corinthians (10:1-4 *B*), Paul solved the riddle of the limitation of Moses' nature:

I want you to know, brethren, that our fathers were all
under the cloud, and all passed through the sea, and all
received the Baptism of Moses in the cloud and in the sea,
and all ate the same spiritual food, and all drank the same
spiritual drink. For they drank from the spiritual Rock
which was always near them: and the Rock was Christ.

Because of his discipleship at Jethro's place, Moses had learned to direct his glance into that region of the cosmos into which the Christ, who had departed the Osiris sphere in heaven, had now moved. Moses looked into the realm of the earth forces: the Yahweh sphere. The play of forces between earth and moon was revealed to him as being divinely ensouled. But to penetrate through the reflected images of this sphere to the perception of the Christ being himself, to behold the source of light, the rays

136

of which were reflected back in a moonlike way out of the domain
of the earth forces, this Moses and the people of his time were
not yet capable of doing. Moses could bring about the experience
of the budhi power of Christ, but he neither knew nor recognized
him whose power was bestowed. Moses only perceived the
Yahweh-like reflection; the Christ being himself remained
concealed to him.[91]

> He who led Moses, who appeared to Moses in the burning
> bush, He who led the people through the wilderness and
> caused water to flow out of the rock, He was the Lord,
> Christ! But the time was not yet come; Moses himself did
> not recognise Him; Moses thought He was another. This
> is what is meant by Moses not having believed in Him
> who had commanded him to strike the rock with his staff.

The divine pronouncement at the spring of Kadesh was not
meted out to Moses as a punishment for a wrong-doing. The
failure of consciousness in face of the Christ being is the destiny
of that particular time, not a weakness of the single human being.
Nevertheless, at no other point does the tragic limitation, which,
because of its share in the dying-away clairvoyance of old, was a
part of Moses' consciousness, come more clearly into view. The
serpent of ancient vision, whose head he crushed in taking hold
of the staff, stung him in the heel, made him weak in regard to
the hard mineral earth element that Moses now confronted as if
it were an impenetrable wall (see Chapter 1.9). His heel limped
as did that of Achilles, his contemporary in Hellas; for his
consciousness was still tied to forces which, because they belonged
to the past, now died out and could not be borne into the future
unchanged.

> That Moses relied completely upon an old clairvoyance,
> that in his case the new intellectual power was still
> clairvoyant, is also . . . shown to us where it was to be
> decided whether he was to lead the people across into
> Palestine. These people were to be led across as those,
> who, through their whole blood-configuration, were to
> inaugurate the intellectual culture. What Moses possessed
> in the way of clairvoyance, could give the impulse — but
> could not in itself be that culture. For this culture was not
> to be a clairvoyant one; it was to appear specifically as

137

something new over against old clairvoyance. Therefore, we see how Moses felt called upon to lead his people up to a certain point — but could not himself lead them into the new land.[92]

The limitation imposed on Moses' soul could also be described in the following way. Above all else, he had use over the gift of retrospection, the faculty of reverse prophecy, penetrating into far-distant primeval ages; he did not possess the gift of actual prophetic preview, seeing forward into the future. The expression, 'Moses and the prophets', designates the duality of spiritual review and prophetic preview, as well as the onesidedness of Moses' nature. In order to recognize the Christ in the rock of the spring-miracle, Moses would have had to be a representative of actual prophecy as well, since, at that time, Christ was still the one to come in the distant future.

Moses had instructed the Israelites in the annual sacrifice of the lamb. The offering of the ram-force, of Isaac, which shone on the human brow in the two-petalled lotus flower as the last gift of clairvoyance, had to be renewed ever and again. But with his Zeus-like, majestic horns of light, Moses himself was the last great human ram. The sacrifice of the ram was finally solemnized on Moses himself. His death in the wastelands of Mount Nebo was the great sealing of the Passover festival, the exodus from Egypt.

The death of Moses is a sublime, silent myth. Looking westward across the meadows of the Jordan into the land of the promise, but, in this glance, losing himself in the vastness of the occident that henceforth would become the stage of history for mankind, the hundred-and-twenty-year-old Moses stood alone on the desolate, barren summit of the mountain. There, far away from any living soul, he breathed his last. In the form of the old mountain-giants, the primordial beginnings took him, the old man from the mountain, unto themselves; the mountains of which he had written that in their realm the Elohim created the world.

In Egypt, monuments for the great leaders of the populace were erected around their own earthly bodies in the mummy coffins. In person or in thought, anybody could visit the graves that contained their preserved bodies. Had he remained a son of Pharaoh, a specific record, linked to a splendid mummy coffin, would have come down through the ages as Moses' grave. Now, a mystery surrounds Mount Nebo, the unknown mountain with the unknown grave, not dug by human hands, a secret that expresses the exact reversal of the Egyptian mummy tradition and the mood it evokes. The grave of Moses that is nowhere, is the key to his spirit that is everywhere. Was it only a man who departed the earth there, or was it a force of nature that sank back into nature's primordial foundation?

2.14 Sinai and Damascus

The Letter of Jude (9) in the New Testament elevates the Nebo myth to a dramatic, apocalyptic scene in the spirit realm by showing us how the archangel Michael struggles with the devil for Moses' body. We are confronted here with an imagination quite similar to the one in the Edda, which describes how the long-hidden Vidar appeared on the battlefield of the gods' twilight and, as the avenger, fought the Fenris Wolf for the body of his father Wotan (Odin).

The apocalyptic picture refers us once again to the secret of the etheric body that Moses bore. By virtue of the superhuman formative-forces body of Zarathustra, Moses carried a precious treasure of mankind's spiritual guidance in the sheaths of his being. In the figure of Moses, divine powers of providence wove a force into the human etheric body that was to make it able to endure and survive the span of time during which it would be incapable of perceiving the spheres of the spirit. Until Moses' age, the human etheric body, as bearer of clairvoyance, was permeated by the sunlight of the spirit. Then, a time began in which man's etheric body became darkened because of the extinction of etheric clairvoyance and thus eluded consciousness. It submerged into the dark mineral tower of the physical body. But one day, the etheric streaming mobility is to be liberated again by the luminous staff of Moses. Then, the etheric body will once again be filled with light; a new etheric clairvoyance supported by the ego will free itself from the physically bound shadow-world of the intellect. The etheric body of Moses will arise in new form.

Over the body of Moses or Wotan, Michael, the messenger of the sun, fights with the sinister Ahrimanic power for the spirit consciousness of man. Will the clairvoyance of old fall prey there to the poison of illness and sin? Or will it survive the cosmic winter under the protection of benevolent powers as the sun-seed of future conscious vision?

When the resurrection of the human etheric body and clairvoyant consciousness begins — and spiritual research states that this will begin after the first third of the twentieth century — then the rock wall will become transparent before which Moses' consciousness still had to fail. Rudolf Steiner never tired of proclaiming the new etheric clairvoyance, in the light of which the Christ being becomes visible, and of preparing the way to it:

Something else had to arise in place of the earlier clairvoyance . . .[93]

. . . In earlier times men did not perceive, did not think with the physical body only, but they perceived and thought with the etheric body. What was perceived in the etheric body was experienced consciously in the astral body as Astrology. But in modern Astronomy everything is a matter of calculation. The etheric body must be revitalised, and this is connected with the new revelation of Christ. When the etheric body is re-vitalised, man finds Christ . . . it is essential that this vitalising of the etheric body shall take place.[94]

It was the fruit of his Damascus experience that enabled Paul to solve the mystery that remained hidden to Moses, namely, that the spiritual rock was Christ. Just as Moses was the last in ancient clairvoyance, so Paul was the first in the new etheric vision. Before the gates of Damascus, being as one born prematurely, far ahead of his time, he was given the first human share in the mystery of the second coming of Christ. Paul experienced the stone tablets of the commandments becoming transparent for etheric light. Through the physical rock, he looked into the countenance of him, of whom he could then say that he was the spiritual rock.

At Mount Sinai-Horeb, Moses with his waning vision beheld the stern moonlike Yahweh through the fire of the bush and the mountain's summit. Before Damascus, at the edge of the oasis abounding in springs, which was felt to be a reminiscence of paradise, Paul, as the first of the new vision, beheld the redeeming Christ through the veil of the sense world. These two scenes belong together as exactly mirroring correspondences, a fact that Rudolf Steiner often pointed out. Before Damascus, the tragedy of the Moses' consciousness found its redemption. From now on, the element of the cloud, which was the rightful spiritual home of Moses, was accessible again in a spiritual sense. The curtain was drawn away from the ethereal sphere and the Christ appeared in heavenly clouds. On a higher level, the mystery of the cloud column was renewed, which had led the people through the desert. The Israelites had to discover the earth in their desert. We men of the present have been led into the wasteland of materialism and its temptations in order to penetrate again from there to heaven, to the experience of the etheric world.

Finally, the spiritual pattern that links the thornbush experience of Moses with the Damascus experience of Paul is confirmed to us even by a look at the map. The geography of the Holy Land is symbolic and transparent for many secrets of history. The Kadesh-Sinai area is located the same distance southwest of the Dead Sea as Damascus is northeast of the Sea of Galilee. A significant symmetry is discernible around the topography of the Jordan. The lunar landscape of the Judean Desert, overlaid with the forces of the earth's interior, continues in a southwesterly direction into the netherworld of biblical Sinai. The sunny scenery of Galilee with its paradisal reminiscences leads in a northeasterly direction to the oasis of Damascus. At Sinai, human consciousness died away. At Damascus, the first rosy dawn of its resurrection lit up.

Joshua – the Judges – Ruth

3. Battles and Premonitions of the Messianic Future

3.1 Joshua and Jesus

In his oracular style, Johann Georg Hamann, the magus of the north, once put the correspondence between the sequence of figures in the Old and New Testaments into the following formula: 'The Hebrew household was none other than the archetype of a transcendental history, the horoscope of a celestial hero.'[95] The fact that the figures of the Old Testament, with their deeds and destinies, are images projected on to the earth of the heavenly destinies of the Christ-being, the celestial hero, moving towards the earth, is nowhere true in greater measure than in Joshua's case. Joshua is a Messianic prophecy become form, even to the saviour's name that Moses gave him; Joshua and Jesus are the same word and signify 'helper and bringer of salvation'.

The Old Testament begins in the style of a saga of the gods. Well into the story of Moses, this mythological element, that still looks up into cosmic heights, continues. Beginning with the Book of Joshua, the style of a saga of heroes moves into the foreground. While Moses was still the great teacher, the mediator of divine revelation, something he could not be without intimate association with the beings of the higher world, Joshua was now the militant man of action, who was drawn completely into the sphere of the will. Joshua was the heroic leader of the Old Covenant. His courage and initiative extended far beyond human levels, but the superhuman divine element did not confront him from outside as was the case with his great predecessor Moses; in him, it worked as intensified human will.

For customary interpretation and feeling Joshua is ranked far behind Moses. This, however, does not tally with the opinion prevailing in the biblical books. For them, Joshua was the one privileged to accomplish what Moses was unable to do, because of a tragic limitation of his nature. Moses led Israel away from Egypt; insofar, his mission was a negative one. Joshua, on the other hand, guided the people into the promised land; he brought the benefit and blessing of positive fulfilment. In Moses' case, nevertheless, his work stands outside his person in history; it extends far beyond himself. In Joshua's case, by contrast, person and work are identical; what is great and mighty in him is first of all his own personality and nature. He harboured in himself a mystery of embodiment, something took on form in him.

The sequence of the great individualities of the Old Covenant exhibits the laws and will of providence in many different ways. At the beginning stand the *fathers*. They were the inaugurators and bearers of a heredity from which not only the chosen people, but the Messianic lineage was to emerge. The fathers are followed by the *leaders*: Moses, Joshua, the judges up to Samuel. It is significant that they did not belong to the Messianic hereditary lineage. Their contribution to the history of the Israelites was not a bodily but a soul and spiritual one. Finally comes a third age: the era of the *kings*. Beginning with David and Solomon, they again belonged to the Messianic line. They were at the same time fathers, for, physically, they continued the lineage that started with Abraham, Isaac and Jacob: the build-up of the Messianic corporeality, purified of all atavistic remnants. On the level of soul and spirit they further developed the culture which had been inaugurated in the era of the leaders. The two streams converged and, although only for a brief period until the division of the kingdom, brought about a great unity of the hereditary and cultural tasks within the totality of the Israelites.

The duality of the Israelite-Jewish mission must be understood from the direction of the last fulfilment. A physical vessel and a soul vessel, in which he would be able to dwell, had to be fashioned for the Messiah who was to come. This is why the Messianic future required both a bodily and a soul preparation. The former took place in the carefully guided heredity stemming from the fathers in the tribe of Judah. The latter was brought about more from outside through the influence of other cultures and differing racial qualities. It is here that the leaders coming from the other tribes, hence not Jewish in the specific sense, had their place between the fathers and the kings.

In the specifically Jewish stream, a physical corporeality was built up step by step, from which the remnants of clairvoyant spirituality left over from the old sun and linked to the body, were distilled out more and more completely. The solar visionary power of ancient time was active in man as long as his corporeality retained its etheric transparency and porous plasticity. As his physical organism became harder and denser, man lost the light of vision, although he gained a new form of consciousness in its place. A process took place in the human being that can be illustrated by a comparison. If one applies a thicker and thicker coating to one side of a glass pane, its clear transparency is lost; instead, it assumes the character of a mirror. It exchanges its likeness to the luminous sun for that of the moon that only reflects a light not her own. It was the eugenic mission of Jewry to produce a corporeality that was no longer sunlike and transparent for the spiritual nature of the world and no longer permeated by spirit itself, but that could instead confront the things of the world moonlike as does a mirror and in this way could create the prerequisite for clearly contoured sense perception and intellectual knowledge.

Nevertheless, the time was to come when the completely sunlike Messiah, the Christ, was to enter from the spiritual cosmos into the human configuration, which had become a lunar vessel. In order that the sun spirit could inhabit the earthly moon dwelling, foreign to its nature, a soul form had to be fashioned that would be capable of being the mediator between the two by virtue of its kinship with the sun. A culture and a sentiment had to be nurtured within the people of Israel, whereby a path was prepared for a solar content to enter into the lunar vessel.

This was why, in the middle period, the time of the leaders, the return of the solar branch of the people was brought about, which had once been eliminated from the physical development of Israel. 'From outside', with the help of those leaders who did not belong to the Messianic lineage, contributions were made to the Israelite culture by the once rejected stream of Ishmael, Esau and Joseph. Moses, the Levite, was the greatest bearer of the purely cultural reattainment, brought about completely from outside. He transmitted the contribution of Joseph by means of the initiation he received from the Egyptian culture, the contribution of Hagar and Ishmael at the Arabian mystery site of Jethro.

Among the successors of Moses, the principle of reattainment continued in a less visible manner. The outward reattainment was replaced by a reflection of the sun-related impulses entering on more inward paths. Joshua and the judges were not teachers but warriors. In them, the folk components that had once been distilled, returned not as cultural creation, not as teaching and work, but as substantiality through individual human beings. Those were men in whom certain sunlike soul forces of the past were simply present again in changed form. The stern continuance of the Jewish hereditary mission had been safeguarded to the extent that it could no longer be disturbed by an appearance of the same soul forces that earlier would have contaminated the bloodline — soul forces represented in personalities from the non-Jewish tribes of Israel. Without suffering any impairment, the corporeal, moonlike character of the individuals had to prove itself compatible with the solar soul pattern of the whole people that gained form in individual leaders. It was as if those who had been cast out were allowed to come home in altered and yet once again human form. In Samson, the solar impulse of Esau seems to reappear; in Joshua, the Adonis-nature of Joseph. Perhaps the law of repeated earth lives was indeed one of the ways in which this more essentially human return took place. The Jewish legends seem to probe for the secrets concealed here by saying that Joshua, who came from the tribe of Ephraim, hence was a descendent of Joseph, was the reincarnated Joseph.[96]

Concealed behind the duality of Israel's physical and cultural tasks that approach each other was something closely connected with what has just been indicated, namely the continuously progressing interplay between the individual souls and the folk spirit of Israel. In order to be servants and carriers of the first ego-impulse, the individual members of the people had to bear the moon character by means of the 'I'-form, separated from the cosmos, of their bodies. On the other hand, Michael, the arch-angel of the sun, made himself the guiding folk spirit of the whole, thus preparing the path for Christ's human incarnation. The moon vessel was not only overshadowed by the sun-substance, because the Messianic spirit of the sun was itself on the way to the earth, but also because its archangel had chosen as its body the people of Israel.

A number of images from the Old Testament designate the path of a sublime, holy development.

Abraham bowed before the priest of the sun spirit who emerged from the background of the mysteries and from whose hand he received bread and wine. There, still separated, the moon stream of the people, about to come into being, and the sun mystery confronted each other. The sun initiate directed Abraham to his moon task.

In the scene of the sacrifice on Mount Moriah, Isaac underwent the sacramental offering of the solar part of his nature in order to be capable of being father to people of a lunar character. But thereby a solar radiance overshadowed him that was prophetically transparent for the Messianic future of the sun. A first ray of the Christ dawn touched his figure from afar.

Jacob, sharing completely in the moon nature himself, struggled with the sun-archangel Michael at the Jabbok ford. As Jacob received the name Israel, the nascent nation received its folk spirit. Henceforth, like an eagle, Michael spread his sunlit wings over the people, who went forward on their lunar path.

From here, the moon stream of the Messianic heredity took its separate course through the tribe of Judah. But, because of this, in the figure of Joseph, the Adonis among the sons of Jacob, the people seemed privileged to be in a specially transparent proximity to the sun mystery hovering above them. The corporeal stream and that of the sun culture separated from one another. Although he did not belong to the fathers, Joseph drew all the people, among them Judah who had once betrayed him and was the bearer of the Messianic heredity, to himself in Egypt into the sphere of the ancient Egyptian sun wisdom. Dreamlike images of bread and wine moved through the soul realm of the people, as if the sacramental blessing of the sun were already drawing near in the light-filled sphere of the clouds, the dimension of the folk spirit.[97]

Centuries went by until Moses led his people through the desert. By means of the establishment of his commandments, he affirmed the individual moon character among the Israelites; at the same time he unlocked dimensions of mankind that extended far beyond the sphere of the folk spirit. But then, as the people crossed over the threshold of the promised land, the impulse of a higher will moved through their whole configuration as if the folk spirit were coming into its own. As if through a multitude of sunflares, this will ignited Michaelic courage and self-aware enthusiasm for the future in the Israelites. Michael, the people's archangel, was tangibly close; and a sun hero led the militant procession in whom the Michaelic genius itself seemed to have become man: Joshua.

The Bible relates that when he had led the people across the Jordan, Joshua had a grand vision: a tall, masculine spirit form stood before him with a drawn sword in its hand. It revealed itself to him as the leader of the heavenly host as well as of the people of Israel (Josh.5:13-15). To Joshua, this experience signified more than an image that arose and then faded again. It was a transformation and fulfilment of his very own being. When the archangel said to him, '. . . I have now come', this announcement was like his moving into Joshua's being. The genius could remain with its people through the radiant soul of Joshua.

The light that Isaac was not yet allowed to harbour in himself, but which nevertheless shone over him after his sacrifice; the being that Jacob still had to fight free of, despite the fact that he thereby achieved a higher union with it; in Joshua, this being descended a step nearer the sphere of the human soul. Joshua was a Messianic prophecy become form, for the influence of the archangel Michael over his soul is related to Christ's incarnation in the future bearer of the Joshua-Jesus name as the early morning dawn is to the sunrise.

148

3.2 The 'Son of the Fish'

In the Bible, Joshua carried the added name of 'Ben Nun', 'son of the fish'. This was by no means a family-name that would indicate how Joshua's father was named. It was a mystery name, like the name Joshua itself, which he who originally was called Hosea received from Moses. In Egyptian cultic language, the word *nun* already existed. There, it signified the deity of the primeval waters from which the earth's creation solidified. Perhaps the words, which sound alike in Egyptian as well as in Hebrew, were related to each other; perhaps Joshua had brought the name 'Ben Nun' along from Egypt where, like Moses, although considerably younger, he may have had a certain share in the mysteries. In any case, the image of the fish must be comprehended in the context of the ancient practices of initiation, where it was related to the image of the primordial waters.

This can also be derived from a most curious legend, by means of which men of old sought to interpret the riddle of the Joshua being in imaginative manner:[98]

> The father of Joshua, the son of Nun, dwelt in the region
> of Jerusalem, and his wife was barren a long time. The
> devout man prayed for his wife and God heard his prayers.
> But when the woman was with child, the just one fasted
> and cried day and night without cease. The woman was
> cross about that and said to him: You should rejoice that
> God has heard your pleas. The man did not reply to her.
> But when she spoke to him about it daily and implored
> him with her words, he opened his heart to her and related
> to her that it had been told to him from heavenly heights
> that his son would one day kill him. The wife accepted his
> words in good faith, for she knew that truth always issued
> forth from his mouth.
>
> When she had given birth to the child, she saw that it
> was a son. She took a small chest, sealed with clay and
> tar, laid the child in it and threw it in the river. But the
> Lord sent a large fish, and it swallowed the chest with the
> child in it.
>
> It happened that the king prepared a great feast for his
> princes and his courtiers, and the fish was caught that had

swallowed Joshua. It was brought before the king, cut open, and lo, a little boy lay within, crying. The king and his princes were astonished, and the king gave orders to fetch a woman who would suckle the babe.

Thus did Joshua grow up in the house of the king, and the king appointed him his executioner. It came to pass that the just one, the father of Joshua, had trespassed in the eyes of the king, and the latter ordered the executioner to behead the man. According to the laws of the land, however, wife, children and the possessions of the executed one became the property of the executioner.

When, after this, Joshua approached his mother to lie with her, milk poured from her breasts and streamed over their bedding. Joshua was greatly perturbed over this and took his spear to pierce and slay the woman, for he took her to be a witch. In this moment, the woman recalled the words of her husband, the just one, and she said to her son: What you see is no witchcraft; it is the milk with which you were to be suckled, for I am your mother. And she told him everything that had taken place. Immediately, Joshua desisted from her. Now he pondered what he had heard, namely that he had been discovered inside a fish. Woe to him that he had not known that the condemned man had been his father! And he did penance.

Therefore he was called the son of Nun, for in Aramaic, *nun* means 'fish'. But the scouts whom Moses had dispatched, called him 'Beheader,' because of his earlier deed that he had done to his father.

This legend gathers a great number of mythological motifs into one: the image of the basket of Moses, the myth of Jonah and the whale, the Oedipus tragedy, and the legend of Judas Iscariot, which also resembles the Oedipus tragedy; everything comes together in order to illustrate the centrally human significance of the Joshua figure. The story of the abandonment of the babe in a basket on the waters of the stream brings to expression, as it does in Moses' case, the early reawakening of the initiation undergone in past incarnations (see page 30). The Osiris-Adonis initiation, already indicated in the image of the basket or chest, is underlined and made concrete through the similarity with the story of Jonah. The whale, which, according to the Old Testament, swallowed the prophet Jonah for three days, is nothing else but an imagination for the depths of the earth itself, the earth that floats within the primal waters. Into its grave, the pupil of initiation was submerged in the mysteries of Asia Minor during the temple sleep lasting three days. The resemblance of the Joshua legend to the Oedipus and Judas legends shows us that Joshua was already a modern human being. In him, the destiny of ego-man, 'he who slays his father and weds his mother', moved forward mightily, because the paternal principle of universal life dies in him, and the maternal principle of universal love degenerates into egotism.

The pivotal point of the legend is found in the image of the fish that harbours the boy for a while in its belly. From it, Joshua received the name Son of the Fish. In one respect, this image belongs together with the symbols of the bull and the ram that we have discussed in connection with Moses and his Egyptian environment (See Chapter 1.12). Bull, Ram and Fishes are three constellations of the zodiac following one upon the other. From the beginning of the Egyptian-Babylonian era onward, the point of the vernal equinox passed through these three signs. In the third post-Atlantean cultural period (2901-747 BC), for which Egypt and Babylonia were the stage, at the beginning of spring, the sun shone down upon the earth from the constellation of the Bull (Taurus). In the fourth, or Greco-Roman, period (747 BC - AD1413), the vernal sun moved through the constellation of the Ram (Aries). In the fifth, the present period (since 1413), the vernal sun rises in the constellation of the Fishes (Pisces). Moses, the man of the Ram, was ahead of the Egyptian age. Aaron, the man of the Bull, stood by his side as a bearer of forces from the past. But another helper stood beside him, a bearer of faculties that were to become mankind's property only in a distant future: Joshua, the 'Son of the Fish'. The Taurus-sun had implanted the magic word power in man's larynx; Aaron was bearer of this talent. The Aries-sun caused the birth of thought on the human forehead; Moses was its herald and first-born. One day in the future the sun in Pisces was to accompany a resurrection of the human etheric body. Embedded in a new streaming and flowing of his etheric formative forces, man was then to resemble a fish moving through the water full of life. Owing to his kinship with the sun, Joshua carried within him an early radiance of this progressing life force.

Moses, the embodiment of the turning point of the age, stood between Aaron and Joshua, the representative of the past and of the future. As Aaron was Moses' mouthpiece, Joshua was his hand. Aaron translated Moses' visionary thoughts into magical and priestly words; Joshua transformed them silently into the impulse for deeds. As a hero and commander, Joshua was victorious over the army of the Amalekites, while Moses, supported by Aaron and Hur, lifted up his hands in prayer in the form of the cross. More is revealed in a quiet scene in which Joshua, as the 'chosen' servant of Moses (Num.11:28), is in the domain of the sanctuary: 'Thus the LORD used to speak to Moses face to face, as a man speaks to his friend. When Moses turned again into the camp, his servant Joshua the son of Nun, a young man, did not depart from the tent.' (Exod.33:11). What did Joshua do as a guard in the holy of holies? Did he hold back antagonistic forces by the heroic will of his spirit, where the altar of Yahweh was erected above steaming vents in the earth's ground?

The future, which Joshua realized ahead of time through the power of the sign of the Fishes, was the age in which the Christ-being already began to pour its life into human souls. Early Christendom has designated the Christ with the fish-symbol again and again on countless alabaster slabs sealing tombs in the catacombs, as well as elsewhere. Christ was the true Joshua, the actual 'Son of the Fish', and because of this, Joshua was a prophecy of the coming of the Messiah.

3.3 The destruction of Jericho

The crossing of the River Jordan under Joshua's leadership was enveloped in such sensations of the deity's nearness for all the people that they felt themselves transported as if into another world. Although it was a quite natural occurrence, the passage through the stream nevertheless awakened not only the image of the miraculous crossing of the Sea of Reeds, but more than that, it aroused the feeling of being in reality a participant in a sequence of events taking their course in the spiritual worlds. The stream became the threshold to a new world, a new life. Despite this, the Israelites did not feel themselves any the less on solid ground. On the contrary, they must have experienced a quite novel sure-footedness. Not only could they now leave behind the desert with its subterranean gorges and craters, but, attaining the fulfilment of a forty-year-long yearning, a hitherto unknown energy filled them. Were they transported into the world of the heavens, or did a celestial force descend to them, permeating them and ensouling this side with the grandeur of the beyond?

Not far from the location where the Jabbok flows into the Jordan, the river had already once been a threshold in the age of the patriarchs. There, the archangel Michael had stepped into the path of the returning Jacob. In that early morning scene, Jacob had struggled to receive the archangel's blessing in entering into the domain of the conscious, free deed. This power was now bestowed abundantly on Joshua and the people. The archangel did not allow it to be wrested away from him. He did not confront the people as their antagonist, but as their helper and fulfiller of goals. Was not the uplifting experience of the present pervaded by an undefinable, distant presentiment? Here, a human being would one day receive the baptism at the hand of another human being, who would appear in his age like an earthly emissary and representative of the archangel. A highest divinity would then not only hover over the human being but would come into incarnation fully and completely.

Jacob had named the location by the river 'Peniel', 'the countenance of God'; Joshua called the site of the Jordan crossing 'Gilgal'. This word conjures forth a whole wealth of ancient experiences of civilization. Gilgal means 'wheel of the sun', and basically denotes the stone circle made with menhir-like stones; for Joshua had twelve stones erected in a circle at the site where the Jordan had been crossed.

Stone-circles, like menhirs and dolmens, are among the impressive monuments of ancient sun worship;[99] to this day, dating from the very beginning of European epochs, they are found in Ireland, Scotland, England, in Brittany, but also in more southern areas, significantly also in northern Galilee and east of the River Jordan. The play of light and shadow, of physical and spiritual sun forces, was for the Druids of the north and the corresponding priests of the southern peoples a golden portal for looking into what 'holds the world together in its innermost essence'. The stone circles are not to be pictured at rest in static immobility. Physically, the stones stood there of course, without moving. But not only did the shadow of the stake, rising in the centre, move like a sundial from stone to stone, circling along with the sun; above all, the supersensory formative forces of nature had to be imagined as being in the most active motion at such a location. A wheel goes round and round at the border between the sensory and the supersensory world, and its spokes take hold of the soul and cast it from one side of life over to the other. Gilgal, the sun-wheel, was a site of translation by virtue of nature's forces. What the Israelites experienced when, led by Joshua, they crossed over the threshold of the stream was as if the wheel of destiny had taken hold of them and had transported them into another sphere. As a monument, not only of a physical event, but of a mighty spiritual 'having been moved', Gilgal, the mystery-filled stone-circle, now stood within the river bed close to the shore, the ever flowing waves of the Jordan streaming over it. It stood at the site, where, carried by the priests, the Ark of the Covenant had waited during the people's passage. Just as the holy altar had stood at locations in the desert, where the forces of the earth's interior moved about, so here, it had been the centre of swirling forces of divine courage, and the image of the stone-wheel now took its place. In Gilgal, an intensified Peniel had come into being.

The threshold-crossing had been a God-given one. But now it became a matter of struggling and fighting for each further step on the continuing way, with the newly received strength. The land of the future had been reached, but it was still the stage of spiritual forces of the past that had fallen into decadence. A spiritual as well as a physical confrontation had to ensue in all directions. To begin with, the world of Jericho stood in the way of the people. The obstacle was more than a fortified city that was difficult to conquer; the Israelites came upon a zone, impenetrable in a spiritual sense. There, between the river and the eastern hills of today's

Judean Desert, a broad strip of sense-dulling, abundant fruitfulness spread out in the wide Jordan flatland, from north to south, almost reaching the northern end of the Dead Sea. Situated nearly 400 metres (almost 1300 feet) below sea level, this sub-tropical garden of abundant vegetation was covered with a magically sweet, humid oppression of which, at the time of Antony and Cleopatra, distinct and extensive traces still existed.

The Israelites could not have encountered a more pronounced contrast to the barren Sinai Desert. This was the secret of Jericho: it was the last remnant of the oppressively rich world of Sodom and Gomorrah.

In prehistoric times, the whole broad depression in the earth, occupied today by the southernmost part of the Jordan Valley, the Dead Sea and the Wadi el Arabah (Arava Valley), had been a lush magical garden-land. The forces of subterranean fire and gases had brought an end to the humid, abundant life: Sodom and Gomorrah were transformed into the wasteland of stone and brine, of which the Dead Sea is a part. In Jericho a subdued strip of that destroyed life had remained. In the desert the people had experienced the powers of wrath that had destroyed Sodom. Now they confronted a last Sodom-like place.

Jericho means 'city of the moon' (from the Hebrew word *yareach*, moon). Moon forces held sway there. But as yet, they were not effective in the manner of the moon that is separated from the earth, in the manner of a clear mirror of sunlight and aid to the human intellect, which gives rise to mental reflections of things in the brain. The moon forces of Jericho were effective instead in the manner of a remnant of the moon that had not yet departed the earth. Their effect was sultry and intoxicating in a dull sense, causing an intensified form of what they still call forth today as sleepwalking. Following a different interpretation of the name, Jericho was often designated in former times as the 'city of palms'. Both designations point to the truth. The second name refers to the magically enticing luxuriance of the tropical vegetation at the edge of the desert.

Jericho's culture and the character of its inhabitants must have matched that of the environment. A residue of the magic Sodom-decadence must have survived there. If Rahab, the woman who sheltered Joshua's scouts in her home and concealed them from their pursuers, was designated as a harlot, this probably permits us to look from one direction into the life and activities of decadent sexual cults that dominated ancient Jericho. The Israelites would have encountered an intensification in Jericho of what had confronted them as temptations in the land of the Moabites under Balaam's influence through the Midianite temple harlots. Rahab must be pictured as a *qedesh*, a cult prostitute, and her house as the site of one of those degenerate cults. But a spirit spoke out of Rahab's soul to the scouts that was capable of rising above the environment, freeing itself of the confines of Jericho; this spirit could thus recognize Israel's divine mission and accept it.

The Bible describes Jericho to us as surrounded by a wall that prevented the people of Israel from entering; a number of imaginative pictures follow that permit us to experience the dramatic collision of two different spiritual streams. For seven days, Joshua ordered the priests to circle around the city, carrying the Ark of the Covenant to the sound of the holy temple trumpets. For six days, the magic circle was drawn around the city once each day, but seven times on the seventh day. Then, to the battle cry of Israel, the walls of Jericho tumbled down; the fortification that had placed itself in Joshua's way had fallen.

A miracle had thus taken place. But once again, an apocalyptical, not a physical event was referred to. What was effective were not the material silver trumpets and their sound, but the spiritual power, for which they are a symbolic picture in the same sense as are the seven trumpets in the Apocalypse of St John. The nocturnal lunar world of Jericho was confronted by a mighty, infectious sun impulse. The Michaelic folk spirit of Israel, the archangel of the sun, had now really gained entrance into the people led by Joshua. In the sphere of the folk soul, a sunrise took place with irresistible force. Sun power arose 'as does a hero.' In the spirit realm, this sunrise was accompanied by the sounds of trumpets that could burst open rocky portals and shatter walls. The sun arises in the manner in which Goethe describes it at the beginning of the second part of the *Faust* drama:

> Hearken! Hark — the Hours careering!
> Sounding loud to spirit-hearing,
> See the newborn day appearing!
> Rocky portals jarring shatter,

> Phoebus' wheels in rolling clatter,
> With a crash the light draws near!
> Pealing rays, and trumpet-blazes . . .

Did the procession of priests with their daily circling of the city not follow the circle that the sun draws across the sky, finally culminating through a rhythmic intensification of time in a breakthrough into timelessness? Magic circles of the radiant sun broke the magic spell of the shadowy moon.

The effects of the Michaelic spirit, brandishing swords of light, were directed at the people of Jericho, not — as one might think by misunderstanding the imaginative description — at the stones of the city-wall. It is perhaps correct to imagine that the inhabitants of Jericho were blinded and confused by the sun-imbued appearance of the Israelites and the sounds of the circling procession of priests; reeling from all these impressions, they gave up their watchfulness and will to resist and thus forfeited the advantages that the walls of the city offered them. It might be possible that a miracle occurred similar to the one that took place in the year 1241 after the Battle of Wahlstadt. The Mongolian hordes of Genghis Khan had penetrated into Europe at that time on a broad scale. No army was able to offer them resistance. The fighting force of the German princes that faced them in the area of Liegnitz (now Legnica in Poland) was overrun despite its bravery. However, the victorious army of the Mongols all at once began its withdrawal. The peril of Asian invasion was turned back. But by what means? The weapons of Europe had not been capable of this. Only one explanation remains, namely that the Mongols in their atavistic spirituality were frightened of the spirit of central Europe which was coming to expression in early urban culture. The people of Jericho may in like manner have been frightened by the spirit of the Israelites encircling the city. The lunar dream dispersed before the resounding might of true sunlight. Without applying military means in the external sense, the Israelites became masters over the strange city.

It must have been especially the impulse of stern formative energy of Israel's soul realm which carried the seed of doom into the chaotically proliferating world of ancient abundance. In the image of the trumpet sounds, all apocalyptic texts of the past speak to us of the forces of sound ether that represent the actual source of form in the supersensory realm.* Greek mythology relates that when Cadmus founded the city of Thebes at the site of his victory over the dragon, the walls of the city with its seven gates were not built by human labour but by the sounds of harps. This meant that the chaotic power of the dragon, the ancient, unbridled force of nature, was confronted in the first Greek urban constructions with a bright, light-filled form impulse. The music of the harmonies of the spheres in the supersensory realm of sounds was transposed into the form-language of architecture, of which it was later said correctly that it was 'frozen music'. Just as the walls of Thebes were built by the power of sound that is concealed in the light of the sun, so the walls of Jericho were brought to the point of collapsing. A new spiritual will to build made its appearance in the figure of Joshua.

The fate that befell Jericho because of the Israelites was like the final step in the destruction of Sodom and Gomorrah. Since a spirituality and culture had developed there that would have been poisonous for the future evolution of humanity, nothing of it could be allowed to remain. The city was levelled, and all its cultic wealth was put under a ban, subjugated to a form of exorcism in order henceforth to be considered sanctified for the Yahweh worship. But one person from the tribe of Judah broke the stern commandment of the ban and appropriated a valuable Babylonian coat, and also took a silver and a golden staff from the treasures of Jericho. Right away, the Israelites behaved as if their benevolent angel of the sun had left them, and their courageously forward-moving will of destiny weakened; alien tribes threatened to become master over them. How could this happen?

What had taken place did not merely count for a theft. The perpetrator was named Achan, the 'serpent'. The name already indicates that this was a person who still wanted to nurture the ancient clairvoyant faculties in his nature and was therefore fascinated by Jericho's spirituality. If mention is made of a Babylonian coat and stolen silver and gold, this points to soul-spiritual forces and traditions of Jericho that Achan intended to incorporate surreptitiously into the Israelite development. This betrayal could

---

*The vibrating plates of Chladni are a physical illustration, by means of laboratory experiments, of the formative forces slumbering in sound.

only be atoned for by mercilessly re-establishing the purity of the Israelite impulse. Nevertheless, a quintessence of Jericho's life was incorporated into the Israelite future, particularly with a view to the Messianic mission of the people. The harlot Rahab was not only spared during the destruction of the city, but even accepted into the blood-relationship of Israel as one of the matriarchs of the Messianic lineage. When Rahab had said to the two scouts of Joshua, 'the LORD your God is he who is God in heaven above and on earth beneath', she had intuitively recognized the Messianic mission of the chosen people, and she had pointed prophetically to the divine being that was on its way down to earth from heaven (Josh. 2:11). She had thereby united herself with those who, as a people, were to form the earthly vessel for the human incarnation of the Messiah. As Salmon's wife and mother of Boaz (Matt.1:5), she was now included in an especially close form in the Messianic stream of heredity.*

The conquest of Jericho signified the final end to the smouldering afterglow of the Lemurian fire of Sodom in the Sinai territory. The people transformed this fire into an inward element, destroying the latter's creation by means of their own spiritual power. From the subterranean forces of the desert, which had held the people under their spell for forty years, the Israelites, bearing within them the fruit of the desert, fought their way clear. Now, they themselves were a brightly burning flame that lit the spirit of egohood.

3.4 The world of the Canaanites

After crossing the Jordan and erecting the stones at Gilgal, Israel had to do battle with forces of the past as well as the future. The battle against Jericho had been against a past reaching back far beyond Egypt and Babylonia. Now, battles of a completely different nature had to be waged against the Phoenician-Canaanite

---

*The legends state[100] that Joshua himself became Rahab's husband and begat Boaz with her. It also says that Rahab was the reincarnated wife of Potiphar. Through her marriage with Joshua, who had been Joseph once upon a time, a part of the Egyptian destiny had been turned in a positive direction. But this tradition is probably misleading. Salmon may have been Salma, one of the two scouts, to whom Rahab offered shelter in her house.

inhabitants of Palestine, who were still under Egyptian sovereignty.

Usually, quite inadequate ideas have been formed concerning the Canaanites. Misconstruing the imaginative descriptions of the Bible, people have seen primitive savages, or barbarian heathens in them, as they saw bedouin-like nomads in the Israelites.

In reality, the inhabitants of Palestine were at that time nations with an advanced culture, endowed with an energetic and far-reaching will for civilization. Either they themselves still belonged to the Phoenicians, or they were at least related to them and participated in the latter's worldwide commerce and their trade, spanning oceans and continents. The Phoenicians were emissaries and go-betweens not only between the worlds of Egypt and Babylonia, but between all the cultures of ancient humanity. All over the ancient world, as maritime voyagers and colonists, they sought to translate the heritage of their great past into new progressive impulses.

The tribes from whose name the word Palestine has derived were the Philistines, a group of a more northern origin, who had linked up with the Phoenicians and had migrated from other parts of the eastern Mediterranean shortly before the age of Moses, settling in the fertile coastal areas in the western part of the land. People frequently think of them in a manner that obstructs a realistic historical view. The story of Goliath suggests that the Philistines had been clumsy giants. In reality, they were a nation with an advanced culture; and unusually tall stature can no more be assumed in their case than in that of another people, from whom the German word, *Hüne*, (man of near-gigantic proportions) derives, namely the physically rather short Huns.

The Bible shows us a number of encounters by the Israelites with giants; not only among the Philistines but also, for example, among the Amorites, 'giants' existed. Even their kings, Og and Sihon (Josh.2:10), bore names that indicate the giant-element. The imaginative picture of the giant reflects a condition of consciousness more than one of corporeality. It refers to people whose etheric bodies still extended far beyond the physical bodies. The giant-element was found in the formative-forces or life-body, not in the physical body. Old magically clairvoyant soul potentials were still active among those peoples who are described as giants in the Bible, and it was just these supersensory forces that were the cause of the frequently over-ripe culture of these nations.

Now, the Phoenician-Canaanite tribes pose a riddle to us. Their nature appears to have been dominated by a strange contradiction. On one hand, untimely clairvoyant soul-forces extended into their being. On the other hand, we see them rush impatiently into the progressive modern mode of civilization. How is it possible that they were simultaneously 'giants' and modern men of their age? Among the Philistines, the character of forward-striving activity was underscored especially by the fact that they could all have been designated as 'sons of the fish'. The deity, Dagon, to whom their worship was directed and for whom they built imposing temples in Ascalon (Ashkelon), Gaza, and other towns by the sea, was represented in the figure of a giant fish. This did not only signify that Dagon was experienced as the protective spirit of the Philistine coastal region and maritime activity. Like the picture-image of the big fish in the Jonah myth and the Joshua legends, it pointed to an initiation practice that was to bring about the connection with the forces of progress and the future which originated in the constellation of Pisces. This was the characteristic feature of the world of Canaan, something that appears at first to us like a contradiction. There, the giant-forces of the past did not manifest as tranquil revelation and wisdom but as a will impulse towards the future. Unchanged elements of the past were to be transferred forcibly into the future. Nations lived here who disdained to find their way 'through the desert' into the land of egohood. Without giving up the ancient treasures, they wanted to force the new world. The age of the 'I' of man was arising ever more powerfully and in Palestine awakened an almost ecstatic drive and instinct. But the 'I'-impulse made its appearance there in the form of the giant. The new clothed itself in the old that it was supposed to replace, and the old behaved in the manner of the new. A caricature apppeared of the same will which in Joshua, the true 'Son of the Fish,' and the people led by him, was alive in pure form blessed by Michaelic power.

The same puzzling, contradictory make-up of Palestine had confronted the Israelites once before in an important symbol. The Bible relates that, upon their return, the twelve spies sent by

161

Moses to Palestine, Joshua among them, brought back a gigantic cluster of grapes. If this image had contained nothing more than the promise of fertility in the land ahead of them, the Israelites could not have been so shocked by it. The huge cluster of grapes was more of a cosmic riddle than a miracle. In it, the symbolism continued that arises in the stories of Noah. The Manu-Noah of Atlantean prehistory had been designated as the first planter of grapes for the reason that he laid the foundation of future 'I' development.[101] In antiquity, wine was, after all, the gift of nature by means of which the ego — still hovering above the human being — was led down slowly into the soul and corporeal sheaths and into the pulsing blood. In the element of Dionysian intoxication, the ego came closer to incarnation, leaving behind the divine heights. Noah was the great forerunner of Dionysus in earlier developments, which then culminated in the evolution of Israel.

The universal change came over humanity in the age of Moses. The 'I' had arrived at the human forehead, carried down by the contracting etheric body. The age of Dionysian intoxication as a preparation for the 'I' was gradually coming to an end. A healthy further development of the human being demanded that the harmonious Apollonian path of thought increasingly complement and replace the ecstatic Dionysian path of impulsive will. Moses was one of the great forerunners of Apollo, of the calm, luminous ego in thinking.

It was an impulse of Noah, occurring at the wrong time, that the Israelites encountered, when the spies showed them the land ahead of them in the Dionysian image of the grapes. They could not help but feel that they were facing a world of Dionysian giants.

Again, with this, the contradictory nature of Canaan was indicated; just as between the symbols of the giant and the fish, so, between those of the giant and the grape, a polarity and tension existed. The correctly interpreted ego impulse had to lead to the point now where men ceased to be giants; but here, held back in Dionysian intoxication, it lived in such a manner that not only did it allow them to remain giants, it intensified the magic giant-nature and made it unrestrained.

The spies' grapes subtly point back to another Palestinian cultural stream. There, long ago, the king of Salem, Melchizedek, had gone to meet Abraham, who was returning from battle, bestowing on him the sacrificial symbols of the sun mysteries, bread and wine. What had become of the Melchizedek stream in the eight hundred years that had gone by between Abraham and Joshua?

Of the five Palestinian kings, whom Joshua had to fight against soon after the destruction of Jericho, Adoni-Sedek, king of Jerusalem, ranked first. His name is closely related to that of his great predecessor. Melchizedek means 'King of Justice', Adoni-Sedek, 'Lord of Justice'. Joshua therefore had to do battle against the successor of the one before whom Abraham had bowed. The stream that once flowed out of such a holy source had become decadent and useless. Salem-Jerusalem was no longer the holy school for Israel that it had been in the days of the patriarchs; it had turned into the Israelites' dangerous adversary. How is this to be understood? We have already spoken several times of the 'death of Osiris', as a process that brought about the twilight of Egyptian spiritual life. Osiris, the ego-bearing son of Isis, disappeared from the sun spheres on high, where he had appeared to the Egyptian initiates; henceforth, he had to be sought in a different region. The myth relates that the body of Osiris, who had been slain by Typhon, was immersed in the waters of the Nile in a coffin-chest. The river carried the coffin northward to the sea; it finally washed ashore in Byblos on the northern Levantine coast, north of present-day Beirut.

Large segments of the ancient world have interpreted this tradition to mean that, in a mysterious manner, Osiris, who had disappeared from Egypt, had now established his domicile in Palestine and Syria. Phoenician-Canaanite Palestine had believed that it was to take the place of Egypt as the abode of Osiris, whom one now called Adonai, Adonis, or Baal, the Lord; in the Baal-Adonis worship, the Osiris secret was to be nurtured further. The king, Adoni-Sedek, of Jerusalem, who confronted Joshua, revealed through his name that he was one of the advocates of this claim. In reality, however, the transition of a sublime divine being from one spiritual sphere of the cosmos to another lies behind the image of Osiris' death. It signified a misunderstanding and coarsening of what had in reality occurred to assume that Osiris merely moved from one land into another. The Israelites, who, under the leadership of Moses, did not immediately depart for Palestine but first moved into the desert, where the actual new sphere of Osiris could be discovered in the Yahweh experience, were faithful followers of the vanishing Osiris and pioneers preparing his future realm of activity. When Joshua led the Israelites west of the Jordan into the territory of the Phoenician-Canaanite tribes, a falsified and a true Osiris-Adonis stream clashed with each other. Baal-Adonis wanted to deny Yahweh-Adonai entrance into his land. In the conflicts with the Canaanites, Joshua's people encountered a spiritual decadence that was opposite that of Jericho but no less dangerous. In a mistaken way, Jericho sought to retain forces of the past from ages that had run their course long before the awakening of the ego. In an erroneous way, the Canaanites wanted to force and anticipate the ego's future.

A most unusual difference existed between the gods of Egypt and Babylonia and those of the Palestinian nations preceding the Israelites. The Egyptians and Babylonians looked up into the expanses of the star-studded cosmos and there encountered an immense variety of divine beings. The Canaanites turned mainly to the same entity regardless of whether they called it Osiris, Adonis, Baal, Tammuz, Dagon, Dionysus or some other name. Nevertheless, they underwent only a seeming transition to a monotheistic form of religion. From the celestial multitude of the gods of antiquity, they selected one single being and placed it in the foreground. In particular, they laid claim to the ego-bearing being whose light had been extinguished for the vision of the Egyptians. Isis, who, in Egypt, had turned into the mourning widow, was permitted by the Canaanites to remain shadow-like by the side of Osiris-Adonis in the figure of Astarte (Ashtaroth). Thereby, the Canaanite religion possessed a powerful ego- and will-nature without treading the paths of ego-evolution that led through the soul's impoverishment. They confused the divine predecessor of the ego with the ego itself and because of that remained in the sphere of the 'giant' and Dionysian intoxication.

What means for revitalizing the dying forces were at the disposal of the Canaanites? The Phoenician-Canaanite world subsisted by the misuse and betrayal of the mysteries. The Osiris initiation, in which the neophyte was led through death and rebirth to the universally extended realm of Isis and her continuously born son, had been bestowed on a select few in ancient Egypt only after long preparation. The world of the Baal-Adonis cult was based on the fact that the foundation for this initiation was prepared high-handedly. People no longer imposed on themselves strict conditions and preparations in order to attain initiation. Instead, during the great folk festivals, while the coffin of Adonis was submerged in the water for three days, the principle of initiation was symbolically brought as closely as possible to even the unprepared masses of the people. Widespread, intentional disclosure of the once customary concealment took place; impure egotistic instincts laid claim to the spirit nobility that previously was only accessible to a highly purified soul. Instead of the genuine sun radiance of the higher ego, the true Osiris light, being ignited as of old in the disciple's soul, the Dionysian ecstatic ego was enkindled by means of initiation and cultic rites.

In Joshua's age, as many forms of the false Osiris principle existed in Palestine as did Canaanite tribes. The cult of the anti-ego intensified even into the black-magical blood-lust of Molech worship. As the twelve tribes of Israel confronted the multitude of their opponents, who were their actual counter-images, the people of Israel awakened in a variety of ways to their potential as the true vessel of the ego deity that worked in that age.

The cluster of grapes, fetched by the twelve spies, was certainly a picture of the spiritual and religious condition of Palestine at that period. We behold in it an imagination of the Dionysian decadence of ecstasy that had usurped the symbols of bread and wine since the time when Melchizedek had carried them forth to Abraham as unassuming holy signs of the pure sun mysteries. Adoni-Sedek, the first of the kings against whom Joshua had to do battle, did not bring forth bread and wine as did his lofty predecessor. He too stood under the sign of the giant grape that had frightened the people in the desert.

From this point, we understand the deeper meaning of a scene which was to take on the greatest significance for the Israelites' settlement in Palestine. The inhabitants of Gibeon came to Joshua in a strange disguise to petition him for a treaty. Like beggars, dressed in torn rags, they carried upon their asses old, mended wineskins with spoiled wine and dirty sacks with mouldy bread.

What was their intent? At first glance one might believe — something the biblical text seems to suggest — that the Gibeonites wanted to deceive Joshua, whom they feared, with a ruse, and win him over to their side. But the central significance that Gibeon in particular was to assume subsequently for Israel's destiny allows for a different interpretation of this scene. Did not the Gibeonites present a quite honest and truthful symbol for the extinction of the Melchizedek mysteries? Was it not just this that distinguished them from the rest of the Canaanites that, instead of clinging to the vanishing old faculties by means of ecstatic intensification, they were prepared to resign themselves to the spiritual impoverishment that appeared over the whole world? Once, bread and wine in Melchizedek's hand had reflected the still radiant light of the spiritual Osiris sun. Now, bread and wine were in danger of becoming powerless and dim. Dusk had broken in upon the sun mysteries and one had to look out for the bearer of the new light. Was Gibeon perhaps the site of a sun mystery which, just because of its inhabitants' attitude, retained its genuineness and was spared the decadence of the surrounding world, because it honestly admitted the cosmic twilight and privation into which it had been included?

3.5 Gibeon

The treaty between Israel and Gibeon caused the outbreak of a war. Five Canaanite kings, led by Adoni-Sedek of Jerusalem, moved their armies against the city of Gibeon in order to punish it for its alliance with the Israelite strangers. Joshua acknowledged the treaty obtained seemingly by artifice, but in reality based on a significant spiritual accord, and moved with his army to the aid of the besieged Gibeonites. Soon the ranks of the five kings reeled before Joshua's onslaught and were vanquished. In a miraculous way Joshua was able to gain complete victory despite the fact that night was closing in. He uttered a strange sentence in the hearing of all the people: 'Sun of Gibeon, stand still, and moon of the Valley of Aijalon!' It then remained light until Joshua and his people could return to their camp after having won the victory (Josh.10:12 B). What happened because of this battle?

It is important to gain a clear concept of the location and

significance of the city of Gibeon. Not far north of Jerusalem there rises a tower-like mountain summit. Although it is not the highest elevation in that region (being 885 metres, 2935 feet) its slender, high-rising shape dominates the surroundings of Jerusalem. Not only is there a marvellous view from up there: westward into the fertile plane of Jaffa and beyond it over the Mediterranean Sea, eastward into the world of the rocky mountain-wastelands on both sides of the Jordan, southward to the prominently situated city of Jerusalem, northward into the fields of Samaria and the snow-covered summit of Mount Hermon; from Jerusalem itself as well as from the roads that lead towards the city, the eye is drawn again and again toward this wondrous mountain-top, crowned with a tower, as upon a landmark of this region. This is Mizpah, the 'heights of the lookout', of great importance in Samuel's age. On its summit, Samuel was subsequently buried, and the grave, revered by all the people, made it an even holier site. Thus, its significance remained in effect through the centuries, and even today it is as if something of the solemn royal splender of David's age had adhered to this height.

At the foot of the mountain, Gibeon, 'the city of heights,' was located. We must assume that a close connection existed between Gibeon and Mizpah. Mizpah was the sanctuary that towered over all the surrounding land including the city of Jerusalem.*

The land abounded in 'holy mountain summits', on which, in pre-Israelite times, services to the gods had been performed. But Gibeon 'was the greatest high place' in the land (1Kings 3:4 *B*). Following the indications contained in the biblical books, we can imagine how this summit once looked. Up there, 'the great stone which is in Gibeon' (2Sam.20:8) rose up — a giant menhir, perhaps representing the centre of a stone circle (gilgal), that kept alive the memory of ancient Druid sun cults.

The city of Gibeon with its mountain sanctuary poses a formidable riddle within the Old Testament descriptions for the reason that its pre-Israelite religious and historical development passes without any break into the era of Israel. The tribe of Benjamin, in whose region Gibeon was located, relinquished the city to the

---

*Gustaf Dalman equates Mizpah (Nebi Samuil) with the mountain of Gibeon. Many other scholars share this opinion but without drawing the consequences from it.

Levites, thus making it into a city of priests. Soon after Israel's entry into Palestine, we note that important scenes in the life of the Israelite nation take place on this summit. There, the people looked for and found presence of mind in the life within the boundaries of the Canaanite cults (Judg.10:17; 21:1). For holy gatherings of the people, the assembly came up to the Lord in Mizpah (Judg.21:5). In Mizpah, Samuel called the Israelites together for the mighty judicial statements (1Sam.7:5), and there he introduced to them Saul who had been anointed king (1Sam.10:17). Most surprisingly of all, during the first period of the kingdom we find the tabernacle, together with the altar of burnt offering, originally placed by Joshua in the Samaritan city of Shiloh, in the high place at Gibeon: 'For the tabernacle of the LORD which Moses had made in the wilderness, and the altar of burnt offering were at that time in the high place in Gibeon' (1Chr.21:29). Even in the age when the Ark of the Covenant had already found its place on Mount Zion, the tabernacle remained on the height of Gibeon. Solomon himself offered up a sacrifice there and because of it had a decisive dream-revelation (1Kings 3). Only when the temple was erected, was the height of Gibeon replaced by Mount Moriah as the dwelling place of Yahweh.

This is all the more strange since, on the other hand, it is clearly discernible that the city of Gibeon, located in the midst of Israel's territory, retained political independence as well as its pre-Israelite religious character up to the time of the kings. An attempt by Saul, whose hometown was Gibeon, (1Chr.8:29–33), to interfere in this had to be bloodily avenged by David upon the request of the inhabitants (2Sam.21). Even today, the village of El Jib, which is situated at the site of ancient Gibeon, makes a quite antiquated impression despite Jerusalem's vicinity.[102]

All this indicates that Gibeon must have been the one Palestinian mystery site that Joshua did not have to oppose; instead, he could relate directly to it and ally himself with it. Although even Jerusalem had fallen victim to decadence since the days of Melchizedek, one sun sanctuary nearby had nevertheless remained pure, having carried the spirit of the old Melchizedek mystery through the ages of twilight, until Joshua, the bearer of a new sunlike impulse, came along and once again lit the dying light. When the Gibeonites brought forth spoiled bread and wine in their beggars'

168

garb, this not only indicated an honest admission of their own privation but also a homage before the one who was bringing help, whom they were ready to serve.* When Melchizedek came forth to meet Abraham with bread and wine, Abraham bowed before him; now, those who bore the bread and wine bowed to him whom they went out to meet. And for the first stages of its Palestinian destiny, Israel found a spiritual guiding centre.

Accordingly, the figure of Joshua represents an important stage in the religious relationship with nature. By virtue of his discipleship of Jethro, Moses was still completely integrated with the weaving of the forces of nature on sanctified mountain heights. On Mount Sinai-Horeb, he received his revelations from the earth's fire. Later, after Elijah, the prophets of Judaism arose as radical opponents of the sanctuaries on mountain summits, doing away with them everywhere. In between stood Joshua, still allied with the holy heights. In the fire that was first kindled on the ancient altar of rock slabs on the summit of Mizpah — partially preserved even today — the Sinai fire lived on as in a reflected memory. And later, when the tabernacle with the altar of the burnt offering received its place up there, the telluric fire of Moses' age intensified inwardly until finally the Temple of Solomon was constructed and the prophets urged the replacement of all external offerings — except for those on the rock of Moriah — with the heart's attitude of devotional sacrifice.

At no other moment did Joshua appear more radiantly as the sun hero and warrior, than when, as victor over the five kings at the foot of the city of Gibeon, he called out the mantric sentence (Josh.10:12 *B*) 'Sun of Gibeon, stand still, and moon of the Valley of Aijalon!' It has often been thought that the Bible wanted to dish up the incredible miracle tale that upon Joshua's command the sun and moon had interrupted their celestial course here. But the biblical text itself indicates that the sentence which Joshua uttered was not coined by him. Joshua quoted it from an old, holy book, the *Sepher Hayashar*, the 'Book of Those who See God.'† It is an ancient mantric word that Joshua called out to his

---

*The Bible does in fact indicate that the Gibeonites entered into a relationship of service to Israel as 'hewers of wood and drawers of water' (Josh.9:12).

†The traditional translation is 'Book of the Just.' The title employed by us here is rendered analogously to the book's title given by Rudolf Steiner.

people. The misunderstanding to which this scene has fallen victim is moreover caused by the fact that it is translated: 'Sun, stand thou still at Gibeon!' In reality, it is not the physical sun, making its way across the sky, that is being addressed, but the 'Sun of Gibeon.' It was the spiritual being of the sun that was revered and experienced as the source of revelation in the sun mystery of Gibeon.[103] It is an old ritual expression, by means of which the sun priests of Gibeon entered into a relationship with the divine powers, that was called out by Joshua, who wanted thereby to attain for his people the same relationship which hitherto the Gibeonites had been privileged to experience.

In the Provençal descriptions of the battles that Charlemagne had to fight in Spain against the Moors, a scene occurs that can remind us of the victory of Joshua at Gibeon. After Roland's death, the army of the Frankish king was on the verge of defeating the Moors, when night fell. Had they interrupted pursuit of the Moors, the enemy would have been capable of renewed resistance despite defeat. Charlemagne prayed and addressed his army, inciting them to such visionary enthusiasm that, while the Arabs were enveloped in nocturnal darkness, the Franks believed that the sun, in order to aid them, was standing still in the sky. It was light as day for them and they could attain total victory. It is possible that before the gates of Gibeon a similar soul experience took place, touched off by the ancient sun-invocation. Joshua proved himself to be master over the inner sun forces of his people. He was able to call them forth to bright life. The Michaelic power of the sun archangel, communicated to the people as their folk spirit, arose as a radiant inner light in the people's awareness following Joshua's words. The Israelite folk came into its own, spiritually, in the encounter with the Phoenician-Canaanite nations.

Today the site of ancient Emmaus (El Qubeibeh) north-west of Jerusalem, where the two disciples had the encounter with the resurrected Christ as told in the Gospel of St Luke, is still wondrously enveloped by the solar landscape of Gibeon. Far across the land, in the midst of the sun-drenched green chain of hills that slowly sweep down to the wide Mediterranean Sea, can be seen the Valley of Aijalon, the 'valley of deer'. And inland, in the mountains shining in golden-brown colours and continuing further into the grey desert of Judea, Gibeon is situated with the towering lookout of Mizpah. Emmaus lies in the middle between Aijalon and Gibeon, both of which still belong within the closer radius of this region. Perhaps it was here where Joshua called out the sun mantram to the victorious Israelites.

When the two disciples recognized the Christ, they had an experience of the spiritual sun. When the physical sun had set below the horizon of the sea, they entered the house of Cleopas, and the bread that was broken suddenly shone with the spiritual sun force of the consecrated host. The question can come to mind whether it was a hint of the sun sanctuary of Gibeon that came to the fore, as it did twelve hundred years earlier in Joshua's victory achieved at the same location.

3.6 The twelve judges

Upon the entry into the Promised Land, the destiny of Israel under Joshua had something of the secrecy and momentum of a new beginning, of a sunrise. The blissful enthusiasm of a first love, the invigorating nascent state of Michaelic life held sway in it. The people's entry into the land on this side of the Jordan must have seemed like an earthly reflection of the archangel's entrance into their communal soul. It was an experience of Immanuel: the awareness of 'a god in our midst.'

After Joshua, the sun-warrior, had died in his city of Timnath-serah, the 'home of sun radiance,' a time of proving their worth commenced for the Israelites. The divine momentum made way for human toil. The people had all at once been allowed to see and to take hold of their own higher being. Would they now be able to hold on to what they had achieved, to develop it further out of their own strength?

The apportionment of the land to the twelve tribes took place by no means in a coincidental or arbitrary manner. Each tribe was assigned a region as its domicile which corresponded to the tribe's specific character. This was made possible by the fact that the cosmic differentiation of the land into the most varied kinds of landscape corresponded to the human differentiation of the people into twelve different branches. As the focal point for traces of all great epochs of earth evolution,[104] Palestine encompasses in richest contrasts a suggestion of all significant expressions of scenery possible on earth. The people of Israel, on their part, bore within themselves a trace of all of humanity's nuances. The land and the people fit so well together because both were a reflection of the twelvefold starry zodiac with its all-embracing multiplicity.

The twelve tribes of Israel, however, did encounter inhabitants already settled in the Palestinian territory. These Phoenician-Canaanite peoples were also not arbitrarily spread over the various regions of the land. Their multiplicity, related also to the cosmic manifoldness of the Jordan area, corresponded to the multiplicity of the Israelite tribes. All the streams contained in the Israelite folk confronted their counter-images, and each was settled in that area which embodied the same cosmic nuance as they did in a giantlike Canaanite-Dionysian manner. The Israelite tribes were in a certain sense confronted with their doubles in order to find and work out their own true being.

How must Israel's living together with the folk groups, previously settled in Palestine, be pictured? The Israelites' initial appearance under Joshua's leadership had had the effect of an outbreak of a storm; in any case, it had brought about the possibility of settlement in most of the regions. Only a few localities, — for example Jerusalem, which was an ancient city having already been mentioned under this name in Babylonian records of earlier centuries — shut out the Israelites. Almost everywhere else, however, the previous Canaanite population remained alongside the new arrivals. Although the biblical report states that Joshua had finally subjugated thirty-one kings — and legendary tradition stresses the human totality of this number by saying that all the nations of the world, thirty-one in number, had had colonies in Palestine[105] — it is also emphasized that the victorious Israelites did not expel their opponents (Judg.1:27-33). A cultural and social mingling between the victorious and the defeated came about which in some of the tribes probably also led to miscegenation.

It was most difficult for the Israelites to find the right religious direction in face of the impressive cults of Baal and Astarte (Osiris-Adonis and Isis), which were observed among the now neighbouring Canaanites. The difficulty of remaining aware of the difference is often underestimated, because the devotion of the age of the Jewish prophets is usually predated to this much earlier period. It was not until half a millennium after Joshua that the clear-cut contrast arose between Judaism and paganism, habitually presupposed in reading the Old Testament. It only came about because the two tribes of Judah and Benjamin, living in Judea, separated from the rest of the Israelite folk. Only this later stream, the actual Jews, developed — in correspondence with the desert-character of their domicile — the religious attitude that turned completely away from nature, and whose prophets went about abolishing all the holy high places and the other nature sanctuaries. The other ten tribes always remained more closely related to paganism. At the time of Joshua, and in the immediately ensuing period, even the tribe of Judah did as yet not possess the religious attitude exclusively directed to the inner being. Therefore the Israelites, along with the Canaanites, made use at that time of the same holy mountains, trees and grottoes for their veneration of God. No sharp, external line divided the Canaanite and the Israelite cults. After all, Joshua himself had erected holy stones on sanctified heights, and even Solomon still made sacrifices on the holy summit of Gibeon. In addition, the sight of the tabernacle and the Levite ritual conducted in it, dating back to Mosaic inauguration, remained accessible only to the directly neighbouring tribes of Israel after settlement in the land. Most of the tribes were in fact dependent on contact with foreign cult sites. The Israelites could distinguish themselves religiously from their surrounding world and find their own Yahweh-path only by their inner spiritual attitude, which was averse to ecstasy or at least toned down the ecstatic element. It is therefore not surprising that the Bible has to report again and again that Israel went astray on the path of foreign gods: 'And the people of Israel did what was evil in the sight of the LORD, forgetting the LORD their God, and serving the Baals and the Asheroth' (Judg.3:7).

The Yahweh worship's unique characteristic consisted in the fact that it imbued its adherents with an alert intellectual consciousness of self that did not cease except during sleep. The ego felt itself appealed to with every directive and commandment. It signified a danger to be inattentive and dreamy, for then it was not possible to comply in a strict sense with the challenges of the commandments. As protector and keeper of the still fragile ego of man, Yahweh was the 'inner judge,' the one who gave inward direction to each individual. The Phoenician-Canaanite cults brought about states of intoxication, interruptions of self-awareness by means of their Dionysian elements of ecstasy. Who was then the guide of the human being? It was in any case not one's own 'I', or a divine power working in the sense of man's own ego. Some alien, cosmic power of superhuman dimension became the 'Baal', the ruler over man. Increasingly, these 'giant forces' had to turn into demonic nonentities who hollowed out the being of man. They were not Elohim, divine creator powers, but *Elilim*, idols, literally translated, 'nothingnesses'.

Obviously, so long as the ego impulse was still young and delicate, however, it was difficult to acquire the capability of distinguishing between the spirits, to perceive the element of ego-likeness or ego-antagonism. How were the Israelites aided against the suggestive ecstasy surrounding them?

As if called up by invisible powers, figures of leaders appeared one after the other, who, by means of the ego impregnation of their own nature, could judge the right directions, could be 'judges' of their own people in the sense of the ego-imbued Yahweh consciousness. It would be erroneous to think that the 'judges' were individuals who handed down judgments and presided in a court, in face of whom, therefore, all those had to tremble who broke the law. Here, the emphasis is not on the moral sense of the word 'judge', but on that of the soul realm, where one must judge the direction in which to go (see also p. 122).

This is the reason why the Old Testament calls the judges 'saviours' as well, the bearers of divine healing forces; this is why it can say of Othniel, the first judge: '. . . the LORD raised up a deliverer for the people of Israel, who delivered them . . . The Spirit of the LORD came upon him and he judged Israel' (Judg.3:9). The Baal ecstasy is a fever that is cured by one who restores the soberly awake state of mind. The suggestion of magic is a spell that is lifted by one who reinstates the ego in its inner position of rulership. Israel's judges in the period following Joshua were personifications of the ego impulse, aids of egohood, leaders in ego development.

The Bible lists twelve judges without specifically stressing their number: Othniel, Ehud, Shamgar, Deborah, Gideon, Tola, Jair, Jephthah, Ibzan, Elon, Abdon and Samson. Through the silent language of its composition, the Bible thus indicates the law of the inner course of Israel's history.

In Joshua's figure, the spring sun itself had risen radiantly — the victory over Jericho was in fact an Easter event. Subsequently, it was as if the sun, moving around the heavens in the year's circle, shone through the twelve constellations of the zodiac, one after another, each time in different colouring and power. The archangel of the sun, Michael, who had now made himself the soul and guiding spirit of the people, moved from tribe to tribe, hovering in turn over each of the twelve leading figures, ensouling and inspiring them and, through them, lighting up Yahweh's ego-path for the people of Israel. Although the origin of the twelve judges did not correspond exactly to the twelve tribes, nevertheless, the judges were obviously representatives of the twelve soul-nuances encompassing the people. This is how, when need arose, a helper and leader was always present, not elected or called by men. Inasmuch as through each of the twelve judges one twelfth of the people arrived in a specific way at the experience of 'God in our midst' (Immanuel), the counter-images of the Israelite tribes, represented in the Palestinian tribes, were confronted with corrective and repulsing elements. Each of the twelve judges had to carry out a confrontation with a different Baal tribe. The Israelite history of the age of the judges resembles the hand of a clock, which, reflecting the sun's course, runs a circle through all twelve positions.

3.7 Deborah, Gideon, Abimelech

A number of dramatic events pass before us that are imbued in each case with something like an archetypal image of human destiny.

At one time, Israel was hard-pressed by Canaanite peoples. The hostile army was led by Sisera, a mighty, magical personality. A woman-judge was active in Israel at that time, the prophetess Deborah. Her name means, 'bee', and is therefore synonymous with the name given, for instance, by the Greeks to their Ephesian priestesses. We see that in one of its branches Israel still headed, in this period, in directions like those customary since earliest ages in several of the pagan nations of the Mediterranean region. Use was made of the sibylline powers of the female nature in order to receive revelations from the spiritual worlds.[106] Following a spiritual inspiration, Deborah appointed a man from the north of Galilee, Barak. He had to call together an army on Mount Tabor, and moved with it against the hostile troops. In the Jezreel Valley, on the field of the great Egyptian Battle of Megiddo, this onslaught took place. Sisera was gripped by a great fear. He felt as if those who were storming down from the summit of the ancient holy mountain of divine sun worship* into the valley were the heavenly hosts themselves, who were angered at him. And above the heads of the armies, something actually took place, for which the onslaught of the Israelites was an image. What had already bestowed the inner character to Joshua's battle at Gibeon was repeated: a battle of the gods above the heads of human beings brought about the decision. After the victory had been won, Deborah expressed that in a hymn of triumph: 'The kings came, they fought; then the kings of Canaan fought at Taanach, by the waters of Megiddo; but they did not win the victory. From heaven they were fought against; the stars from their courses fought against Sisera.' (Judg.5:19f *B*). The frightful vision of the gods breaking in upon them put Sisera's troops to flight. Without a battle, Israel gained the victory. Sisera came to a gruesome end in the house in which he believed he could hide. A woman drove a nail through his head, setting a ghastly symbol for the step towards the Calvary (the place of the skull) of intellectual consciousness, which the Canaanites were not willing to take.

This second, and outwardly seen, smaller battle of Meggido is even more clearly an apocalyptic event than the first one, through which Thutmose III established the basis for the Egyptian empire. Something of the spiritual battle of Armageddon affects this confrontation in a direct way. Here at this site, humanity

---

*The location and nature of the 'Mountain of Transfiguration' is a sure indication of the fact that already in ancient times a sun sanctuary existed on that summit.

approaches closely to the threshold of the spiritual world and the powers guarding it. A few centuries earlier, Thutmose III had fought his way out of the unity with and protection of these forces guarding the threshold, turning to purely terrestrial warfare and striving for power. The battle between Sisera and Barak makes it evident that the world of ancient spirituality, represented in Sisera, is not only abandoned by the benevolent gods but crushed. Israel, on the other hand, is allowed to be the hand and weapon of the Michaelic powers at the threshold of Armageddon. Sun-imbued forces work through the will of the Israelites. A first step is attained in the reversal of the battle of Megiddo into that of Armageddon. In the battle indicated by the Revelation to John (16:16), spiritually advancing mankind will itself fight its way back one day into the realm beyond the threshold.

By the side of Barak, the Israelite's military commander, the Bible also lists Lappidoth, Deborah's husband. Lappidoth means 'burning torches', and Barak signifies 'lightning'. Even in the names, the fact is expressed that here, human beings are permitted to become instruments of divine powers. The celestial fire of the burning bush and the lightning-power of Sinai have become man. What still worked externally at the age of Moses, begins now to become a factor of man's inner being. A further step in the Messiah's journey to earth is felt when the people of Israel appear as if ensouled by a victorious cosmic power. The human incarnation of the Messianic force is preceded by its incarnation in a whole people.

In subsequent times, the Midianite-Ishmaelite tribes, in whose region the Israelites had sojourned during the forty-year-long desert journey, came increasingly to the fore as oppressors of Israel. Only a few decades had gone by since Midian, in the person of Jethro, had been Israel's teacher, and already, an unbridgeable chasm gaped between the inner directions of will on the two sides. The Midianites stood still and fell into unbridled decadence, whereas Israel, led by the Michaelic light, underwent an almost precipitous development.

Gideon is called upon for the spiritual and militant confrontation with the friends turned into foes. He himself is predestined by his character of soul to experience and activate the earth's forces, with whom the Midianites had religious associations and to whose sphere Moses found access through Jethro.

The Bible describes how Gideon had a spiritual encounter when he sorted the wheat from the chaff on his father's threshing-floor. The image of the threshing-floor, however, refers to high-lying rock-sanctuaries. We shall deal with this in more detail in the story of Ruth, which takes place at the threshing-floor belonging to Boaz at Bethlehem, and later, in the description of David's story, where the 'threshing-floor of Araunah' the later site of the Temple, is an important element. At the high place of Ophrah, in front of the holy oak, before the stone altar of Baal and the wooden column of Astarte, Gideon was carrying out a cultic rite, when an angelic being appeared to him. In order to determine what kind of spiritual power was approaching him, he fetched offerings, poured them out over the rocky altar, and lo, a column of fire and smoke shot up out of the cracks of the rocks. Half-volcanic earth-forces slumbered here in the mountain's interior and could be brought to the point of appearing in solfatara-like phenomena. The fire of Sinai, from which Moses received his revelations in Midian, was active also here and addressed Gideon, who thereby perceived that the angel of Yahweh was beckoning to him.

Enabled by this experience to distinguish clearly between Baal, the deity of the earth's surroundings, and Yahweh, the god of the earth-forces, Gideon destroyed the symbols of the Baal and Astarte worship on the holy high place and erected an altar to the Yahweh divinity, on which he enkindled his offerings with the wood of the Astarte image. This ignited the torch of battle. The Midianites were provoked and drew near with their army. The Bible describes this whole course of events in half-imaginative pictures that require translation in every case into a physical, historical representation. Subsequently, the imaginative character of the pictures and with it their miraculous strangeness increases. In order to attain certainty concerning his mission and the outcome of the battle, Gideon asked twice for a sign. During the night, he placed a ram's fleece on the threshing-floor; the first time, the dew was to wet the fleece and leave the ground around it dry, the second time, the dew was to wet only the ground around the fleece. Both times, the deity complied with Gideon's request and let the dew fall as he had specified. Do we really confront the toying with an oracle here, which a too patient deity is willing to enter into? The ram's fleece on a high place of sun worship is the same image that arises to Greek vision as the Golden Fleece, brightly shining in the sun. Inasmuch as Gideon made use of it, we recognize in him one who continued on with the Mosaic consciousness. He was capable of visionary thinking and thinking vision in which the ram power of the forehead found the transition from ancient clairvoyance to thought. With this consciousness, Gideon, like Moses, looked half clairvoyantly and half in thought into the activity of nature forces, deciphering from them the signs according to which he directed his actions. This made him capable of battle against people, who, through their traditions, were close to living and reading in the sphere of the earth's forces.

Finally, Gideon selected suitable companions for the impending confrontation. Their number and the usefulness of their weapons was not his concern. They had to be persons who in turn had a quite special relationship to the earth-forces. If the Midianites were to be overcome, it had to be clear that this did not come about because of external superior man-power, but because of a spiritual superiority (Judg.7:2). As the Bible relates, Gideon tested those following him by the manner in which they drank the river's water. He was to reject only those who drank in the manner of dogs, who, without scooping water out with their hands, bent down to lap up the water. This signifies that these still possessed a direct, instinctive relationship to the forces of earth nature. Of the great number of men, only three hundred remained in the end.

When Gideon had the camp of the Midianites surrounded, they were just telling each other their dreams. Owing to their delicate sense of intuition, the superiority of the spirit leading the Israelites and the hopelessness of their resistance had come to their awareness in a frightening way through a number of images in their dreams signifying disaster. When Gideon's small band then approached the camp from all sides with burning torches and the sound of trumpets, the Midianites' fear was so great that here too, the Israelites attained complete victory without having to fight. In revealing itself to them, the Michaelic spirit power

179

fought for Israel by intimidating and breaking the will of the enemy.

Figures like Deborah and Gideon were able to show and embody to their people the ego directed by Yahweh, despite the fact that their nature too was tinged by an after-effect of humanity's ancient forces which determined their place in the unity of all the tribes and streams of Israel. It is therefore not surprising that their spiritual leadership was in close proximity to all manner of aberrations, for, after the victory, even Gideon fashioned a sun symbol from the golden head-pieces of the subjugated Midianites, which he then placed in the central position of the cultic worship on the rocky heights of Ophrah.

None of those who had been called upon to be judges succumbed to *one* particular temptation. Not one of them, who received the ovations of the people, had himself proclaimed king and inaugurator of a dynasty. Each knew with every fibre of his being that the divine, guiding power of the people made use of him, not because of any virtue that derived from heredity or could have been passed on to descendants. A feeling must have been connected with this, of the folk spirit's hovering in turn over all the tribes and spiritual characteristics of the people of Israel. So, each judge knew that after him would come a bearer of completely different forces, destined for a task differing utterly from his own. When the people said to Gideon: 'Rule over us, you and your son, and your grandson also,' he rejected this suggestion and replied, '. . . the LORD will rule over you' (Judg.8:22).

After Gideon's death, however, Israel had to bear the consequences of dynastic aberration. Abimelech, Gideon's son (by a concubine) from Shechem in Samaria, had himself declared king by the inhabitants of Samaria under the ancient holy oak of Shechem. So as not to have to contend with anybody having the same right to the crown, he had all the sons of Gideon, seventy in number, slain. Only Jotham, the youngest of the Gideonites, escaped the slaughter. It was then Jotham, who, with the force of a prophet, spoke to the people on the top of the holy Mount Gerizim. By means of a fable, he called for spiritual self-reflection and thus banished the danger that threatened the direct link of the people to their divine leading power by means of the interference of royalty. He told them: The trees once wanted to anoint a king over them and first approached the olive tree, then the fig tree and finally the vine. But none of them wanted to abide by their will. Only the bramble, whom they chose in fourth place, was prepared to become king of the trees. With this, Jotham not only stated something concerning the usurper Abimelech; more than that, he described in picture-form the descent of wisdom in humanity in general. The olive tree radiates primordial wisdom of the gods. The fig tree is the symbol of initiation, in which humanity found refuge when the primal revelation dimmed away. The vine brought Dionysian-ecstatic spirituality that only for a time could serve the preparation for the ego impulse. The bramble, finally, is the image of man who is completely impoverished in regard to divine wisdom, so that he can discover his earthly ego. Thus, through this fable, Jotham demonstrated the condition of mankind. No doubt could remain that Abimelech's action was an outrageous presumption of man estranged from God. How could man, turned into a bramble, dare place the royal crown upon his head!

Jotham predicted that the bramble would be consumed by fire. Man had even lost the non-consuming spiritual fire that Moses still beheld in the burning bush at Mount Horeb. Jotham's prophecy came true. In the same place where, in the age of the patriarchs, the gruesome drama of Dinah had taken place, Abimelech and those who had made him king destroyed each other in apocalyptic drama. In the midst of the fires that consumed Shechem, Abimelech perished, crushed by a millstone that a woman dropped on him from a tower.

Abimelech's death, similar to that of Sisera, evokes the apocalyptic images of a day of judgment. In Sisera's case, the image of the forehead pierced by a nail reveals the tragedy of those who are not of their own free will ready for, or capable of, the development of thought-imbued consciousness. Here, in the image of the millstone, we behold matter's reaction to him who is unable to place spirit and matter into the correct relationship. An image confronts us that visionary traditions have always drawn when they wanted to describe the downfall of impure, egotistic impulses. In the Revelation to John (18:21), the angel casts the millstone into the sea and thereby unleashes the tempest in which Babylon, the great harlot, perishes. Grimm's fairy-tale, 'The Juniper Tree', shows us the end of the evil step-mother in the midst of consuming fire in a similar image:[107]

> 'Well,' said the woman, and sprang to her feet and her hair stood up like flames of fire, 'I feel as if the world were coming to an end! . . .' And as she went out at the door, crash! the bird threw down the millstone on her head, and she was entirely crushed by it . . . and smoke, flames and fire were rising from the place . . .

Abimelech's presumption was more than a passing episode. In it, a new level of mankind's Fall made its appearance, and apocalyptic, cosmic wrath was the response to it by the forces of destiny.

3.8 Jephthah's Daughter

The traditions outside the Bible go out of their way, especially in regard to the era of the judges, to emphasize the correspondences between Israelite and Greek history. We cannot give much credence to them, but as a whole they must be considered as indicating the parallel course of the first Occidental and the last Oriental culture. It is said, for example, that at the time of Othniel, a smith in Athens invented the saw; at the time of Ehud, Hercules freed Theseus; during Shamgar's reign, Argos was destroyed; under Deborah's tenure, Miletus was founded. When Gideon was judge, Paris was supposed to have kidnapped Helen and choir-song and trumpet are dated simultaneously with the death of Hercules and the destruction of Troy by fire with the age of the judge Abdon.[108]

Now there is one parallel which, regardless of whether it coincided exactly as to the date in time, was of the greatest cultural and historical significance: the sacrifice of Jephthah's daughter in Israel corresponds in all details to Iphigenia's sacrifice in Greece.

The narrative in the Book of Judges describes a tragic destiny to us, the execution of which contains weighty riddles. As judge over the Israelite tribes, Jephthah had to wage war against the Ammonites. Prior to the battle, he made a vow: If victory is to be his, he will offer as a sacrifice to the deity the first thing that he beholds of his property upon his return. News of his victory preceded him, and, adorned in festive garments, his daughter came to meet the returning victors at the head of a group of young maidens. Shocked, her father watched her approach: She herself was the sacrifice that he had to offer up on the altar in obedience to his promise. After a grace of two months, which, as the Bible relates, she spent on the holy heights in mourning, the sacrifice was carried out. Do we really confront the fact of a bloody human sacrifice here? Has the suggestiveness of the black-magical neighbouring cult, the gruesomeness of the Molech worship, infiltrated Israel and even its leaders? Or is a special imaginative mystery concealed here?

The apocryphal tradition tries to find a deeper meaning in the sacrifice of the maiden. It states that Jephthah's daughter made use of the two months' grace to go to all the wise men of the people and to become their disciple. The sacrifice offered up to the divine world was supposed to have been her soul that she had thus turned into the very essence of wisdom existing on earth. When she was lifted on to the altar, the voice of the deity was heard to say: 'Her death is a precious gift to me, for the wisdom of all wise men indwells her.'[109] But this legendary description remains a groping attempt at interpretation. Although it allows us to sense distantly a meaning in the sacrifice of the maiden, it does not solve the gruesome riddle of a human sacrifice.

Another tradition can be recognized faintly in the text of the oratorio, *Jephtha*, composed by Handel in 1752. The English libretto was written by Dr Thomas Morell following Italian sources which in turn were based on still older traditions. When the maiden had been led to the sacrificial altar, an angel appeared who restrained the priests and announced that the meaning behind the oath was not the bloody sacrifice. The daughter of Jephthah was to dedicate herself to divine service as a priestess:

Thy daughter, Jephtha, thou must dedicate
To God, in pure and virgin-state for ever . . .
The holy spirit, that dictated thy vow
Bade thus explain it and approves thy faith.

This description suggests a comparison with Isaac's sacrifice in which an angel called a halt to the proceedings that were about to take place. And it is just this tradition that reveals the kinship and sameness of meaning with the scene in the Iphigenia mystery by means of the name that it gives to the maiden. Here, Jephthah's daughter bears the name, 'Iphis,' which resembles closely the name Iphigenia.

By being considered together with the two other scenes of human sacrifice, the Hebrew and the Greek, the sacrifice of Iphis begins to become transparent. In none of the three cases is a bloody human sacrifice offered up. In Isaac's and Iphigenia's cases, this is stated within the mythical description itself; instead of Isaac, a ram is sacrificed, instead of Iphigenia, a hind. In the case of Jephthah's daughter, the biblical report does not contain a corresponding substitution. Nevertheless, just as in both the other myths of sacrifice, it is a matter of a soul and spiritual deed of sacrifice. Iphis is the Iphigenia of Israel. If we are able to comprehend the meaning of the Greek sacrificial myth, the riddle of Jephthah's daughter will be solved as well. The Greek myth shows us the fleet of the Hellenes in the harbour of Aulis, prevented from departing to Troy by the lack of wind, brought upon them by the wrath of the gods. The battle against Troy has as its goal the spiritual independence of Greece, and with it that of Europe, from the magic priest-cults of Asia. If the gods prevent this battle for freedom, they reveal thereby that they do not attribute to the Greek people the maturity necessary for independence. From the old seer, the Greeks hear that there is a way to change the gods' mind: the sacrifice of Iphigenia, the daughter of King Agamemnon. The maiden is made ready for sacrifice on the altar. But while the people believe that she is undergoing death by sacrifice, she is transported by the goddess Artemis to the temple at Tauris where she is anointed as a priestess. In her place, a hind is offered up. The anger of the gods is now appeased, the wind swells the sails, the voyage to Troy commences, the path to Europe's freedom is opened.

Is the anger of the gods concerning past misdeeds merely silenced by the sacrifice of Iphigenia? No, the conditions for future independence are fulfilled as well. This is the positive gain of the sacrifice brought by the Greeks with the daughter of the king. A priestly stream is inaugurated in which Iphigenia is the first priestess, through which Greece attains an actual right to separate from Trojan-Asiatic tutelage. By means of Iphigenia's sacrifice, the Greek people find a source of inward intensification for their own culture.

Rudolf Steiner once spoke about this meaning of the Iphigenia myth and by its means pointed out a law which had to be adhered to in all ages during the establishment of an external culture:[110]

> In the civilisation which the ancient Greek associated with the names of Agamemnon, Odysseus, Menelaus, we find the external civilisation which we know today, untouched by forces of clairvoyance. It is a civilisation whose knowledge of nature and her laws is assumed to be as useful for finding a philosophical basis for the secrets of existence as it is for making armaments. But men no longer feel that this kind of mental culture requires a sacrifice . . . that in order to achieve it they must offer sacrifice in a deeper sense to the higher spiritual Beings who direct the supersensible worlds . . . The ancient Greek did notice that this external culture involved sacrifice; it is the daughter of the human spirit who in a certain way has to be sacrificed ever anew. And he represented this perpetual sacrifice demanded by intellectual culture as the sacrifice of Iphigenia, daughter of Agamemnon . . . If nothing but that external culture were given to mankind, then under its influence men's hearts, the deepest forces of souls, would have withered away. It is only because mankind retained the feeling that it should make perpetual sacrifice and should single out, set apart from this general intellectual culture, rites which, not superficially, but in a more profound sense, may be called sacerdotal — it is only because of this that this intellectual civilisation has been saved from drying up completely. Just as Iphigenia was offered to Artemis as a sacrifice, but through her sacrifice became a priestess, so in the course of bygone millennia certain elements of our intellectual civilisation have had repeatedly to be cleansed and purified and given a sacerdotal-religious character in sacrifice to the higher gods, so that they should not cause the hearts and souls of men to wither up. Iphigenia represents the perpetual sacrifice which our intellectuality has to make to the deeper religious life.

It is most revealing that the Old Testament has its Iphigenia

figure during the age of the judges. Until then, the destinies of
the people had not really been guided by human beings but
directly through the leading powers of the spiritual world. Moses
still had use of the clairvoyant talent of revelation. Joshua was
the bearer of a sunlike inspired will. And the judges, chosen by
the divine power itself and called forth to their mission, were
nothing but embodiments of the closeness to the spiritual world
in which the people still found themselves. During the episode of
royal rule by Abimelech, lasting three years, an impending age of
profane, external cultural developments was clearly felt. Jephthah
was a leader-figure who had originally been lifted up on the shield
by the people themselves, and only later, through supersensory
experiences, became 'Israel's judge' in the actual sense. The
sacrifice of Iphis therefore represents the deed out of the soul
sphere of the people, which, ahead of time, at the onset of a
culture directed by men, created the compensation and safeguarded the cultivation of a priestly, religious life of devotion
alongside the necessary external development of culture.

Although the inauguration of the priesthood and ritual of Aaron
and Levi had taken place through Moses within the confines of
the Sinai-Horeb revelations, what good was the institution of this
priestly service, if it only remained as if placed above the life of
the people without their souls finding a vivid relationship to it?
In Iphis, Jephthah's daughter, the impulse of a personal,
devotional life took on form within the Israelite folk development.
When we are told that during the time remaining to her before
the sacrifice, she went to all the wise men of the people to learn
from them, we see beginning in this 'the sacrifice of modern
intellectuality to the religious deepening of the human heart.'[111]
The insight dawned that it would be wrong to employ all the
intellectual and soul forces of the people in building up an external
culture. Iphis means 'noble', Iphigenia is 'the one of noble birth'.
The noblest part of the spiritual life present within the people was
drawn out of the cultural tasks in the foreground and, as the
spiritual quintessence of the culture, was used for inaugurating a
priestly-religious realm of inwardness. This is the meaning of the
sacrifice of Jephthah's daughter, the Iphigenia of Israel. Under
the pressure of warlike problems, before the eyes of all the people,
an impulse and a stream were inaugurated that signified an ensoul-

ing of the ritual life established by Moses, as the figure of a noble woman made the sacrifice of dedicating herself to a quiet, virginal-priestly life of wisdom.

In its imagery, the Bible indicates that the sacrifice of Iphis found lasting continuation: 'And it became a custom in Israel that the daughters of Israel went year by year to lament the daughter of Jephthah the Gileadite four days in the year.' (Judg.11:39f). The discreet activity of a community of anointed maidens, which may have been a correspondence to what Rome possessed in the order of the Vestal Virgins, henceforth weaves into the Israelite development. Only on certain days of the year, this community emerged out of seclusion and presented the admonishing image of Jephthah's daughter before the people in ceremonies of a sombre festival of sacrifice.

3.9 Samson

The story of Samson is one of the most puzzling chapters in the Old Testament. A human being grows up, whose birth was accompanied by divine signs and visions; who, while still in his mother's womb, had been dedicated to the Nazirite asceticism; and who then, endowed with superhuman bodily strength, nevertheless appeared to lead an adventurous life of lust. Destined for the office of judge and vanquishing the mighty Philistine nation, he did not seem to cut himself off strictly from the customs and the religion of the Philistines, since he involved himself with Philistine women. What does the Bible have to tell us with this strange and remarkable giant figure who, with forces connected to his growth of hair, tore apart a lion, slew a thousand foes with the jawbone of an ass, lifted the city gate of Gaza and carried it up to the mountains of Hebron, situated a great distance away; and who, deprived of his strength and eyesight through a woman's cunning, perished finally as the slave of his enemies, although he succeeded in drawing many Philistines along with him into death when, with a last expenditure of his strength, he brought about the collapse of the palace in which he had had to amuse the people as a blind fiddler?

Modern theology confronts this tale helplessly. It has really not advanced beyond the question of whether Samson was a historical or a mythological figure. If he is viewed as a historical personality, then, in the customary manner in which biblical descriptions are interpreted, it is impossible to avoid fashioning an image of him in which coarse, barbaric features predominate despite the allowances believed necessary for miraculous stories. Most scholars have indeed relegated Samson to the realm of legend, which is synonymous with denying his historical existence. They arrived at this view the more they considered the striking parallels between the Samson story and some of the sagas of gods and heroes of antiquity, and the more they paid heed to the 'solar motifs', the relationships to the sun and its course, which in fact do surround the Samson figure in great numbers and seem to suggest the humanization of a sun deity.

As follows from the methods of our descriptions up to now in all instances, we must consider it misleading to pose the alternative that something is either historical or legendary. Genuine myths and sagas are not fabrications. While the traits that are designated as saga-like and therefore unhistorical are not recapitulations of external events, they do picture the supersensory and inner soul experiences of the personality in question and are therefore no less true and historically accurate than what is customarily acknowledged as 'genuine history'. Genuine sagas, such as those contained in the biblical books, are historical texts which, by means of their imaginative style, can include the non-physical, the spiritually historical sets of facts as well. One must only strive to find and utilize the key to imaginative language. Where it approaches the description of Samson's destinies, the Book of Judges seems to touch actually upon a vortex of supersensory life. For this reason, the imaginative pictures deviate in a specially pronounced way from the outer historical reality.

At first glance, Samson appears in the biblical description as an 'uncivilized, ferocious man'. But he is that only in the same sense as Hercules who, in Greek and later in humanistic symbolism, was depicted as the son of gods, swinging his club and dressed in a lion's skin. As Jephthah's daughter is Israel's Iphigenia, Samson is Israel's Hercules. And if we can discern the historical and spiritual truths of the Hercules (or Herakles) myth, we have at the same time the key to the Samson figure.

At the beginning of the twelve labours that Herakles is charged with, there stands the struggle with the Nemean Lion. Samson's destined tasks also begin with his conquest of the lion in the vineyards of Timnah. Both Herakles and Samson are able to break the shackles, which fall away from them as if singed by fire, and then, freed, they cause devastation among their adversaries. Herakles tears off the bonds as he is being dragged to the sacrificial altar by King Busiris in Egypt. Samson does the same when his people have bound him in order to deliver him to the Philistines, the angry lords of the land. Both Herakles and Samson succumb to feminine allure. The Greek hero becomes entangled in disgraceful humiliation when, in woman's garb, he has to spin before Omphale, his mistress. Twice, Samson allows a Philistine woman to elicit his secret from him and thus comes under the power of his opponents. Finally, both Herakles and Samson appear to be closely connected with the symbol of the pair of columns. On his westward voyage for the apples of the Hesperides at the end of the world, Herakles erects the two tall columns. Samson, the blind fiddler, tears down the two columns of Dagon's temple so that all the people are buried under the debris of the structure. Earlier, he had already carried the gate of Gaza, constructed of two columns, up to the top of the mountain.

In the destinies of Herakles, especially in his 'twelve labours', the sequence of an inner path clothed in imaginative descriptions is easily recognizable. Certain soul forces and abilities are acquired which then appear in the imaginative image as supernatural strength of body and bravery. For the purpose of providing the key to the mythology of the people of antiquity, Rudolf Steiner points to the saga of Herakles with other examples as well:[112]

> The twelve labors imposed on Hercules are seen in a higher
> light when one reflects that before the last and most
> difficult one he was initiated into the Eleusinian Mysteries.
> At the command of King Eurystheus of Mycenae he was to
> fetch Cerberus, the hound of hell, from the nether world,
> and take him back there again. To be able to undertake
> a journey into the nether world, Hercules had to be an
> initiate. The Mysteries led man through the death of the
> transitory and thus into the nether world; through initiation
> they wished to save the eternal element in him from des-

truction. As a mystic he could overcome death. Hercules overcame the dangers of the nether world as a mystic. This justifies the interpretation of his other deeds as stages of the inner development of the soul. He overcame the Nemean lion and brought him to Mycenae. This means that he became master of the purely physical force in man; he tamed it. Next he slew the nine-headed Hydra. He overcame it with firebrands, dipping his arrows in its gall so that they would never miss their mark. This means that he overcame lower knowledge, the knowledge of the senses, through the fire of the spirit, and out of what he had gained from this lower knowledge he drew the strength to see the lower world in the light belonging to the spiritual eye. The other labors can be interpreted in a similar way.

The solar interpretation has often been applied to the Herakles myth, and it was believed that in the twelve labours a legendary rendition could be rediscovered for the sun's passage through the twelve constellations of the zodiac. With that, it was thought that the earthly human value and historical reality of the Herakles figure would have to be surrendered completely. Now, a close connection exists no doubt between the Herakles myth and the mysteries of the sun's effects; but cannot the stages of experience pertaining to a human soul development be reflections of celestial stations of the sun? Indeed, with this we discover the compatibility and identity between myth and history, between cosmic and earthly human reality.

This is also the case with the biblical Samson myth. The name itself refers to the sun. It actually means, 'bearer of the sun'. Many features of the story of Samson can be interpreted in a solar sense. In the scene where Samson tears the lion apart and afterwards takes honey from its carcass, we can, for example, see a reflection of the passage of the sun in high summer through the constellation of Leo, which causes the ripening of the aromatic element in earth nature. But this is just the significant aspect of the Samson figure that here, because of a certain inward sequence of experiences, cosmic forces become active in a human being. The Bible speaks of Samson, because in him a separate stream of the Israelite spiritual life intervenes for the first time in the cultural development.

The daughter of Jephthah embodies the beginning of a religious stream of wisdom and devotion, separated out of the external cultural life. The stream that emerges out of seclusion in Samson is that of the Nazirites. During the forty-year-long desert journey, Moses had already established this community resembling a religious order (Num.6), which, on a broader basis, nurtured and aspired to the same goal as the later, more severely restricted order of the Essenes and Therapeutics. It was the task of the Nazirites to reactivate and perpetuate again and again those forces that had been systematically distilled out of the line of heredity and the bodily organization of the tribes of Israel, namely the faculty of clairvoyance and prophecy.

As a whole the people of Israel had to renounce the light of ancient clairvoyance in favour of the capability of thinking. But a segment of the people, singled out into a kind of order, were to keep alive a spark of this light as in an eternal lamp and bear it forward into the future. This light, cultivated in this circle, was to make possible at all times the prophetic prospect of the Messianic future in order that the people could always be reminded and exhorted concerning their highest spiritual mission. In the great figures of the prophets of later Judaism, who enkindled the torch of Messianic prophecy over and again for the Israelites, Naziritism found its richest, greatest continuation and fulfilment. The first great Nazirite was Samson, the last was John the Baptist.

Rudolf Steiner characterized this exceptional stream by detailing the exercises carried on within it:[113]

> In point of fact, right through Hebrew history, some individuals were, by certain methods, prepared to be able to understand the Christ Event. In the earliest times there were only a few of these men, but they and their way of life must be closely studied if we are to realise what careful preparations were made for the coming of Christ, how the Hebrew people, with the qualities they had inherited from Abraham, were rendered capable of a prophetic understanding of how the human Ego would be brought to man through the Saviour. Those men who were prepared so as to be able to recognise and understand, by *clairvoyance*, the significance of the Christ, were called

Nazarenes [Nazirites]. These men were able to perceive *clairvoyantly* all that had been prepared from the earliest days of the Hebrews, in order that, out of and through this people, the Christ might be born and understood. In a mode of life compatible with the development of clairvoyant insight, these Nazarenes were bound by strict and strenuous rules. These rules, since they belonged to quite another age, differ considerably from those essential for the attainment of spiritual knowledge to-day . . . Nobody should imagine that methods which in earlier times led to clairvoyant knowledge of Christ would have the effect of leading a man of the modern age to the same momentous recognition.

In the first place Nazirite rule prohibited the partaking of grape juice, alcoholic beverages and dishes that had been prepared with vinegar. Furthermore, everything belonging to the animal kingdom had to be avoided. The Nazirites were vegetarians in the strictest sense of the word. Finally, an important rule was to leave their hair uncut as long as they were in the preparatory stage of their seership.

Such rules had the purpose of returning to the condition prior to the moonlike hardening — something that was still possible in those early times because of the still pliable bodily organization of man — which, coming about in the course of humanity's evolution, had caused the loss of ancient clairvoyance. By the avoidance of everything that had the effect of making one more strongly a part of the earth and thus causing the etheric body to shrink down to the form of the physical body, that ancient condition could still in some degree be restored so that the corporeality was porous for the sun forces and therefore itself sunlike and clairvoyant. In a certain respect, the effects of the Fall upon the physical human being were undone. Wine worked to make the ego stronger and extinguished the old clairvoyance for the reason that something other than the pure sun force brings about its ageing. Rudolf Steiner stated[114] that the Nazirites knew:

that in the grape the plant-forming principle has overstepped a certain point, namely the point where the sun-forces alone are working on the plant. In the grape there are at work, not the sun-forces alone, but something

192

that develops inwardly and has already matured by the
time the sun-forces are weakening in the autumn.

Particularly a meat diet carries forces into the human being
which press inward, because in it, not only ethereal sunlike effects
such as in a vegetarian diet, but also soul elements are active.
The Nazirites arranged their diet in such a way that they impregnated their organism with pure sun forces and thus led it back
indirectly to its own paradisal sunlikeness. The wearing of long
hair served the same goal, for at that time it was still a means
against the hardening of the human organism.

Strange as it may sound, in our hair we have a relic of
certain rays by which the sun-forces were once instilled
into man. What the sun in earlier times thus instilled into
man was something *living* . . . in ancient time it might
have been quite possible, by leaving the hair uncut, to
receive certain forces into one's being . . .

. . . Such then, was the purpose underlying the
Nazarene custom of allowing the hair to grow long.[115]

In the configuration of the people of Israel, members of the
company of Korah were quite the opposite of the Nazirites. Korah
means 'bald-head'. Just as the long hair was an expression of their
spiritual aims among the Nazirites, so was the tonsure-like shaved
head among the people of Korah, who also formed a kind of
order or lodge. The Nazirites sought to preserve the link with the
pure sun-forces that enkindled seership in the human being. The
people of Korah had an extreme, modern disposition; and the
intellectual hardening of the human being, the organism that is
emancipated from the cosmos and has become a mirror apparatus
for thoughts, was the principle of their endeavours.

This duality had effects even upon the monastic streams of
Christianity. The monks and clerics of the Eastern Church have
retained the Nazirite rule not to shave their hair to this day,
whereas in the Western Church monks and priests join in the
Korah tradition with their rule of tonsure. This is why Orthodox
monks retained for a long time a cosmic, visionary strain in their
religious devotion, whereas the Roman monastic orders early
made themselves bearers of the intellectual development of
culture.

They were forces of old cosmic vision which Samson, as the

long-haired one, had at his disposal and which vanished for him when, during sleep, his hair was cut. When the Bible describes Samson as the one who could avail himself of gigantic physical strength, it only draws an imaginative picture for the forces of the ancient clairvoyance that were dependent on the body and which Samson had revived anew in himself through the Nazirite asceticism. In all its parts, the Samson saga requires translation out of the images seemingly depicting coarse, external facts into a description of the ethereal, supersensory forces that were cultivated among Nazirites.

Samson's birth was surrounded by miracles similar to those of Isaac and the later ones of John the Baptist. The barren one gave birth and angelic visions called forth in the parents the awareness of predestination. The Greeks experienced those among their leaders as demigods, in whose conception and birth divine forces played a part; therefore, in Herakles, for example, whom they viewed as a son of Zeus and a human mother, they considered the superhuman element more than his human nature. The Bible describes the secret of births, in which a divine and a human element work together, with the greatest discretion. But it does place the figures, whose birth was surrounded by miracles, closely together and pictures all of them as extending far beyond the level of men. Through his sacrifice, Isaac relinquished the sunlike, divine portion of his nature. Samson and John the Baptist, on the other hand, stepped into history with prophetic vehemence in a superhuman, mighty manner.

During Samson's age, the seafaring Phoenician Philistines, having recently settled in Palestine along the fertile Mediterranean coast, were masters also over the territories inhabited by the Israelites. Nevertheless, we do not see Samson confronting and radically opposing the Philistines at first. Through the pictures of the biblical descriptions, we see him involved in a succession of spiritual confrontations with the world of the Philistines. The prophetic Naziritism stands up against the magic of the Dagon-Adonis cult. Two streams, equipped with supersensory force, compete with each other.

When Samson first entered the sphere of action of the Philistine cult, he had already performed the first of his Herculean works.

Just as Herakles defeated the Nemean lion in the thirty-day struggle and took possession of the lion-skin that rendered a person invulnerable, so Samson too had vanquished the lion and had made its strength his own. Through the Nazirite restoration of his corporeality to a pure sun force, he had activated the royal force of vision, elsewhere already dimmed down in the human being, to the extent that it could be attained through the bodily element. What would be completely unthinkable as a natural process had thus become a reality of soul: In the carcass of the lion, overcome by him, Samson found a swarm of bees, by whose honey he could nourish himself. These imaginations indicate that out of his physical corporeality, which otherwise consumes the supersensory and turns it into something earthly, Samson could now receive super-earthly gifts:

Out of the eater came something to eat.

Out of the strong came something sweet (Judg.14:14).

The sunlike corporeality did not consume but bestowed nourishment; it did not contract as does all that is grim and bitter, but it expanded and widened out as if consisting of pure sweetness.

Now the imaginative report describes how Samson went among the Philistines and took himself a wife. Since his nature was expanding into clairvoyant magic soul faculties, he felt himself attracted by the Philistine spiritual life as if it were related to him. But what appeared at first as a union was in reality an altercation. Two spiritual streams that were after all incompatible clashed with each other.

The Philistines could not help but express amazement at Samson who was familiar with their initiations without having graduated from their schools. He was a riddle to them. Would they succeed in solving it? The Bible relates the event as if Samson had posed a riddle to those who now were around him, a riddle that related to his victory over the lion and the honey-miracle. Only because Samson suffered a diminution of strength and left himself open to the Philistines as he confronted them, could they hit upon the solution of the riddle. The Book of Judges relates that in the following way: Samson allowed his wife, who was an accomplice of his opponents, to elicit the secret from him.

The riddle, 'out of the eater came something to eat. Out of the strong came something sweet', would be completely insoluble, if

195

the scene with the lion were meant to be a physical event, for it would be unnatural for a swarm of bees to settle in an animal carcass. But the words of the riddle's solution, 'What is sweeter than honey, what is stronger than a lion?' is an even more difficult riddle, if taken literally, than the one posed by Samson. It is comprehensible as a saying of the mysteries: The sun force of the seer is sweeter than honey and stronger than the lion.

What had now taken place in Samson? How did it happen that he exposed a weak spot? Only in the confrontation with the spiritual sphere of the Philistines, Samson became aware of his completely different nature. His supersensory power was not ecstatically unrestrained as was that of the Dagon worshippers. As a member of the Israelite folk, he too had a share in the already acquired ego consciousness that was linked to the power of thought. Living among the Israelites, he appeared related to the Philistines, but among the latter his Israelite consciousness of thought moved completely into the foreground.

This is why, at first, Samson was filled with some uncertainty after having come to the Philistines. The more conscious he was, the more he limited his supersensory power by his awareness. To begin with, consciousness and being stood in opposition to each other. It was not possible to become conscious in thought of the instinctively working faculties without evoking a shadow-like dimming of them. This was why Samson did not have the strength to keep to himself the awareness that made him unsure of himself as well as the knowledge of his own nature.

The myth of Lohengrin touches upon similarities with this part of the Samson story in regard to rules applying to the soul. Elsa von Brabant's tragedy consisted in the fact that she was not satisfied with the being of the spirit-messenger Lohengrin; she had to ask for his name. Afterwards, she knew the name but the real being had become remote to her. What works as an essential force as long as it remains unconscious in the heart, pales to begin with into a mere thought-image, when lifted into consciousness. When Samson allowed his Philistine wife to elicit the secret from him, the tragedy of Elsa von Brabant occurred in himself at the same time. The fateful question resounded in his soul that had to lead to impoverishment. His secret was betrayed. People discerned from where his power was derived.

But Samson's defeat was in reality a victory. His appearance signified the introduction of a fermenting impulse of consciousness into the spirit-life of the Philistines. And this could only bring about obstacles, confusion and chaos in the realm of ecstatic magic. The solution of the lion-riddle was a dangerous stroke of luck for the Philistines, a truly treacherous happening. If the tragedy of Elsa von Brabant already befell Samson himself, it hit even more the Philistines, who, through Samson's wife, had posed Elsa's question. Through Samson, Israel's world of consciousness struck the first blow in the spirit battle against the magic of the opponents.

The damage brought upon the Philistines by Samson's introduction of the intellectual consciousness into their sphere, the faculty of thought-imbued cleverness, is described by the imaginative report in the following way. Samson is supposed to have caught three hundred foxes and, tying them together in pairs, with firebrands attached to them, chased the animals into the cornfields of the Philistines so that everything went up in flames. In order to interpret this strange story, it was pointed out that in antiquity certain tribes actually employed such trickery to do damage to their enemy; that in Rome, for instance, foxes with burning torches tied to their tails were chased through the circus during the festival of Ceres in order to exorcise the bunt, which was called *robigo*, 'red fox', in Latin. In the Book of Judges, this scene must nevertheless be interpreted imaginatively, not physically. The cultic custom of the Romans and the ruse of combat among people of antiquity can well be considered a physical realization of an imaginative picture-experience, which the ancient world knew as a symbol of the dangers that threatened along with the intellect.

Now it becomes obvious that by his gaining a share in the processes of the intellectual consciousness, Samson was in reality not weakened in regard to his visionary power. On the contrary, he had received an impetus for an intensification of it. It increased because of opposition. For the first time, the picture appears of Samson being shackled, an image that returns later several times. Samson's own people brought him bound to the Philistines, the masters of the land, whose anger they wanted to appease. But Samson broke the fetters and stood before them in intensified possession of his faculties. His sunlike, prophetic nature was only the more invigorated by the shackles imposed on him by the head consciousness, already developed everywhere in Israel, and he conjured up increased disaster upon the Philistines.

Here, the imaginative report of the Book of Judges contains an especially puzzling hieroglyph: Samson took hold of a new jawbone of an ass and with it slew a thousand men. It has been taken for an aetiological saga, invented to explain why a certain mountain was called 'Heights of the Ass's Jawbone'.

The imagination of the ass's jawbone can best be understood in reference to the sign with which the constellation of Cancer, in which the summer solstice occurs, has always been depicted. It consists of two curves, of which one comes from outside and curls into a spiral, whereas the other one uncurls and swoops

outward. This sign really expresses the secret of evolution. The past pours into the present, the future is born out of the present; the old is replaced by the new. Nature herself describes this sign at the summer solstice. The old has matured to its greatest development: now the culmination point is passed over and in the external diminution the new sprouts and grows. Samson, like John the Baptist later on, was a man of the summer solstice. He was a bearer of mature, old sun forces. But he also had a share in the new impulse that was entering into humanity, the formative ego-consciousness of thought. The two curves of the sign of Cancer resemble the shape of an ass's jawbone; and the two stars, the 'Northern Ass' (Asellus borealis) and the 'Southern Ass' (Asellus australis) stand in the sky within the constellation of Cancer. The curve of evolution, in the power of which Samson showed himself to be superior to the Philistine magic based on what was past, is that which leads out of the present into the future. Perhaps, standing before the Philistines, Samson really unveiled a prophetic picture of the future — something for which the biblical description could well be an image — which had the effect of an outbreak of an eschatological tempest, an end of a world, upon the listeners.

A scene occurs in the Greek saga of Herakles, where the angry hero purloined the tripod, because the Pythia of Delphi refused the oracle to him, and he himself became a prophet. The corresponding image in the Samson myth is that where Samson carried the gate of Gaza with its two columns up to the summit of a hilltop of Hebron. The secret of the threshold and the portal of the spiritual world pass, in figures such as Samson, out of initiation practices of the ancient mysteries into the realm of individual man. Through exercises and exertion of the innermost will of the spirit, individual human beings could henceforth reach the border between this world and the world beyond, the Pillars of Hercules. In a certain sense, what is said in the Gospel of the last great Nazirite applied even to Samson, the first great Nazirite: 'From the days of John the Baptist, the kingdom of heaven suffers violence, the kingdom of heaven is found through the will.' (Matt.11:12 *B*).

In intensified form, Samson once again underwent the trials brought upon him by his first encounter with the Philistines. According to the biblical description, he again became involved with a Philistine woman and succumbed completely to her allure. She bore a name that expresses the opposite of Samson's sun-name. The word, Delilah, points into nocturnal darkness for it contains the Hebrew word for night, *laylah*. The physical-spiritual strength of Samson suffered damage through the up-and-down, the attraction and repulsion, in his soul that struggled through to awareness. The soul weakened the spirit.

Delilah allowed herself to be used as an instrument of the Philistines who wished to bring Samson's secret completely under their power. Twice, strong shackles were put on Samson by Delilah. Both times he broke the bonds which fell to the ground as if singed by fire, and he achieved increased spiritual power. Finally, as the Bible tells it, Delilah elicited from him the Nazirite secret of the long hair. Just as Kriemhild betrayed Siegfried's vulnerability to Hagen, Delilah here betrayed to the opposing power how Samson's faculties could be overcome. During the night, she called the Philistines who cut off the sevenfold, braided hair of the sleeper. A more superficial interpretation of these scenes would have to ask: Why didn't the Philistines simply kill their sleeping opponent? That would have been just as easy and even easier than robbing him of his hair. We can see that everywhere it is a matter of a spiritual conflict: The Philistines did not want to dispose of an enemy but wanted to employ an alien secret and a foreign power in the service of their own life.

Samson was deprived of his eyesight, bound in chains and forced to do menial services in the prison. Behind the picture of grinding wheat that we find him occupied with, something else is surely concealed. Samson must take the special powers that are his own, which now no longer appear as vision in him, and place them in the service of the enemy.

Then, once again, it becomes quite clear what intentions the Philistines harboured in regard to Samson. During an opulent, orgiastic festival in the temple of Dagon, Samson was brought out of the prison. He was to enhance the celebration by his playing on the harp. What is most probably meant with this scene is an intention to use him as a clairvoyant seer and source of oracles. But Samson had been able to cast aside even the last and most cruel bond. He had grown in inner strength even through the loss of the sun's gifts in the hair and the eyes. The prophetic talent of seership broke through in its former purity despite the fact that it had been deprived of any support in the physical element. A moving picture unfolds: the blind minstrel stood between the two holy columns of the portal and threshold of the Dagon temple. That must have resembled those which, according to Herodotus, stood in the Melkart-Hercules temple at Tyre — one column expressing the nature of day, fashioned of shining gold, the other, the column of night, in a green colour that was phosphorescent in the dark. As if coming from another world, Samson stood upon the threshold and plucked the strings. But the song that he sang contained nothing that satisfied the sensation-hungry, Dionysian-drunk Philistines. The spirit of Yahweh struck its blow of destruction against the magic of Dagon. Apocalyptic terror must have passed through the souls of the Philistines with Samson's song. It made them lose faith in their whole structure of life. The whole configuration of their religious-cultic life collapsed. The two columns no longer framed the portal to an open spirit world. Debris obstructed the path everywhere. Perhaps the temple may have collapsed physically as well, destroyed by the raging mob itself, who, when their orgiastic intoxication had changed into

wrathful insanity, trampled everything underfoot and, deprived
of their senses, rushed upon the roof in such numbers that the
building could not support them.

What kind of song may Samson have sung? Although nothing
can be found in the whole text that would lend the Book of Judges
prophetic character, it has always been counted in former times
among the prophetic books of the Old Testament. One reason
may be that when people still knew how to read the imaginations
of mythology, they saw in Samson the first prophet. The Nazirite
gift of prophecy must have broken through powerfully in this last
act of the Samson drama. In Samson, the clairvoyance cultivated
among the Nazirites emerged militantly on the cultural level. Its
mission was to awaken and keep awake the sense of the Messianic
future. Therefore, to the sounds of the harp, the blind prophet
may have sung a song of the cosmic judgment that had to break
in upon the old magic cultures; he may have sung of the Son of
God who would be born among the people of Israel. Outwardly,
the Philistines remained the rulers of the land. But the spirit-
battle had broken the force of their magic and banished their
demonic element.

In the sequence of the figures of judges in Israel, the Abimelech
episode signifies an important turning-point. The judges preceding
Abimelech used up the forces streaming out of the past. The
judges who stood at the head of the people after this turning-point
embodied potential for the future, hidden streams of development
which henceforth were active in the soul life of Israel. Under
Jephthah and Samson we behold communities resembling
religious orders which, not unlike the later orders of nuns and
monks, began or unfolded their fermentative activity. Jephthah's
daughter represented the beginning of a special stream of devotion. The destiny of Samson, Israel's Hercules, was like a dramatic
prologue for the stream of the prophets, which, later on, was to
lead the people to such a high level of spiritual power.

3.10 Bethlehem and Ruth

It belongs to the architectonic wonders in the structure of the Old Testament canon that the historical books leave room exactly in the middle for a very brief text, which, in its marvellously delicate poetry, stands apart from everything that precedes as well as follows it, the Book of Ruth. Just at the point where the mythological style of the hero's saga reaches utmost intensity, the musically pensive calm of a lyrical idyll sets in. The soul of a woman takes the place of the aggressive figures of the judges.

The significance of the time reached within Israelite history finds the most wonderful expression in the uniqueness of the geographical location to which the Book of Ruth leads us: Israel's journey reaches Bethlehem. The path had already passed through many prophetic stations; now it led for the first time to the Messianic site where, one day, the Christ would reach the earth from its journey through the spheres of the cosmos.

We pointed earlier to the miracles of Bethlehem, when we had to describe the area of Hebron and the Mamre grove as the first abode of Abraham in the promised land.[116] Hebron and Bethlehem are the two focal points of a region in Judea where one can clearly sense a mystery even today. In Abraham's age, the appearance of the southern part of the land was changed completely by the subterranean forces of fire and steam that caused the destruction of the area of Sodom and Gomorrah in an after-glow of the Lemurian world conflagration. The Dead Sea came into being in the centre of these world catastrophes. In the farther radius of this 'judgment day', the Judean desert emerged, grandiosely symbolizing the fall into death of all earthly nature. Extending almost up to Jerusalem, it imprinted upon all of Judea a sombre, stern character of death. Only one island of life was spared in the midst of the petrified rigidity. That was the area south of Jerusalem, the focal points of which are Bethlehem and Hebron. All around spread the landscape of the cosmic Fall. On this island, most noticeable still today in Bethlehem and on the shepherds' pasture lands and slopes, a breath of a world prior to the Fall, a last radiance of paradise, remains. We have spoken[117] of the fragmentary remnants of the pre-Lemurian paradisal realm, the 'little earthly paradises', which were still faintly imbued with

reminiscences of the pre-physical Old Sun, the 'great cosmic paradise'. Contrasting with the Judean desert, the territory of Galilee
above all belongs to them. But the two smaller regions are also a
part of them; both are equally far from the Sea of Galilee: the
oasis of Damascus in the north, the area around Bethlehem in
the south. The southern island is a Galilean isle in Judea. With
special cosmic innocence, Bethlehem herself shines forth with her
pasture lands and cornfields.

In the wooded hills and sloping meadows of Arcadia, the
Greeks had a landscape where they felt transported back into the
Golden Age, the paradisal age of the earth irradiated by the gold
of the sun, where they sensed that the blissful innocence of the
shepherds which mankind had lost in the Fall was still alive. It
was believed that, enjoying eternal spring, the shepherds dwelt
there in everlasting youth, beauty and peace, held in the embrace
of the great Mother Nature, not yet abandoned to conflict and
the loneliness of the world.

Bethlehem was and is the Arcadia of the promised land, the
site of pastoral life in the midst of Judea. The stories of David's
childhood in Bethlehem's meadows and of the shepherds to whom
the angels appeared during the night of Christmas have a mood
that must be connected instinctively with the name of Bethlehem.
For even today, the loveliness of the place is mirrored in the
special beauty, friendliness and cheerfulness of the people living
there. And the prophecy of Micah, which designated Bethlehem
as the birthplace of the Messiah (Mic.5:2), must have been based
on age-old convictions of the people and sages that he who brings
paradise back to mankind would have to be born at the site where
the last reflection of the lost paradise remained alive.

The name of this locality points to another side of its secret.
Bethlehem means 'house of bread'. It probably has this name for
outward reasons as well, for it is situated on an island of fertility
in the midst of a rocky desert lacking any vegetation. But above
all, the name Bethlehem has religious and historical connotations.
More than through any external conditions, the place is given its
soul and character by means of the spiritual secret holding sway
there, of the grain of seed and the ears of wheat.

Traditional theology[118] has also called attention to the importance of the wheatfield and the threshing floor as symbols and

stages of the gods' activity in the religious and cultic life of pre-Israelite Palestine. Theology pointed out that the Canaanite holy high places were in many instances identical with the elevated threshing-floors of the villages in question, or were at least designated as 'threshing-floors' in a figurative sense. At some Palestinian cultic sites, Baal-Adonis can actually be called the 'deity of the threshing-floor'. Repeatedly, at important points within the Old Testament, we come across the mention of threshing-floors that must be considered in this sense as high-lying cultic sites. Gideon received his mission in a revelation on the threshing-floor of Ophrah; David acquired Araunah's threshing-floor in order to construct the temple there. In like manner, Ruth, the gleaner of ears of corn, came to the threshing-floor of Boaz to present herself to him as maid-servant and bride. The image of Boaz's threshing-floor permits us to behold the sanctuary as through a veil from where Bethlehem has its name.

Again, a comparison in Greek spiritual life will help. In Eleusis, the Greeks had a mystery-site, which was ensouled by the secret and fragrance of the grain of seed and the ears of wheat. There too, the external wondrous wheat fields at the coast of the blue Bay of Salamis, to which the holy processional path led all the way from Athens, was only a veil for deeper levels of existence. Men sensed the earth-mother Demeter there, feeling embedded in her lap, and beheld her in the statues that represented her with the ear of wheat in her hand. If Eleusis had not been a special source and centre of life-giving ethereal forces, a place where the goddess Natura revealed herself, people would not have built a temple there to Demeter.

Bethlehem is the Eleusis of the promised land. And if it was possible to sense a trace of paradise there for long ages, this was connected with the fact that here also a source and centre of ethereal forces existed, giving experience of the earth as the great mother of all life and, at the same time, as the guardian of the cosmic condition. The divine of the cosmos in woman, the lofty secret of the virginal mother, held sway there as well as in Eleusis.

Eleusis has the mood of Messianic expectancy in common with Bethlehem. The Greek name, Eleusis, means the same thing as the Latin word, *adventus*, 'the arrival'. At the place of the womb

204

of the great mother, people looked longingly forward to the birth of the cosmic son. The festival of the Eleusinians was held annually as a preparation for the coming of the divine saviour. The secret of death and life was beheld in the scenes of the mystery plays. The lament of Demeter-Ceres over the loss of her daughter Persephone alternated with the jubilation over her return. Concealed behind this rhythmic alternation, and part of the deeper levels of the mystery, were the death and resurrection of Dionysus, as the Greeks called the being of Osiris or Adonis. A subdued form of the Osiris secret was experienced there. Above, in heaven, the god dies; when will he be reborn on earth? The simplest and yet most archetypal concentration of all the mysteries of Eleusis was represented in the grain of seed, which, when it is sown, dies; that it may sprout and grow and arise again. This is why the goddess was depicted with an ear of corn in her hand.

Bethlehem, the house of bread, has also had its Eleusinians. It was the site of an especially important, although quietly concealed Adonis-mystery sanctuary. We find definite traditions concerning this in early Christian times. It was believed that in order to desecrate Christian sanctuaries, the Roman Caesars, particularly Hadrian, had established Mithra grottoes and Adonis temples in many caves at the identical location. In reality, what really happened was probably that at the site where the most profound events of the Old and New Testaments occurred, Canaanite cultic centres had already existed earlier and were subsequently re-established by the Caesars opposed to Christianity. If we know how to read the imaginative language of the ancient holy Scriptures, the Book of Ruth, for example, is a particularly clear indication of the religious-historical past of Bethlehem.

Let us first trace the reports from the early Christian era. St Jerome, who himself chose Bethlehem as his domicile and, in the immediate vicinity of the grotto of the birth of Jesus, pursued his theological studies for forty long years, verified that between the rule of Hadrian and Constantine, a Tammuz-Adonis cult was practised in the same rocky grotto where the crib of the Jesus infant had stood:[119] 'Bethlehem, which is now ours, the most exalted place on earth . . . was overshadowed by a holy grove of Tammuz, who is identical with Adonis; and in the cave, where the Christ-child once whimpered, the dirges over the beloved of Venus resounded.'

The commentaries recorded in reference to the book of the prophet Ezekiel allow us to perceive that the Church fathers possessed a clear conception of the cults which, accordingly, were also practised in Bethlehem. For Ezekiel speaks (8:14) of the Tammuz cult, which, at that time, when the people of Israel were in the Babylonian exile, took place in the temple at Jerusalem. St Jerome states:[120]

> According to a heathen sage, Adonis, the beloved of
> Venus, the supremely handsome youth, was slain and
> then called back to life in the month of June. Therefore,
> in his honour, the people annually celebrated a festival,
> where he was first mourned as dead by the women and
> then praised in song as having newly arisen alive . . . The
> sequence of the death and resurrection of Adonis, the
> mourning and the jubilation, was interpreted in the
> following way. The first has its correspondence in the grain
> of seed which dies in the earth's ground, the second relates
> to the sprouting crops in which the resurrection of the
> perished grain of seed becomes evident.

Some time before Jerome, Origen expressed something quite similar:[121]

> Year after year, the people celebrate commemorative
> festivals there, where the god is first mourned as having
> died, then is praised with jubilation as having risen from
> the dead . . . They say that Adonis is a symbol of the
> fruits of the fields, which are in the condition of mourning
> when they are sown, but which are resurrected and fill
> man with jubilation when they sprout and grow.

Such cults, quite closely resembling those of the Eleusinians, must be pictured as the hidden secret of Bethlehem as early as the period when Joshua led the people into the country. The mystery site of Bethlehem was probably one of those that knew how to guard against Phoenician decadence and with which the leaders of Israel could therefore associate. But most likely it was cultivated in a humble obscurity and did not emerge even so far as did the mystery centre of Gibeon. We must also picture the Bethlehem cult as being enveloped in the paradisal Demeter atmosphere of the locality. Later, destiny brought it about that the now abandoned grotto, in which the Adonis cult had been celebrated in the past, was used as a shelter for cattle. Thus it became the birthplace of the Jesus child. And in the same cave a century later, those who could not comprehend that prophecy and expectation were superseded by fulfilment, renewed the ritual cult which had been but an expression of the Eleusinian longing of pre-Christian humanity. Rudolf Steiner pointed to the religious-historical past of Bethlehem:[122]

> We can now say that it was part of the karma of world
> history . . . that in the place where the Bible with a certain
> truth locates the birth of the Jesus-child — in Bethlehem
> — there was a centre of the Adonis cult. Bethlehem was
> one of the places where Adonis had been worshipped. The
> Adonis who died and rose again was often celebrated
> there, and so was an aura prepared . . . [for the] Being
> who . . . appeared later . . . on earth.

Israel's history had already touched upon the area of Bethlehem when Jacob returned with his people from Mesopotamia. Eleven sons had been born to him in Babylonia, although only one by Rachel whom he loved with all his heart. Now, at the threshold of the house of his father, where he had arrived, Rachel was to become a mother for the second time. But sudden grief clouded the joyous celebration: Rachel sealed the birth of her son with the sacrifice of her own life. This took place in Bethlehem. To this day, close by the gates of the little town, Rachel's grave is revered by Muslims and Jews alike.

Rachel had been like a reflection and embodiment of the eternal in woman. At the well in Babylonia, she had appeared like a goddess in human form to Jacob; hence his servitude of over a decade was only for the purpose of becoming united with her. Her death in Bethlehem also stood like a symbolic sign in Israel's history. When, on the holy high place of Bethlehem, Rachel raised her voice in a cry of pain, the reason was not the pain of birth but a portentous vision of humanity's future. The prophet Jeremiah said: 'A cry is heard from on high, lamentation and bitter weeping: Rachel is weeping for her children; she refuses to be comforted for they have died.' (Jer.31:15 *B*). Rachel's cry of pain is a first, moving Adonaic lamentation. The eternal element of femininity and the paradisal youth and beauty of gods must die in mankind. The death of Rachel at the site where the mother of life was experienced and revered was in itself a prophecy and an apocalyptic event. In Rachel, Demeter, the great mother, becomes the *mater dolorosa*, the mother of sorrows, whose soul is pierced by a sword.

Following this, the Israelites had to undergo difficult and serious paths of destiny. The element of joy and beauty became increasingly alien to them. The people had to relinquish the secret of the eternal in woman and, for the purpose of the ego-consciousness of thinking, which it was their task to develop, had to assume an increasingly masculine character. Israel actually became something like a nation of the eternal element of masculinity. But it travelled through the wasteland of sternness and severity to be able to approach the trial of Messianic fulfilment on the other side.

The Bible allows one of the most beautiful presentiments of future salvation to shine forth from the history of the people by leading us a second time to Bethlehem in the Book of Ruth. The folk with the element of eternal masculinity are gently touched by the rays of the early dawn emanating from the secret of the virginal mother that is newly being revealed. The Moabite woman, Ruth, bore a tinge of the element of eternal femininity into the soul of the people. What died in Rachel seemed to revive anew.

At the time of the judges, when the story of Ruth took place, Bethlehem especially must have withdrawn into quiet seclusion. The larger city of Jerusalem, located nearby, must have had all the attention, since it closed itself off from the Israelites in stubborn hostility. In addition, as the Bible relates, there came a time of famine in the land. In the House of Bread, there was a lack of bread. Had Demeter ceased to bestow her gifts?

It was not a startling event that came to pass because of the famine in Bethlehem. A man and a woman with their two sons migrated to the land of Moab, east of the Jordan. In the foreign country, the two sons took Moabites as wives. Some time went by, and then, as destiny would have it, the three male members of the family died one after the other. Naomi, the mother, decided to return to Bethlehem, where the famine had in the meantime come to an end. She left it to the decision of her daughters-in-law, who had both remained childless, whether to stay in the land of the Moabites and enter into a new marriage. One of them remained, but in the soul of the other, a wondrous, instinctive conviction blossomed forth. It was Ruth, whose pure sensitivity became a perceptual organ for the Israelite mission and future, and for the spirit who hovered over these people. At the moment when she faced the decision, she experienced a reality in comparison to which the affiliation with her own people paled completely. She spoke, 'Your people shall be my people, and your God my God.' Just as did Rahab in Jericho, Ruth, with the sensitivity of her soul, perceived that the divine being, whom Israel served, was on its way to the earth. And she felt herself irresistibly called upon to belong with those who had the task of preparing a place and an abode on earth for this divine being. Thus she moved to Bethlehem with Naomi.

Here, she breathed the atmosphere of the pure, maternal element of the cosmos to which her soul was able to respond with a wonderful echo. We see Ruth striding across the cornfields of Bethlehem as a gleaner of ears of corn. This scene is one of those in the Bible which is most filled with an aroma of soul, and is most lastingly engraved in the hearts of those who have seen it in a picture or have had it described to them in their childhood. The earthy fragrance of ripe wheat wafts from this image; only the scent of Christmas cooking, remembered from childhood, in which a Bethlehem secret is concealed as well, can measure up to it. When Ruth rose and stood erect, the ears of corn in her hands which she had gathered from the ground, was it not as if the goddess, who in Eleusis was represented with the ears of wheat, had herself taken on human form?

The sense for fathoming the Messianic future of Israel, which had caused Ruth to follow Naomi to Bethlehem, must have found a wonderful affirmation and fulfilment in Bethlehem. Did not the being of the Messiah, the Christ, of whom Ruth had said, 'Your God is my God' — the true Osiris-Adonis, drawn close to the as yet pure Adonis mysteries of this locality — hover over the ripe corn of the threshing-floor, as it had earlier soared over the fire and steam of Sinai? If Ruth was willing to give herself to Boaz as a maid-servant and adorned as a bride, did not the devotion and willingness to serve that she felt in regard to the approaching divine being speak in her attitude? In her pure soul, Ruth must truly have experienced 'Eleusis', the coming, the Advent of Christ and her affinity to this secret.

Ruth is the Mary-figure of the Old Testament. In her, Demeter-Ceres became Mary. What Mary later said to the angel, 'Behold, I am the handmaid of the Lord; let it be to me according to your word' (Lk.1:38), was something that already passed through Ruth's soul. Thus, on the threshing-floor of Boaz, within the confines of the sanctuary, she became the wife of Boaz and the mother of the Messianic lineage of David. Invisibly, in soul form, the crown of the *mater gloriosa*, the mother rich in revelation, wove itself around her head.

When, a thousand years later, at the same place, Mary became the mother of the Jesus child in the grotto of Adonis, the secret of Rachel and Ruth became one in her. She became both the *mater dolorosa* and *mater gloriosa*. The death and resurrection of the eternal-in-woman, the virginal, maternal element of the cosmos, took on human form in Mary and thus became a seed for the soul-future of humanity.

In the succession of the biblical texts that follow the Books of Moses, a Messianic, prophetic figure has been concealed. Joshua, the twelve judges, and Ruth, together, appear as a preconfiguration of the same celestial configuration, which later found a fulfilled reality on earth in Jesus of Nazareth, the twelve disciples, and Mary. We have already recognized a Messianic prophecy become form in Joshua, who, ahead of time, pointed to him who would bear the same name as he — Jesus. The judges, whose twelvefoldness is made visible, not coincidentally but in a conscious manner of composition, although with a silent gesture, by the Old Testament texts, appear in a circle as representatives of humanity; just as, later on, the twelve Apostles drew the circle of mankind around the Christ figure. Radiating the maternal secret into the world, Ruth joined the Israelite folk configuration as did Mary, later, join the circle of the apostles.

We may discover the heavenly configuration, which thus fashioned their preparatory and fulfilling human reflection, a degree more clearly through a linguistic relationship in the figure of the Old Testament canon. The Hebrew term, with which the judges are designated, *shophet*, is contained in the name 'Jehoshaphat', which means 'Yahweh is the judge.' Actually, it was as if Jehoshaphat were the name of each of the judges who ruled the people of Israel, for each felt himself to be the exclusive instrument of Yahweh. In reality, Yahweh was the judge of the people who dwelt in direct proximity to God. The Hebrew name Jehoshaphat, however, is identical from a linguistic standpoint with the Indian word 'Bodhisattva', which designates one of the twelve loftiest spiritual leaders of mankind. We can conceive of the judges of the Old Testament as well as the Apostles of the Christian era as reflections of the Bodhisattvas. Now, through the sequence of figures, which one after the other is revealed to us in the Books of Joshua, the judges, and Ruth, an image becomes visible that has often been described out of spiritual research when it was a matter of pointing to the secret of the spiritual guidance of mankind. Around the Christ-being, who represented the central point like a brightly shining spiritual sun, the twelve Bodhisattva figures were gathered in a circle in the spiritual worlds during the pre-Christian evolution of humanity. Sunk in the contemplation of Christ, they interpreted into concepts and teachings for the people of mankind what in the Christ was pure element of force and being. They comprised the sphere of guidance, out of which the destiny of earthly man received its direction in nations and cultures. And within the circle, united with the Being of Christ, in warming, ensouling participation in the translation of being into wisdom, dwelled the virginal, cosmic mother, Isis-Sophia.

The figures of Joshua, the twelve judges, and Ruth, placed together by the canon of the Old Testament, thus create a bridge from the celestial circle of the Bodhisattvas to the Apostles' circle on earth.

Therefore, not only in nature, in history too, 'all things transitory but as symbols are sent', as transparencies for the spiritually substantial and its configurations. In the middle part of its historical texts, the Old Testament describes a portion of mankind's history which, to a special degree, can appear to be peopled by the figures of Providence.

References

1 See Bock, *Genesis*, 20.
2 Lange, *Grab- und Denksteine.*
3 Steiner, *Mysterien* (Feb 5, 1913).
4 Steiner, *Mysterien* (Feb 5, 1913).
5 Gorion, *Sagen*, 4:41.
6 Gorion, *Sagen*, 4:72 & 68.
7 Bock, *Genesis*, 67.
8 Plutarch, *Isis and Osiris*, Ch. 13-15.
9 Steiner, *Antworten* (March 9, 1911).
10 Steiner, *Gospel of St Matthew* (Sep 2, 1910) 41f.
11 Steiner, *Gospel of St Matthew* (Sep 2, 1910).
12 Philo, *Vita Mosis*, 1.5.
13 Bock, *Genesis*, 168.
14 Acts 7:23, 30 and 36. The same arrangement is presupposed everywhere in the copious legendary tradition.
15 Bock, *Genesis*, 89ff.
16 Steiner, *Gospel of St John* (May 25, 1908) 106.
17 Steiner, *Grundelemente* (May 25, 1908).
18 Steiner, *The Bhagavad Gita* (Dec 31, 1912) 66f.
19 Steiner, *Tieferen Geheimnisse* (Nov 23, 1909).
20 Brugsch, *Religion*, 691.
21 Brugsch, *Religion*, 105.
22 Brugsch, *Religion*, 103.
23 *Book of the Dead*, 17.30-38.
24 Steiner, *Tieferen Geheimnisse* (Nov 9, 1909).
25 Gorion, *Sagen*, 4:80-84 & 162-68.
26 Gorion, *Sagen*, 4:178.
27 Gorion, *Sagen*, 4:191 & 201.
28 Steiner, *Antworten* (March 9, 1911).
29 Gorion, *Sagen*, 4:186f.
30 Gorion, *Sagen*, 4:183.
31 Bock, *Genesis*, 116.
32 Steiner, *Tieferen Geheimnisse* (Nov 14, 1909).
33 Steiner, *Mysteries* (Feb 5, 1913) 52.
34 Gorion, *Sagen*, 4:189.
35 Steiner, *Mysteries* (Feb 5, 1913) 52.
36 Steiner, *Lukas-Evangelium* (Sep 21, 1909).

37 Steiner, *Orient* (Aug 26, 1909).
38 Rudolf Steiner describes this in connection with the paintings by Michelangelo of prophets and sibyls on the ceiling of the Sistine Chapel in *Christus und die geistige Welt* (Dec 29, 1913).
39 Steiner, *Christus und die geistige Welt* (Dec 31, 1913).
40 Steiner, *Christ and the Spiritual World* (Dec 31, 1913) 79-81.
41 See Bock, *Genesis*, 34.
42 Steiner, *Christ and the Spiritual World* (Dec 31, 1913) 80.
43 See, for example, Gressmann, *Mose und seine Zeit*. See also the map on p. 79.
44 Bock, *Genesis*, 29-39.
45 Bock, *Genesis*, 29, 39, 131.
46 Gorion, *Sagen*, 4:218.
47 See, for example, Norck, *Wörterbuch*.
48 Steiner, *Antworten* (March 9, 1911).
49 Gorion, *Sinai*, 224.
50 Meyer, *Israeliten*.
51 Steiner, *Deeper Secrets* (Nov 23, 1909) 65f.
52 Bock, *Genesis*, 141.
53 After Gorion, *Sinai*, 226.
54 Gorion, *Sagen*, 1:308.
55 Steiner, *Antworten* (March 9, 1911).
56 Gorion, *Sinai*. The seventh name is missing here, probably because of an oversight.
57 Philo, *Vita Mosis*, 1.10.
58 See Bock, *Genesis*, 165. The apocryphal book, Joseph and Asenath, surrounds this 'chymical wedding' with a great poetic wealth of legends and images (reprinted in Riessler, *Altjüdisches Schrifttum*).
59 Steiner, *Antworten* (March 9, 1911).
60 Gorion, *Sagen*, 4:77.
61 Steiner, *Antworten* (March 9, 1911).
62 Philo, *Vita Mosis*, 1.12.
63 Steiner, *Antworten* (March 9, 1911).
64 Steiner, *Genesis*.
65 Steiner, *Spiritual Hierarchies* (April 18, 1909 eve) 133.
66 Gorion, *Sagen*, 4:74.
67 Bock, *Genesis*, 42f, 63f, 77, 144.
68 Gorion, *Sagen*, 4:75 & 145.
69 Steiner, *Knowledge*, 134-36.
70 Steiner, *Knowledge*, 138-40.
71 Steiner, *Geheimnisse der Schwelle* (Aug 26, 1913).
72 Bock, *Genesis*, 79f.
73 See Bock, Goebel & Heidenreich, *Catacombs*.
74 Steiner, *Outline of Occult Science*, 38-43.
75 Steiner, *Wonders* (Aug 18, 1911) 19.
76 Steiner, *Wonders* (Aug 18, 1911) 33.

REFERENCES

77 Steiner, *Christ and the Human Soul* (July 12, 1914) 16.
78 Steiner, *Gospel of St Luke* (Sep 20, 1909) 116f.
79 Philo, *Vita Mosis*, 2.3 & 4.
80 Compare Frieling, 'Stiftshütte'.
81 Philo, *Vita Mosis*, 2.6.
82 Gorion, *Sagen*, 4:263.
83 Gorion, *Sagen*, 4:326.
84 Steiner, *Gospel of St Mark* (Sep 12, 1912).
85 Philo, *Vita Mosis*, 1.29.
86 Philo, *Vita Mosis*, 1.28.
87 Gorion, *Sagen*, 4:281.
88 Gorion, *Sagen*, 4:214.
89 Gorion, *Sagen*, 4:337.
90 Gorion, *Sagen*, 4:332.
91 Steiner, *Christ and the Human Soul* (July 12, 1914) 15.
92 Steiner, *Antworten* (March 9, 1911).
93 Steiner, *Occult Movement* (Oct 19, 1915) 107.
94 Steiner, *Occult Movement* (Oct 19, 1915) 109.
95 Hamann, *Golgotha und Scheblimini*.
96 Gorion, *Sagen*, 5:15.
97 See Bock, *Genesis*, 175.
98 Gorion, *Born Judas*, 1:65.
99 Bock, *Genesis*, 155f & 165. Also Streit, *Sun and Cross*.
100 Gorion, *Sagen*, 5:15.
101 Bock, *Genesis*, 75.
102 Kittel, *Studien*, 139.
103 See Frieling, 'Josua'.
104 Bock, *Genesis*, 39-41.
105 Gorion, *Sagen*, 5:26.
106 Bock, *Genesis*, 35.
107 *Grimm's Fairy Tales*, 229.
108 Gorion, *Sagen*, 5:35, 46, 47, 53.
109 Gorion, *Sagen*, 5:51.
110 Steiner, *Wonders* (Aug 18, 1911) 16f.
111 Steiner, *Wonders* (Aug 18, 1911) 22.
112 Steiner, *Christianity*, 115.
113 Steiner, *Deeper Secrets* (Nov 23, 1909) 56f.
114 Steiner, *Deeper Secrets* (Nov 23, 1909) 57.
115 Steiner, *Deeper Secrets* (Nov 23, 1909) 58-60.
116 Bock, *Genesis*, 129.
117 Bock, *Genesis*, 31 & 27.
118 Baudissin, *Adonis und Esmun*.
119 Jerome, *Epistula LVIII*.
120 Jerome, *Ezechielem*.
121 Origen, *Ezechielem*.
122 Steiner, *Christ and the Spiritual World* (Dec 31, 1913) 87f.

Bibliography

Baudissin, Wolf Graf von, *Adonis und Esmun*. Leipzig 1911.

Bock, Emil, *Genesis*. Floris, Edinburgh 1983.

Bock, Emil, Robert Goebel & Alfred Heidenreich, *Catacombs, The*. Christian Community, London 1962.

Brugsch, Heinrich, *Religion und Mythologie der alten Ägypter*. Leipzig 1885.

Dalman, Gustaf, *Jerusalem und sein Gelände*. Gütersloh 1930.

Frieling, Rudolf, 'Josua', in *Die Christengemeinschaft*, V.12. Stuttgart, December 1933.

——, 'Stiftshütte (Tempel) als kultische Widerspiegelung der Schöpfung', in *Die Christengemeinschaft*, XII.1. Stuttgart, January 1940.

Goebel, Robert, *see* Bock, E., & R. Goebel & A. Heidenreich.

Goethe, Johann Wolfgang von, *Faust, A Tragedy*. Tr. Bayard Taylor. Washington Square, New York 1964.

Gorion, Micha Josef bin, *Born Judas, Der*. Insel, Leipzig 1916-20.

——, *Sagen der Juden, Die*. Frankfurt a.M. 1913-27.

——, *Sinai und Garizim*. Berlin 1925.

Gressmann, Hugo, *Mose und seine Zeit*.

Grimm's Fairy Tales. Pantheon, New York 1944, and Routledge & Kegan Paul, London 1975.

Hamann, Johann Georg, *Golgotha und Scheblimini*, 1784.

Heidenreich, Alfred, *see* Bock, E., & R. Goebel & A. Heidenreich.

Jerome, *Epistula LVIII ad Paulinum*. Migne 22, Col. 581.

——, *Explanatio in Ezechielem*.

Kittel, Rudolf, *Studien zur hebräischen Archäologie*. Leipzig 1908.

Lange, Hans Ostenfeld, and H. Schaefer, *Grab- und Denksteine des mittleren Reiches zu Kairo*. Cairo 1902.

Meyer, Eduard, *Israeliten und ihre Nachbarstämme, Die*. Halle 1906.

Nork, Felix, *Vollständiges hebräisches Wörterbuch*. Grimma 1840-42.

Origenes, *Selecta in Ezechielem*. Migne 26.

Ostenfeld-Lange, Hans, *see* Lange, H. O. & H. Schaefer.

Philo, *Vita Mosis*.

Plutarch, *Isis and Osiris*.

Riessler, Paul, *Altjüdisches Schrifttum ausserhalb der Bibel*. 2 ed. Kerle, Heidelberg 1966.

Schaefer, H. *see* Lange, H. O. and H. Schaefer.

Spengler, Oswald, *Decline of the West, The.* Allen & Unwin, London 1926-29.

Steiner, Rudolf, *Antworten der Geisteswissenschaft* (Gesamtausgabe No. 60) [1911 March 9]. Steiner, Dornach 1959. (English: *Turning Points*).

——, *Bhagavad Gita and the Epistles of Paul, The.* Anthroposophic, New York 1971.

——, *Bhagavad Gita und die Paulusbriefe, Die* (GA 142) [1912 Dec 31]. Steiner, Dornach 1982.

——, *Christ and the Human Soul.* Steiner, London 1972.

——, *Christ and the Spiritual World and the Search for the Holy Grail.* Steiner, London 1963.

——, *Christentum als mystische Tatsache, Das* (GA 8) [1902]. Steiner, Dornach 1976. (*Christianity as Mystical Fact*).

——, *Christianity as Mystical Fact and the Mysteries of Antiquity.* Steiner, New York 1961.

——, *Christus und die geistige Welt,* (GA 149) [1913 Dec 29 & 31]. Steiner, Dornach 1977. (*Christ and the Spiritual World*).

——, *Christus und die menschliche Seele,* (GA 155) [1914 July 14 & 12]. Steiner, Dornach 1982. (*Christ and the Human Soul*).

——, *Deeper Secrets of Human History in the Light of the Gospel of St. Matthew.* Anthroposophical, London 1957.

——, *Geheimnisse der biblischen Schöpfunsgeschichte, Die* (GA 122) [1910 Aug 26]. Steiner, Dornach 1984. (*Genesis*).

——, *Geheimnisse der Schwelle, Die* (GA 147) [1913 Aug 26]. Steiner, Dornach 1982. (*Secrets of the Threshold*).

——, *Geheimwissenschaft im Umriss, Die* (GA 13) [1910]. Steiner, Dornach 1977. (*Outline of Occult Science*).

——, *Geistige Hierarchien und ihre Widerspiegelung in der physichen Welt* (GA 110) [1909 April 18]. Steiner, Dornach 1981. (*Spiritual Hierarchies*).

——, *Genesis. Secrets of the Bible Story of Creation.* Steiner, London 1982.

——, *Gospel of St. John, The.* Anthroposophic, New York 1977.

——, *Gospel of St. Luke, The.* Steiner, London 1975.

——, *Gospel of St. Mark, The.* Steiner, London 1977.

——, *Gospel of St. Matthew, The.* Steiner, London 1965.

——, *Grundelemente der Esoterik* (GA 93a) [1905 Sep 26]. Steiner, Dornach 1976. (No translation).

——, *Johannes-Evangelium, Das* (GA 103) [1908 May 25]. Steiner, Dornach 1981.

——, *Knowledge of the Higher Worlds and its Attainment.* Anthroposophic, New York 1975.

——, *Lukas-Evangelium, Das* (GA 114) [1909 Sep 21 & 20]. Steiner, Dornach 1985.

———, *Markus-Evangelium, Das* (GA 139) [1912 Sep 22]. Steiner, Dornach 1985.

———, *Matthäus-Evangelium, Das* (GA 123) [1910 Sep 2]. Steiner, Dornach 1978.

———, *Mysterien des Morgenlandes und des Christentums, Die* (GA 144) [1913 Feb 5]. Steiner, Dornach 1985. (*Mysteries of the East*).

———, *Mysteries of the East and of Christianity, The.* Steiner, London 1972.

———, *Occult Movement in the Nineteenth Century, The.* Steiner, London 1973.

———, *Okkulte Bewegung im neunzehnten Jahrhundert, Die* (GA 164) [1915 Oct 19]. Steiner, Dornach 1975. (*Occult Movement*).

———, *Orient im Licht des Okzidents, Der* (GA 113) [1909 Aug 26]. Steiner, Dornach 1982. (*East in the Light of the West*).

———, *Outline of Occult Science, An.* Anthroposophic, New York 1972.

———, *Secrets of the Threshold, The.* Anthroposophical, London & New York 1928.

———, *Spiritual Hierarchies and their Reflection in the Physical World, The.* Anthroposophic, New York 1970.

———, *tieferen Geheimnisse des Menschheitswesen im Lichte der Evangelien, Die* (GA 117) [1909 Nov 23, 9 & 14]. Steiner, Dornach 1966. (*Deeper Secrets*).

———, *Turning Points in Spiritual History.* Steiner, London 1934.

———, *Weltenwunder, Seelenprüfung und Geistesoffenbarung,* (GA 129) [1911 Aug 18 & 19]. Steiner, Dornach 1977. (*Wonders of the World*).

———, *Wie erlangt man Erkentnisse der höheren Welten?* (GA 10) [1904/5]. Steiner, Dornach 1982. (*Knowledge of the Higher Worlds*).

———, *Wonders of the World, Ordeals of the Soul, Revelations of the Spirit.* Steiner, London 1963.

Streit, *Sun & Cross*, Floris, Edinburgh 1984.

Trumbull, Henry Clay, *Kadesh Barnea*, Hodder & Stoughton, London 1884.

218

Index

INDEX

221

INDEX